ZŌGŌNIA

Slice of Death

Written and Illustrated by Tony Moseley

paizo
COMICS

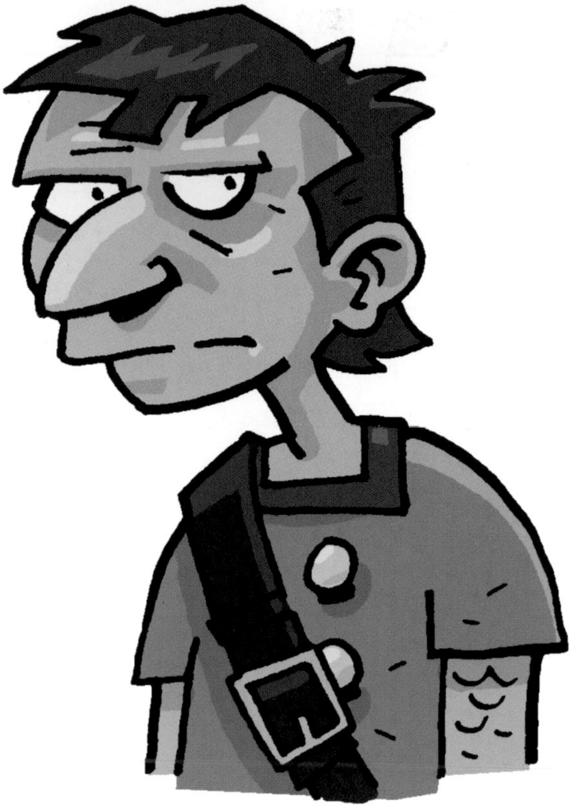

Kev by Kyle Hunter

Graphic Design and Cover: Drew Pocza
Editor: James L. Sutter
Senior Art Director: Sean Glenn
Production Manager: Jeff Alvarez
Paizo CEO: Lisa Stevens
Publisher: Erik Mona

ZOGONIA: SLICE OF DEATH

ISBN 978-1-60125-021-6

Published by:
Paizo Publishing, LLC
2700 Richards Road, Suite 201
Bellevue, WA 98005
www.paizo.com
customer.service@paizo.com

Printed in China.

First printing: March 2007

See ~~No~~ Evil

Since 2001, Tony Moseley's cartoon *Zogonia* has graced the pages of *Dragon* magazine, the longest-running tabletop gaming magazine in history. Cartoons have always played an important role in *Dragon*, shining the continual light of humor on our favorite hobby. Throughout the magazine's 31-year history, cartoons have constantly ranked as favorites in reader surveys, routinely beating out the articles on Dungeons & Dragons that serve as *Dragon's raison d'etre*. In that time, the magazine has launched dozens of extremely popular strips, such as *Fineous Fingers*, *Wormy*, *SnarfQuest*, *Dork Tower*, and *Nodwick*. To this honor roll must be added the magazine's most recent classic strip, *Zogonia* by Tony Moseley. This volume collects the cartoon's entire run, as well as some "lost" episodes and dozens of samples from Tony's spin-off strip, *Mt. Zogon*, which ran in *Dragon's* sister magazine, *Dungeon*.

Zogonia depicts RPG adventurers not as their players imagine them to be—valorous, virtuous heroes saving the world, one dungeon at a time—but as they actually are: brutal, greedy tomb robbers as suspicious of each other as they are of the monsters they murder with impunity. When you strip away the table chatter, the thin veneer of characterization, and the unspoken agreement that in order to keep having fun the guy playing the paladin can't just attack his companions every round for numerous crimes against humanity, you're left with a pretty depressing image: unstable mass murderers covered from head to toe in blood and guts, their rucksacks straining with the load of treasure and coin. There is a very thin line between a criminal and an adventurer, and it takes a genius like Tony Moseley to not only recognize it and find it funny, but to make it funny to us, too.

Steve Martin once said that comedy isn't pretty, and the phrase seems perfect for describing Moseley's cartoon. From the herky-jerky (but utterly proficient) artistic style to the skewed, jaundiced view of humanity present in all of his strips, Moseley shows us the underbelly of adventuring in a way that disarms us and makes us chuckle with knowing twinkles in our eyes. Take a look at the cover of this book. Befitting the name *Slice of Death*, each panel shows a hideous demise, from decapitation by kick to a crushing stone trap to the ever-popular sword slice to the face. These events, horrifying as they would be in the real world, happen on an hourly basis around the game table and no one thinks much of it beyond a mental tabulation of experience points. Tony's three main characters—Kev, Damato, and Dindil—live in a world soaked with the real effects of this existential horror. Unlike in the game, where players move from slaughtering a cave full of orc babies to asking the DM to pass the Doritos, each member of Domato's Delvers is touched by their lethal experiences in a way that often leads to hilarious consequences.

Only in *Zogonia* can you find adventurers contemplating escape from a locked chamber by cutting one of their members into little chunks, to be pushed out a small window and resurrected on the other side. Damato's *Orb of Life* keeps the party alive in the long run, but the relatively easy availability of "back to life" magic means the Delvers constantly bite off more than they can chew. The poor dwarf Dindil most often has to live (and die and live again) with the consequences of this deathstyle, and you can almost see it in his nervous tremors and beady little eyes.

Ultimately, though, *Zogonia* belongs to the party thief (er, "procurement specialist"), Kev. Remember how I said *Zogonia* depicts RPG characters as they actually are, rather than how their players imagine them to be? Kev is the perfect example of that. The ur-adventurer, if you will (and even if you won't—it's *my* introduction). In this regard Kev is a very realistic character. He doesn't want to risk his own neck if he can help it, and he's clearly been changed by his experiences in the dungeon (and I don't just mean changed into a frog, though that does happen, as you will soon see). In one strip Tony even suggests that Kev may be of an evil alignment, which is something almost no decent DM would allow but which a certain type of player often plays anyway, regardless of whether or not his character sheet says "good" or "neutral."

I'm one of those players. I suspect a lot of you are, too.

In the spirit of evil, I give you *Zogonia*. You'll never think of RPG cartoons in the same way again.

Erik Mona
Editor-in-Chief
Dragon Magazine

Creator Commentary: Many of the following cartoons are accompanied by design notes and background information straight from creator Tony Moseley himself. Think of them as a DVD commentary track... just without the DVD.

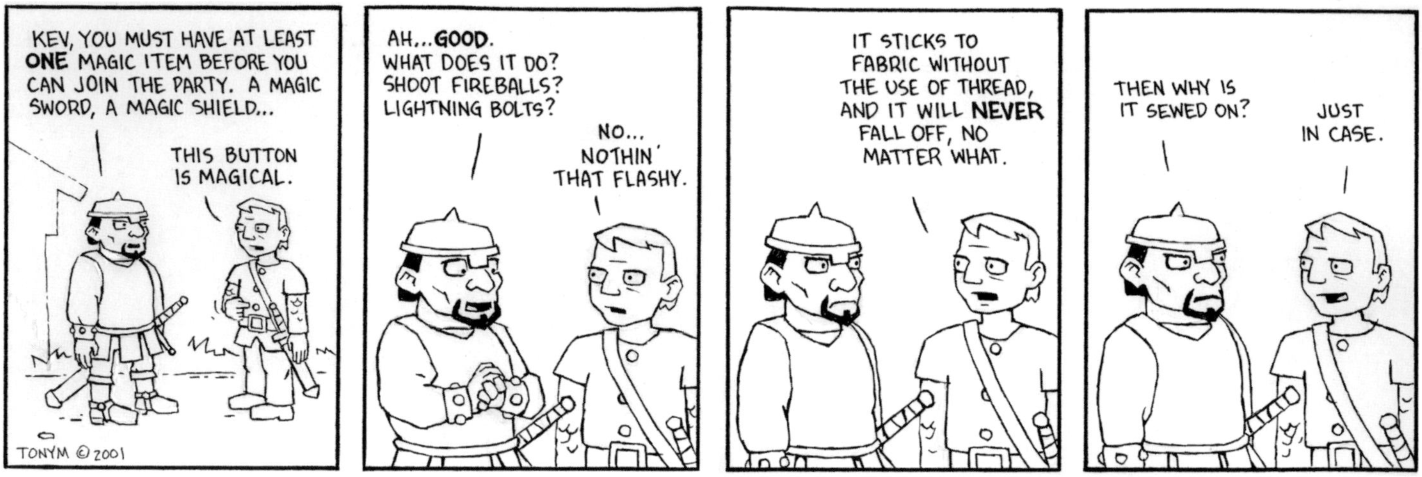
KEV, YOU MUST HAVE AT LEAST ONE MAGIC ITEM BEFORE YOU CAN JOIN THE PARTY. A MAGIC SWORD, A MAGIC SHIELD...
THIS BUTTON IS MAGICAL.
TONYM © 2001
AH,...GOOD. WHAT DOES IT DO? SHOOT FIREBALLS? LIGHTNING BOLTS?
NO... NOTHIN' THAT FLASHY.
IT STICKS TO FABRIC WITHOUT THE USE OF THREAD, AND IT WILL NEVER FALL OFF, NO MATTER WHAT.
THEN WHY IS IT SEWED ON?
JUST IN CASE.

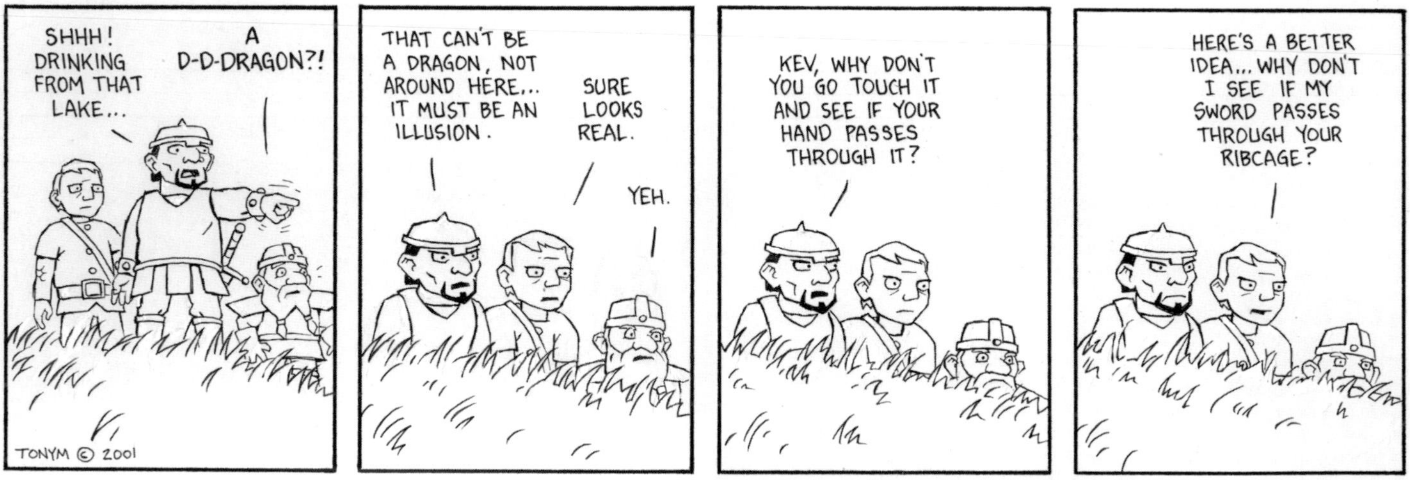
SHHH! DRINKING FROM THAT LAKE...
A D-D-DRAGON?!
TONYM © 2001
THAT CAN'T BE A DRAGON, NOT AROUND HERE... IT MUST BE AN ILLUSION.
SURE LOOKS REAL.
YEH.
KEV, WHY DON'T YOU GO TOUCH IT AND SEE IF YOUR HAND PASSES THROUGH IT?
HERE'S A BETTER IDEA... WHY DON'T I SEE IF MY SWORD PASSES THROUGH YOUR RIBCAGE?

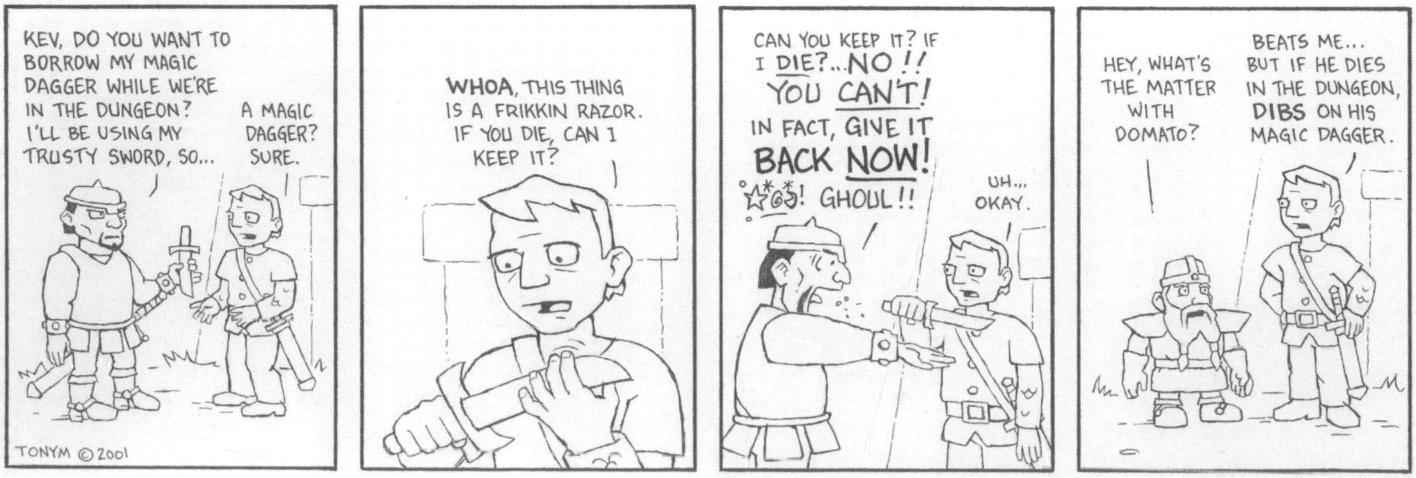
KEV, DO YOU WANT TO BORROW MY MAGIC DAGGER WHILE WE'RE IN THE DUNGEON? I'LL BE USING MY TRUSTY SWORD, SO...
A MAGIC DAGGER? SURE.
TONYM © 2001
WHOA, THIS THING IS A FRIKKIN RAZOR. IF YOU DIE, CAN I KEEP IT?
CAN YOU KEEP IT? IF I DIE?...NO!! YOU CAN'T! IN FACT, GIVE IT BACK NOW!
GHOUL!!
UH... OKAY.
HEY, WHAT'S THE MATTER WITH DOMATO?
BEATS ME... BUT IF HE DIES IN THE DUNGEON, DIBS ON HIS MAGIC DAGGER.

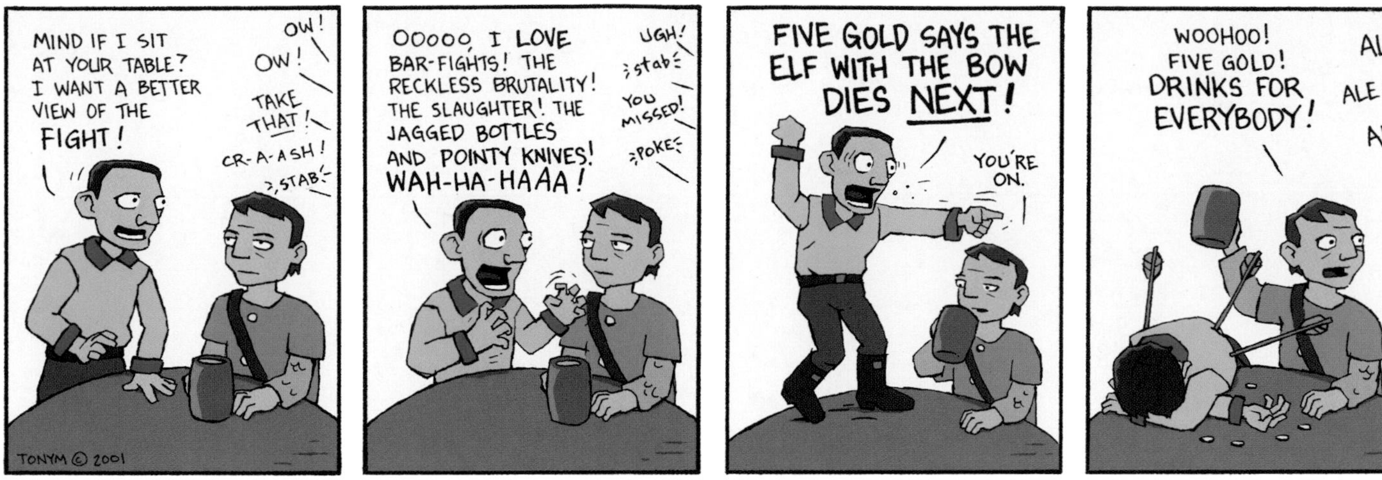

MIND IF I SIT AT YOUR TABLE? I WANT A BETTER VIEW OF THE FIGHT!
OW!
OW!
TAKE THAT!
CR-A-ASH!
STAB
TONYM © 2001
OOOOO, I LOVE BAR-FIGHTS! THE RECKLESS BRUTALITY! THE SLAUGHTER! THE JAGGED BOTTLES AND POINTY KNIVES! WAH-HA-HAAA!
UGH!
stab
YOU MISSED!
POKE
FIVE GOLD SAYS THE ELF WITH THE BOW DIES NEXT!
YOU'RE ON.
WOOHOO! FIVE GOLD! DRINKS FOR EVERYBODY!
ALE!
ALE!
ALE!

The very first Zogonia strip in *Dragon*. In a mere four panels, this strip represents killing, gambling, drinking and a bar fight—the glorious essence of the D&D roleplaying game.

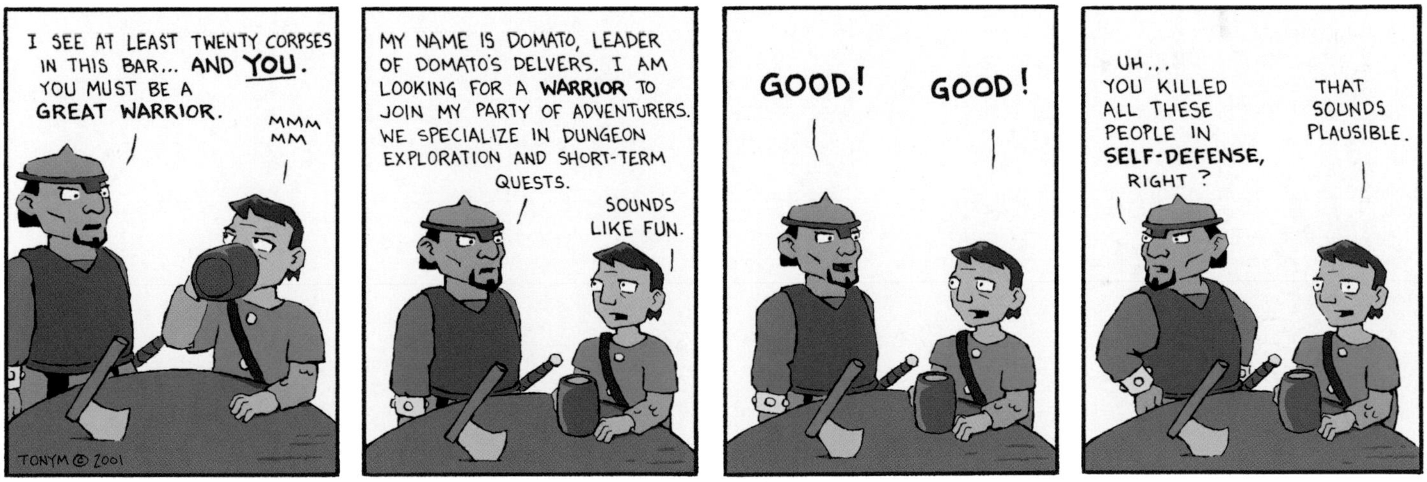

I SEE AT LEAST TWENTY CORPSES IN THIS BAR... AND YOU. YOU MUST BE A GREAT WARRIOR.
MMM MM
TONYM © 2001
MY NAME IS DOMATO, LEADER OF DOMATO'S DELVERS. I AM LOOKING FOR A WARRIOR TO JOIN MY PARTY OF ADVENTURERS. WE SPECIALIZE IN DUNGEON EXPLORATION AND SHORT-TERM QUESTS.
SOUNDS LIKE FUN.
GOOD!
GOOD!
UH... YOU KILLED ALL THESE PEOPLE IN SELF-DEFENSE, RIGHT?
THAT SOUNDS PLAUSIBLE.

In which we learn that 20 dead commoners on the floor will not prevent Kev from enjoying a tankard of ale.

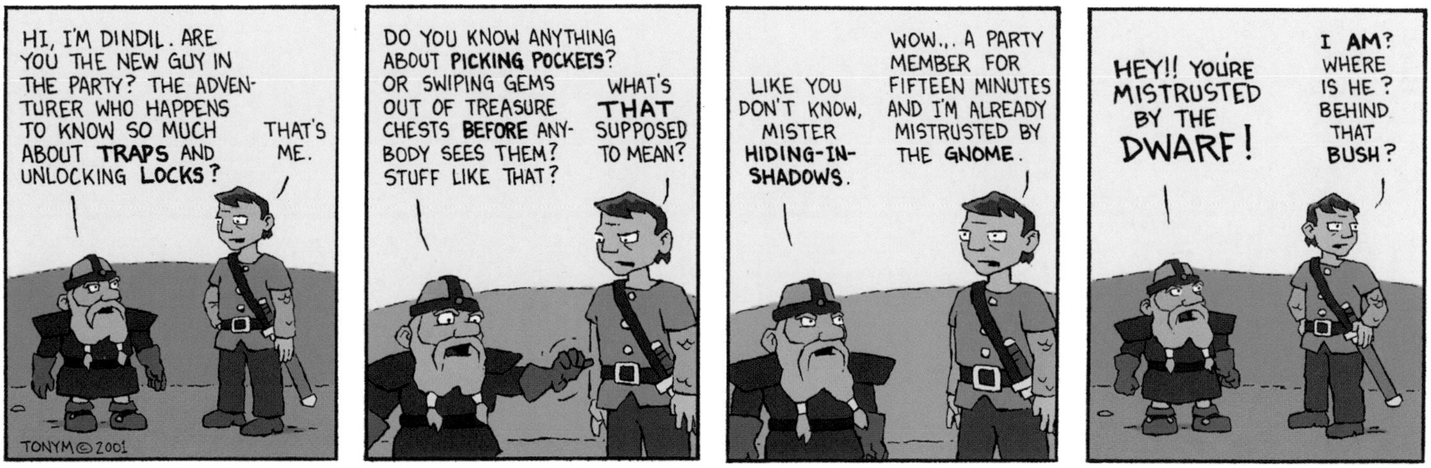

HI, I'M DINDIL. ARE YOU THE NEW GUY IN THE PARTY? THE ADVENTURER WHO HAPPENS TO KNOW SO MUCH ABOUT TRAPS AND UNLOCKING LOCKS?
THAT'S ME.
TONYM © 2001
DO YOU KNOW ANYTHING ABOUT PICKING POCKETS? OR SWIPING GEMS OUT OF TREASURE CHESTS BEFORE ANYBODY SEES THEM? STUFF LIKE THAT?
WHAT'S THAT SUPPOSED TO MEAN?
LIKE YOU DON'T KNOW, MISTER HIDING-IN-SHADOWS.
WOW... A PARTY MEMBER FOR FIFTEEN MINUTES AND I'M ALREADY MISTRUSTED BY THE GNOME.
HEY!! YOU'RE MISTRUSTED BY THE DWARF!
I AM? WHERE IS HE? BEHIND THAT BUSH?

Kev is lucky that Dindil didn't kill him for this insult, as even gnomes are offended when mistaken for a "gnome." Most gnomes prefer to be mistaken for small, effeminate dwarves.

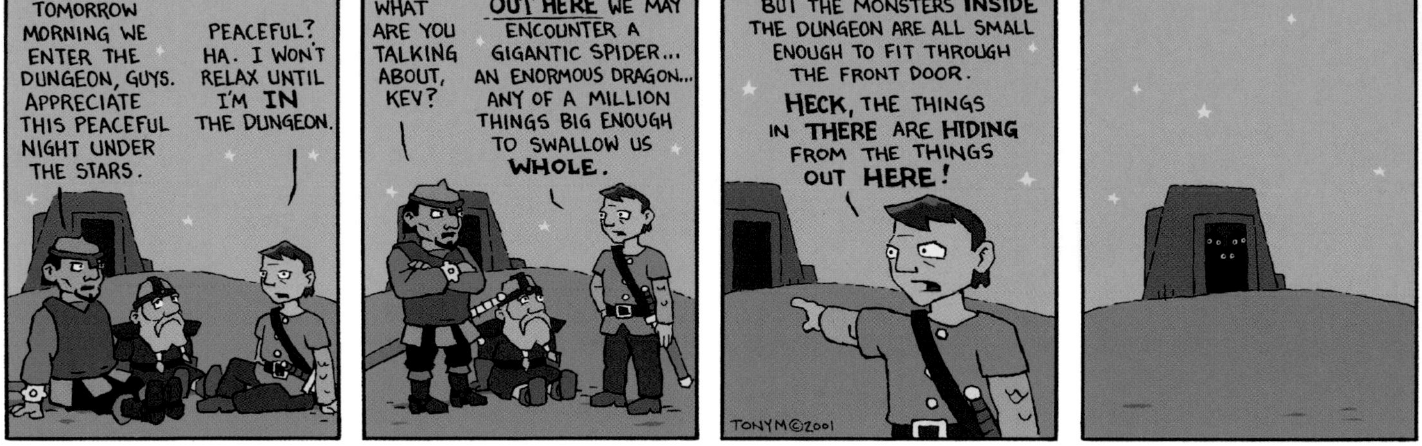
TOMORROW MORNING WE ENTER THE DUNGEON, GUYS. APPRECIATE THIS PEACEFUL NIGHT UNDER THE STARS.
PEACEFUL? HA. I WON'T RELAX UNTIL I'M IN THE DUNGEON.
WHAT ARE YOU TALKING ABOUT, KEV?
OUT HERE WE MAY ENCOUNTER A GIGANTIC SPIDER... AN ENORMOUS DRAGON... ANY OF A MILLION THINGS BIG ENOUGH TO SWALLOW US WHOLE.
BUT THE MONSTERS INSIDE THE DUNGEON ARE ALL SMALL ENOUGH TO FIT THROUGH THE FRONT DOOR.
HECK, THE THINGS IN THERE ARE HIDING FROM THE THINGS OUT HERE!
TONYM©2001

If one is determined to pursue adventuring as a career, then one should never think about how small and chewable one is when compared to dragons and other gigantic beasts.

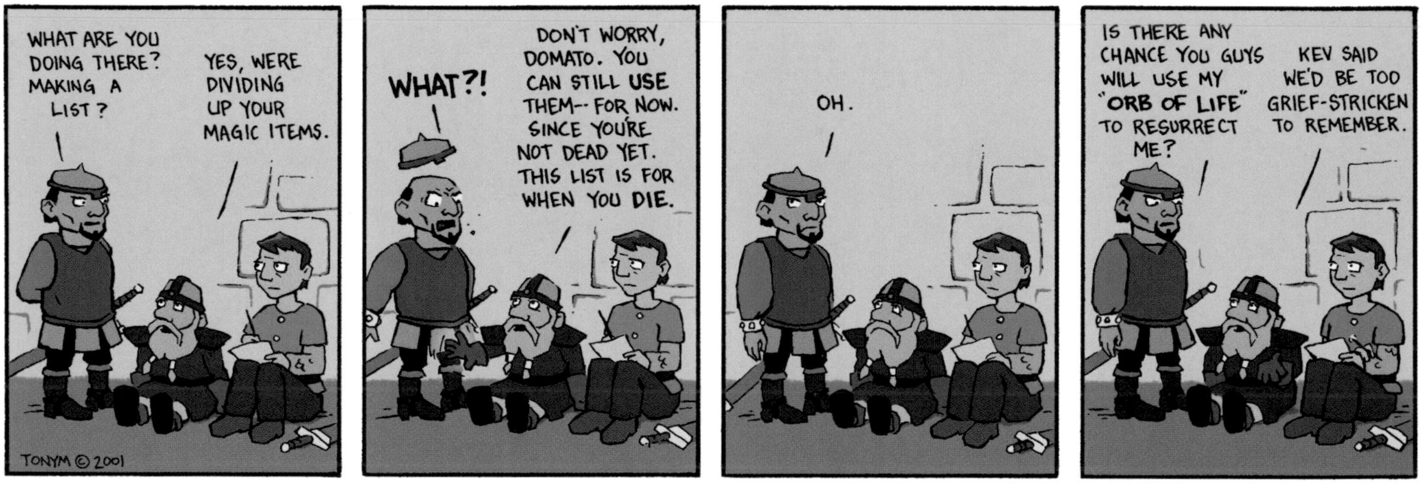
WHAT ARE YOU DOING THERE? MAKING A LIST?
YES, WERE DIVIDING UP YOUR MAGIC ITEMS.
TONYM © 2001
WHAT?!
DON'T WORRY, DOMATO. YOU CAN STILL USE THEM-- FOR NOW. SINCE YOU'RE NOT DEAD YET. THIS LIST IS FOR WHEN YOU DIE.
OH.
IS THERE ANY CHANCE YOU GUYS WILL USE MY "ORB OF LIFE" TO RESURRECT ME?
KEV SAID WE'D BE TOO GRIEF-STRICKEN TO REMEMBER.

A wise man once said, "Every PC should carry an up-to-date will in his or her left boot." To which I add, "...written on a scroll of *resurrection*."

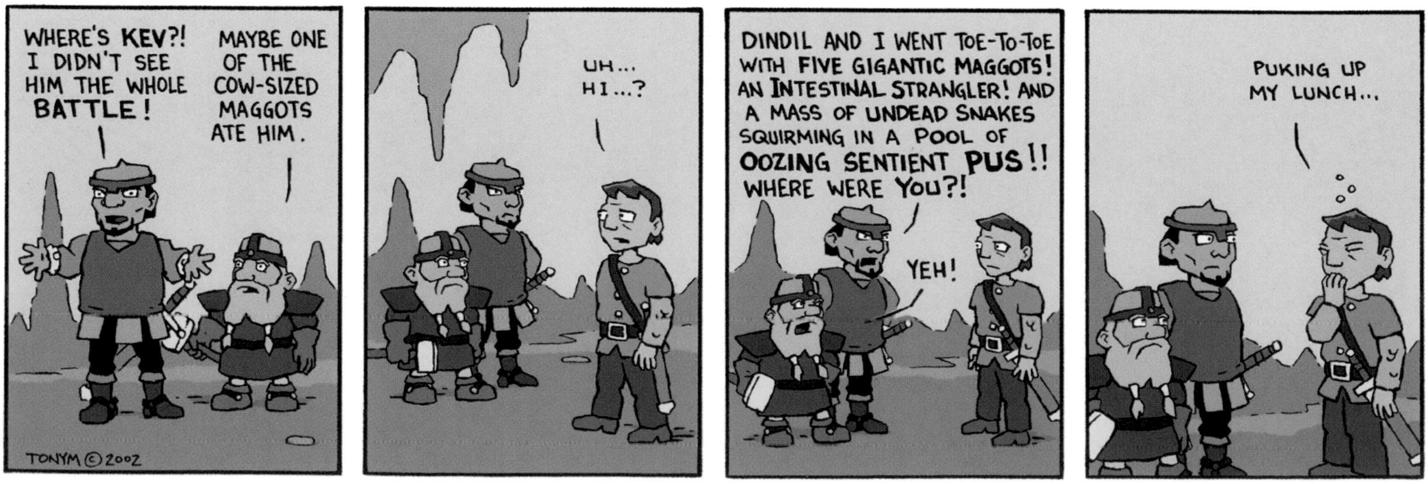
WHERE'S KEV?! I DIDN'T SEE HIM THE WHOLE BATTLE!
MAYBE ONE OF THE COW-SIZED MAGGOTS ATE HIM.
TONYM © 2002
UH... HI...?
DINDIL AND I WENT TOE-TO-TOE WITH FIVE GIGANTIC MAGGOTS! AN INTESTINAL STRANGLER! AND A MASS OF UNDEAD SNAKES SQUIRMING IN A POOL OF OOZING SENTIENT PUS!! WHERE WERE YOU?!
YEH!
PUKING UP MY LUNCH...

Oozing sentient pus? Blecch. What kind of sick, demented necromancer would think up such a thing? Or cartoonist, for that matter...

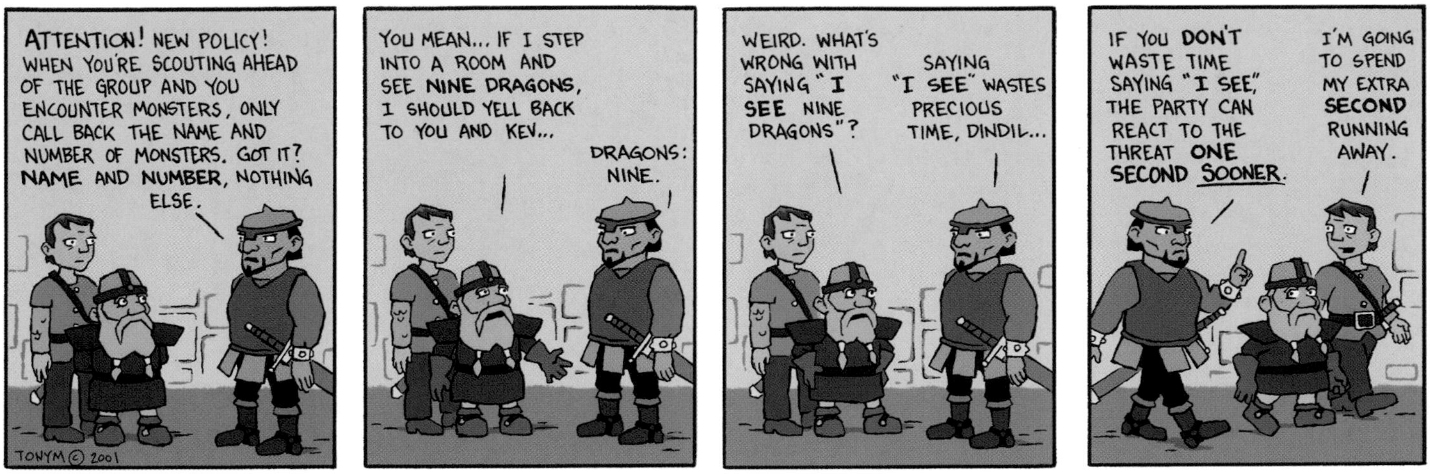
ATTENTION! NEW POLICY! WHEN YOU'RE SCOUTING AHEAD OF THE GROUP AND YOU ENCOUNTER MONSTERS, ONLY CALL BACK THE NAME AND NUMBER OF MONSTERS. GOT IT? NAME AND NUMBER, NOTHING ELSE.
TONYM © 2001
YOU MEAN... IF I STEP INTO A ROOM AND SEE NINE DRAGONS, I SHOULD YELL BACK TO YOU AND KEV...
DRAGONS: NINE.
WEIRD. WHAT'S WRONG WITH SAYING "I SEE NINE DRAGONS"?
SAYING "I SEE" WASTES PRECIOUS TIME, DINDIL...
IF YOU DON'T WASTE TIME SAYING "I SEE," THE PARTY CAN REACT TO THE THREAT ONE SECOND SOONER.
I'M GOING TO SPEND MY EXTRA SECOND RUNNING AWAY.

As the Party Leader, Domato has obliged himself to think up ideas on behalf of the party. Not necessarily good ideas. Just ideas.

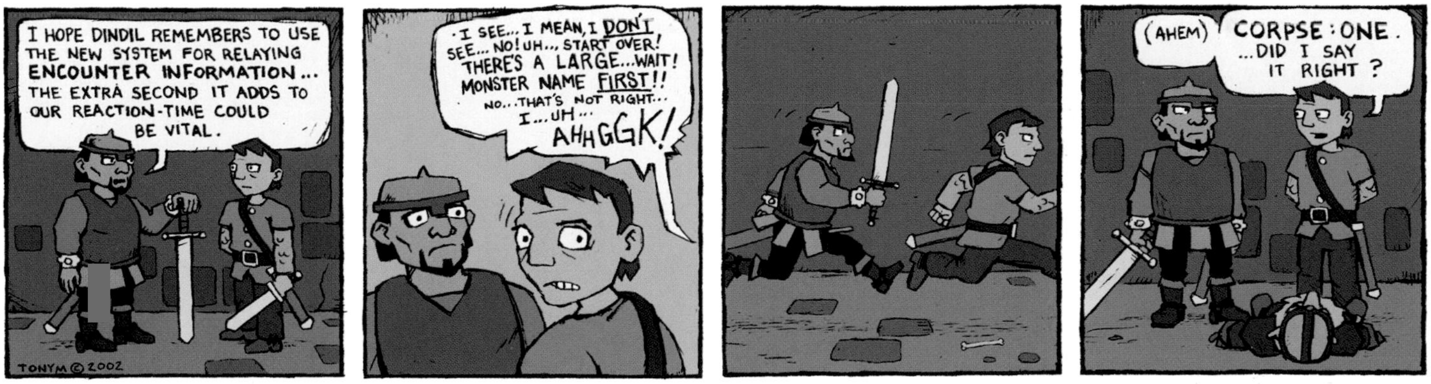
I HOPE DINDIL REMEMBERS TO USE THE NEW SYSTEM FOR RELAYING ENCOUNTER INFORMATION... THE EXTRA SECOND IT ADDS TO OUR REACTION-TIME COULD BE VITAL.
TONYM © 2002
I SEE... I MEAN, I DON'T SEE... NO! UH... START OVER! THERE'S A LARGE... WAIT! MONSTER NAME FIRST!! NO... THAT'S NOT RIGHT... I... UH... AHHGGK!
(AHEM)
CORPSE: ONE. ...DID I SAY IT RIGHT?

The moral of this story: after you kill the scout of an adventuring party, flee before his comrades avenge his death.

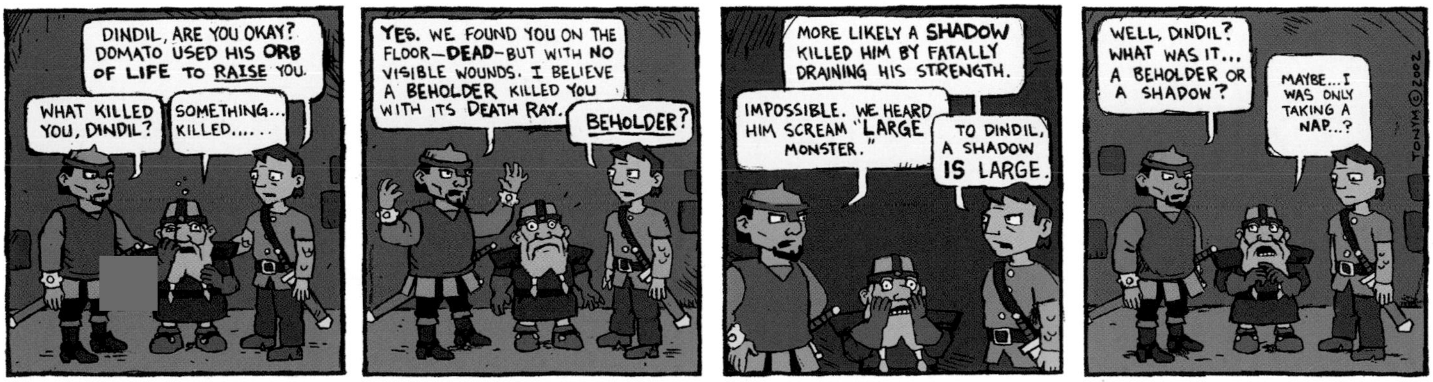
DINDIL, ARE YOU OKAY? DOMATO USED HIS ORB OF LIFE TO RAISE YOU.
WHAT KILLED YOU, DINDIL?
SOMETHING... KILLED.....
YES. WE FOUND YOU ON THE FLOOR—DEAD—BUT WITH NO VISIBLE WOUNDS. I BELIEVE A BEHOLDER KILLED YOU WITH ITS DEATH RAY.
BEHOLDER?
MORE LIKELY A SHADOW KILLED HIM BY FATALLY DRAINING HIS STRENGTH.
IMPOSSIBLE. WE HEARD HIM SCREAM "LARGE MONSTER."
TO DINDIL, A SHADOW IS LARGE.
WELL, DINDIL? WHAT WAS IT... A BEHOLDER OR A SHADOW?
MAYBE... I WAS ONLY TAKING A NAP...?
TONYM © 2002

Domato's *Orb of Life* is an extremely handy magic item, but its operation is costly. Clerics charge Domato several thousand gold coins for every charge they place into it.

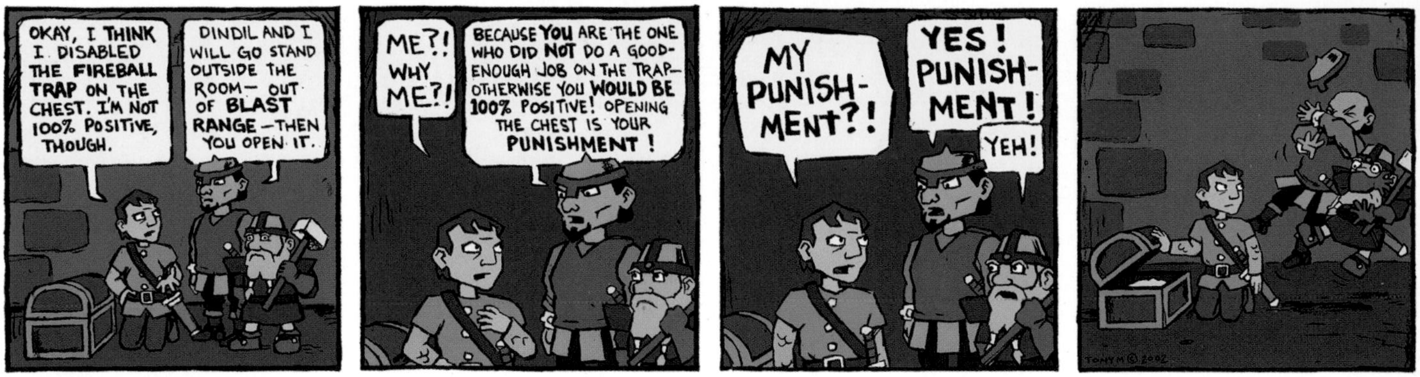
OKAY, I THINK I DISABLED THE FIREBALL TRAP ON THE CHEST. I'M NOT 100% POSITIVE, THOUGH.
DINDIL AND I WILL GO STAND OUTSIDE THE ROOM— OUT OF BLAST RANGE —THEN YOU OPEN IT.
ME?! WHY ME?!
BECAUSE YOU ARE THE ONE WHO DID NOT DO A GOOD-ENOUGH JOB ON THE TRAP— OTHERWISE YOU WOULD BE 100% POSITIVE! OPENING THE CHEST IS YOUR PUNISHMENT!
MY PUNISH-MENT?!
YES! PUNISH-MENT!
YEH!
TONYM © 2002

I'm pretty sure Kev was 99% positive he had removed the trap when he opened the chest. Imagine his surprise, though, if he had actually flubbed the trap-removal! Ha! Maybe next time...

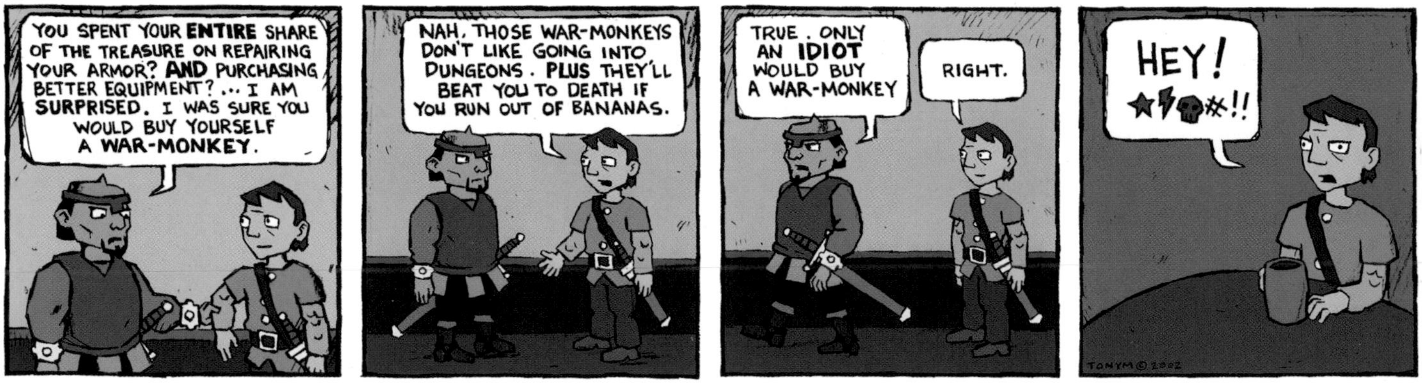
YOU SPENT YOUR ENTIRE SHARE OF THE TREASURE ON REPAIRING YOUR ARMOR? AND PURCHASING BETTER EQUIPMENT? ... I AM SURPRISED. I WAS SURE YOU WOULD BUY YOURSELF A WAR-MONKEY.
NAH, THOSE WAR-MONKEYS DON'T LIKE GOING INTO DUNGEONS. PLUS THEY'LL BEAT YOU TO DEATH IF YOU RUN OUT OF BANANAS.
TRUE. ONLY AN IDIOT WOULD BUY A WAR-MONKEY
RIGHT.
HEY!
!!
TONYM © 2002

Star-lightning-skull-scribble is the Zogonian word for... um... it rhymes with... Screw it. Make up your own cussword.

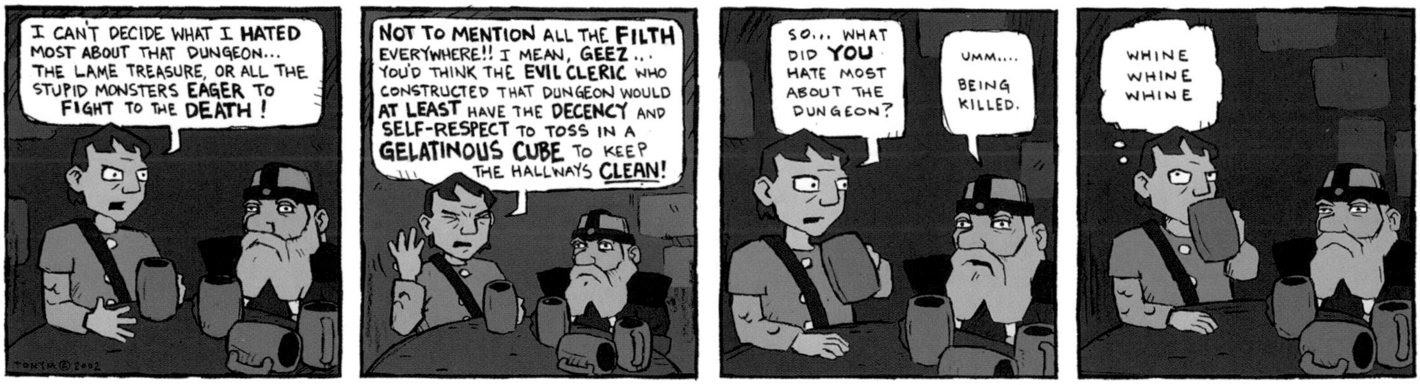
I CAN'T DECIDE WHAT I HATED MOST ABOUT THAT DUNGEON... THE LAME TREASURE, OR ALL THE STUPID MONSTERS EAGER TO FIGHT TO THE DEATH!
TONYM © 2002
NOT TO MENTION ALL THE FILTH EVERYWHERE!! I MEAN, GEEZ... YOU'D THINK THE EVIL CLERIC WHO CONSTRUCTED THAT DUNGEON WOULD AT LEAST HAVE THE DECENCY AND SELF-RESPECT TO TOSS IN A GELATINOUS CUBE TO KEEP THE HALLWAYS CLEAN!
SO... WHAT DID YOU HATE MOST ABOUT THE DUNGEON?
UMM.... BEING KILLED.
WHINE WHINE WHINE

Don't you just hate it when you're complaining about how horrible your life is, and the jerk you're talking to blatantly ignores what you said and starts complaining about how horrible his life is? And so you kick him really hard in the face and he falls out of his chair. And then you remember, while you're looking at him writhing on the floor, that he's actually the one who started complaining first?

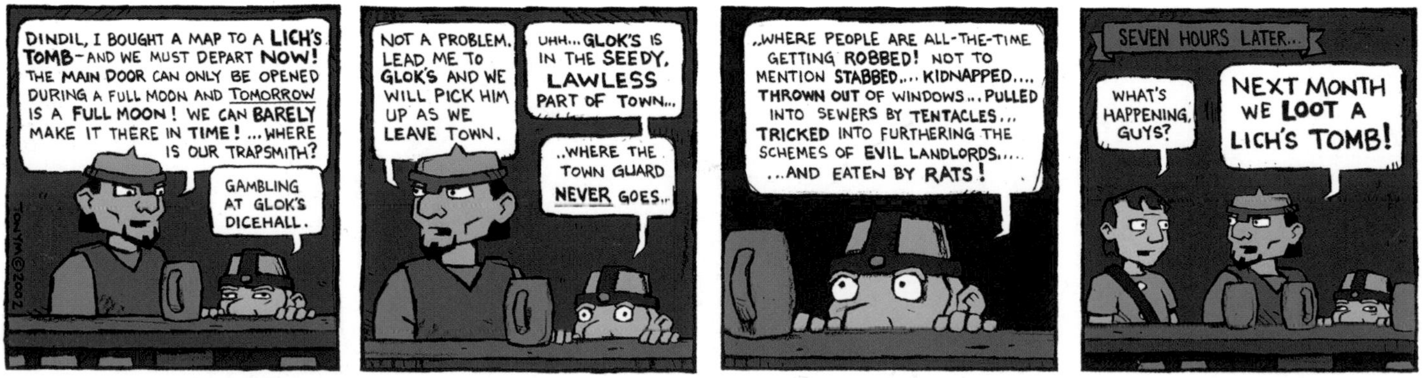
DINDIL, I BOUGHT A MAP TO A LICH'S TOMB— AND WE MUST DEPART NOW! THE MAIN DOOR CAN ONLY BE OPENED DURING A FULL MOON AND TOMORROW IS A FULL MOON! WE CAN BARELY MAKE IT THERE IN TIME! ...WHERE IS OUR TRAPSMITH?
GAMBLING AT GLOK'S DICEHALL.
TONYM © 2002
NOT A PROBLEM. LEAD ME TO GLOK'S AND WE WILL PICK HIM UP AS WE LEAVE TOWN.
UHH... GLOK'S IS IN THE SEEDY, LAWLESS PART OF TOWN...
..WHERE THE TOWN GUARD NEVER GOES..
..WHERE PEOPLE ARE ALL-THE-TIME GETTING ROBBED! NOT TO MENTION STABBED.... KIDNAPPED.... THROWN OUT OF WINDOWS... PULLED INTO SEWERS BY TENTACLES... TRICKED INTO FURTHERING THE SCHEMES OF EVIL LANDLORDS.... ...AND EATEN BY RATS!
SEVEN HOURS LATER..
WHAT'S HAPPENING, GUYS?
NEXT MONTH WE LOOT A LICH'S TOMB!

I love making those little boxes that say things like, "Seven hours later...." They're amazingly powerful tools. Seriously. For example, if I wanted to, I could make a box that said, "One thousand years later..." and all the characters would be *dead*.

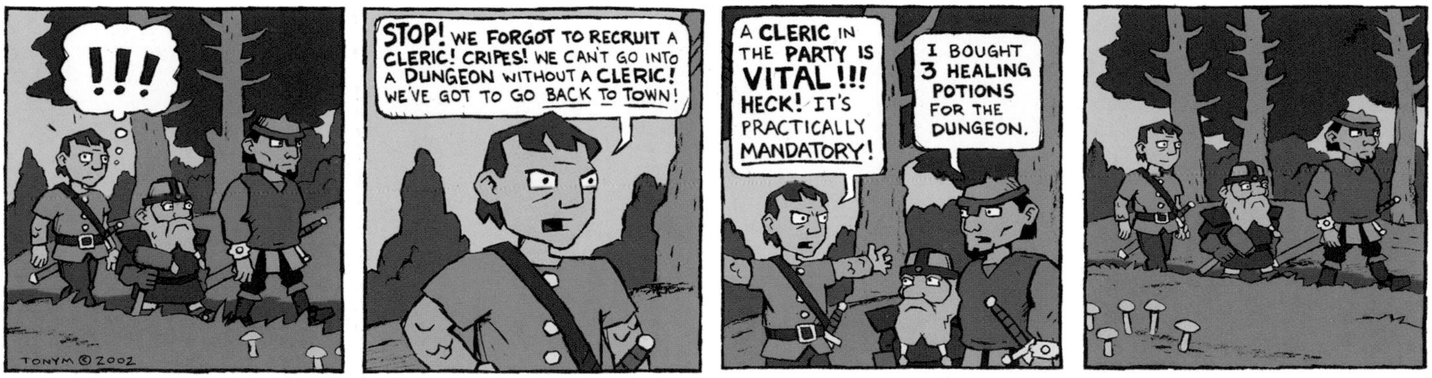
!!!
STOP! WE FORGOT TO RECRUIT A CLERIC! CRIPES! WE CAN'T GO INTO A DUNGEON WITHOUT A CLERIC! WE'VE GOT TO GO BACK TO TOWN!
A CLERIC IN THE PARTY IS VITAL!!! HECK! IT'S PRACTICALLY MANDATORY!
I BOUGHT 3 HEALING POTIONS FOR THE DUNGEON.
TONYM © 2002

In actuality, a cleric is equal to four healing potions. But four is not a funny number, for some reason, so I changed it to three.

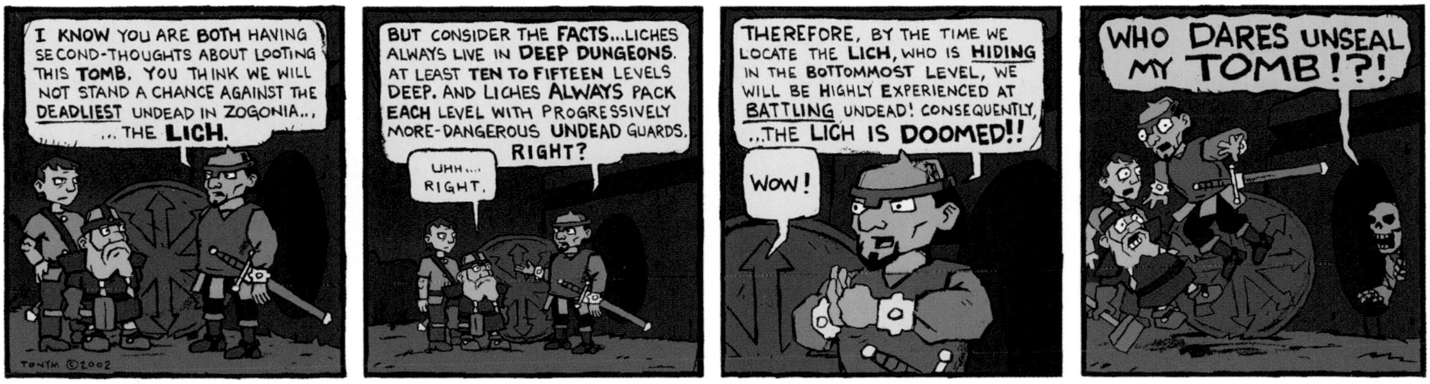
I KNOW YOU ARE BOTH HAVING SECOND-THOUGHTS ABOUT LOOTING THIS TOMB. YOU THINK WE WILL NOT STAND A CHANCE AGAINST THE DEADLIEST UNDEAD IN ZOGONIA... ...THE LICH.
BUT CONSIDER THE FACTS...LICHES ALWAYS LIVE IN DEEP DUNGEONS. AT LEAST TEN TO FIFTEEN LEVELS DEEP. AND LICHES ALWAYS PACK EACH LEVEL WITH PROGRESSIVELY MORE-DANGEROUS UNDEAD GUARDS. RIGHT?
UHH.... RIGHT.
THEREFORE, BY THE TIME WE LOCATE THE LICH, WHO IS HIDING IN THE BOTTOMMOST LEVEL, WE WILL BE HIGHLY EXPERIENCED AT BATTLING UNDEAD! CONSEQUENTLY, ...THE LICH IS DOOMED!!
WOW!
WHO DARES UNSEAL MY TOMB!?!
TONYM ©2002

In this strip, Domato shows us why he is the Party Leader. Domato is adept at using logic to make Kev and Dindil agree with his ideas.

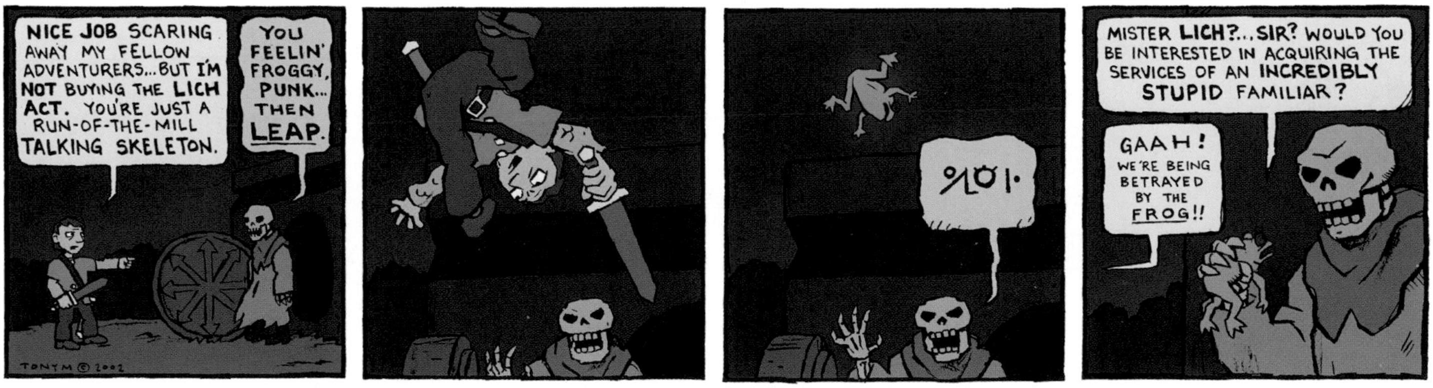
NICE JOB SCARING AWAY MY FELLOW ADVENTURERS...BUT I'M NOT BUYING THE LICH ACT. YOU'RE JUST A RUN-OF-THE-MILL TALKING SKELETON.
YOU FEELIN' FROGGY, PUNK... THEN LEAP.
MISTER LICH?...SIR? WOULD YOU BE INTERESTED IN ACQUIRING THE SERVICES OF AN INCREDIBLY STUPID FAMILIAR?
GAAH! WE'RE BEING BETRAYED BY THE FROG!!
TONYM © 2002

It must be great to be a lich—so powerful, so deadly, so feared. Of course, looking in the mirror must suck eggs.

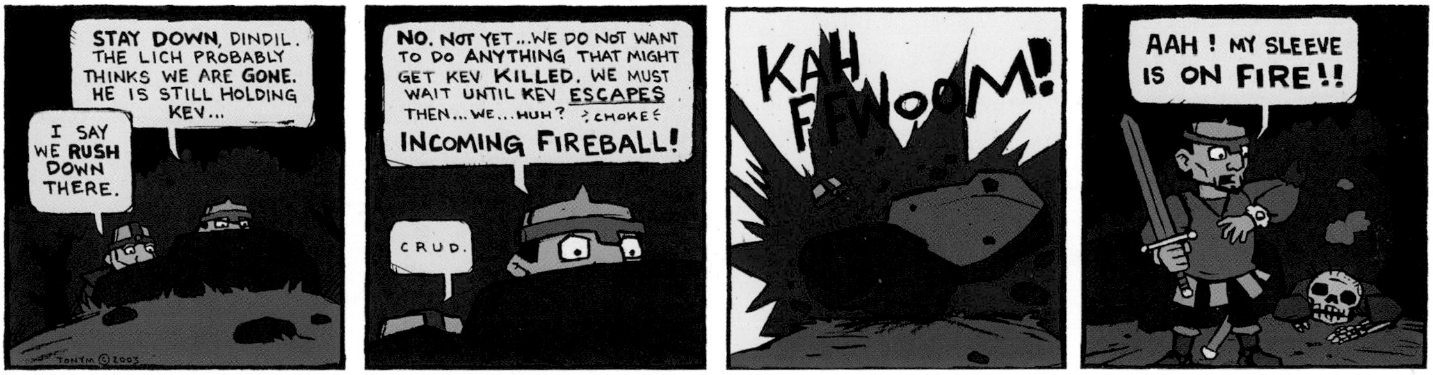
STAY DOWN, DINDIL. THE LICH PROBABLY THINKS WE ARE GONE. HE IS STILL HOLDING KEV...
I SAY WE RUSH DOWN THERE.
NO. NOT YET...WE DO NOT WANT TO DO ANYTHING THAT MIGHT GET KEV KILLED. WE MUST WAIT UNTIL KEV ESCAPES. THEN...WE...HUH? ≥CHOKE≤ INCOMING FIREBALL!
CRUD.
KAH FFWOOM!
AAH! MY SLEEVE IS ON FIRE!!
TONYM ©2003

Fireball is the hand grenade of D&D. This *fireball* must've hit poor Dindil in the chest.

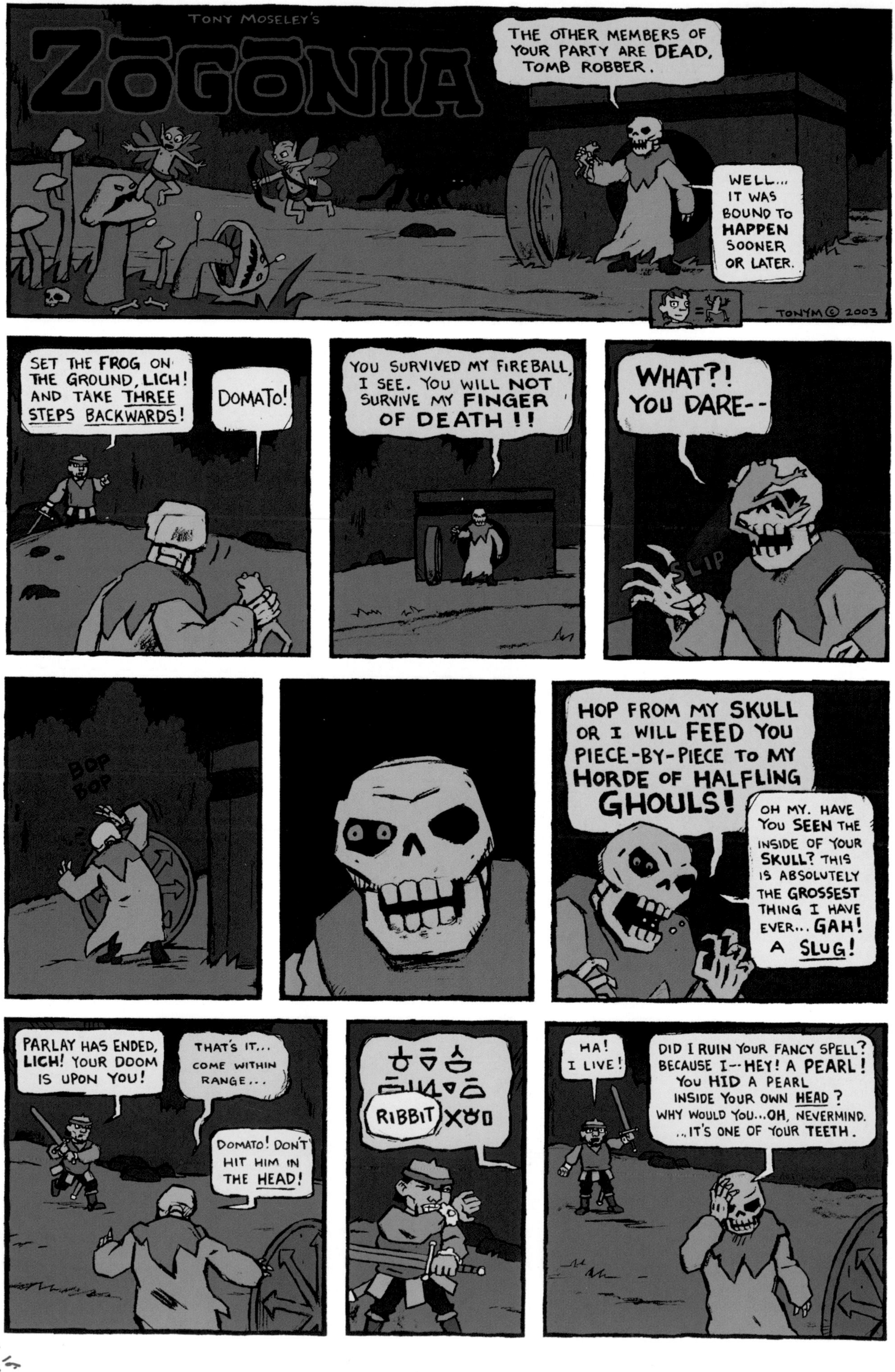
TONY MOSELEY'S
ZOGONIA
THE OTHER MEMBERS OF YOUR PARTY ARE DEAD, TOMB ROBBER.
WELL... IT WAS BOUND TO HAPPEN SOONER OR LATER.
TONYM © 2003
SET THE FROG ON THE GROUND, LICH! AND TAKE THREE STEPS BACKWARDS!
DOMATO!
YOU SURVIVED MY FIREBALL, I SEE. YOU WILL NOT SURVIVE MY FINGER OF DEATH!!
WHAT?! YOU DARE--
SLIP
BOP
BOP
HOP FROM MY SKULL OR I WILL FEED YOU PIECE-BY-PIECE TO MY HORDE OF HALFLING GHOULS!
OH MY. HAVE YOU SEEN THE INSIDE OF YOUR SKULL? THIS IS ABSOLUTELY THE GROSSEST THING I HAVE EVER... GAH! A SLUG!
PARLAY HAS ENDED, LICH! YOUR DOOM IS UPON YOU!
THAT'S IT... COME WITHIN RANGE...
DOMATO! DON'T HIT HIM IN THE HEAD!
RIBBIT
HA! I LIVE!
DID I RUIN YOUR FANCY SPELL? BECAUSE I--HEY! A PEARL! YOU HID A PEARL INSIDE YOUR OWN HEAD? WHY WOULD YOU...OH, NEVERMIND. ...IT'S ONE OF YOUR TEETH.

Surviving a deadly magical attack must be a wonderful, strange experience. The closest contemporary parallel I can think of is being a soldier and having a bullet bounce off your helmet.

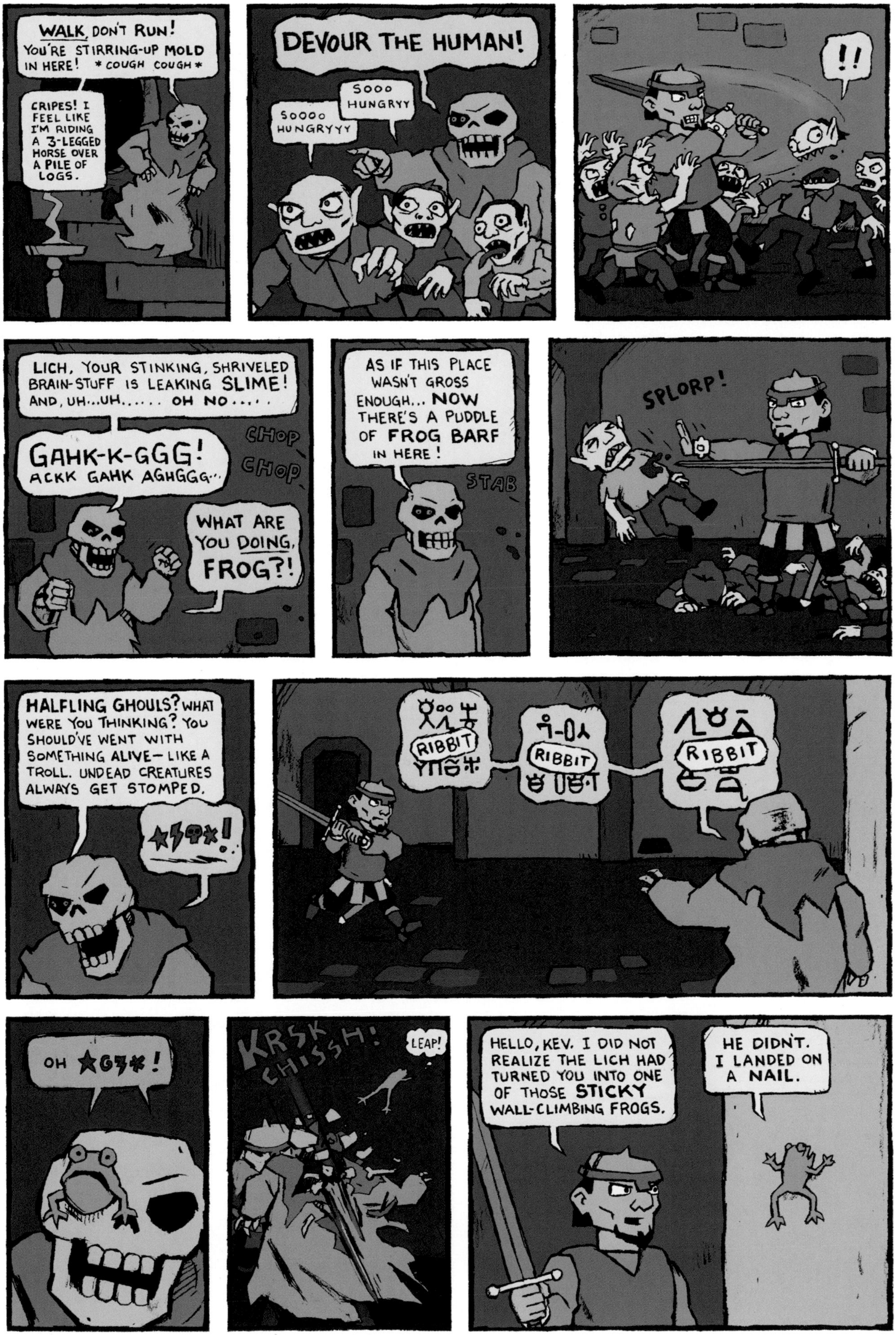
WALK, DON'T RUN! YOU'RE STIRRING-UP MOLD IN HERE! *COUGH COUGH*
CRIPES! I FEEL LIKE I'M RIDING A 3-LEGGED HORSE OVER A PILE OF LOGS.
DEVOUR THE HUMAN!
SOOO HUNGRYY
SOOOO HUNGRYYY
!!
LICH, YOUR STINKING, SHRIVELED BRAIN-STUFF IS LEAKING SLIME! AND, UH...UH...... OH NO.....
GAHK-K-GGG! ACKK GAHK AGHGGG...
CHOP
CHOP
WHAT ARE YOU DOING, FROG?!
AS IF THIS PLACE WASN'T GROSS ENOUGH... NOW THERE'S A PUDDLE OF FROG BARF IN HERE!
STAB
SPLORP!
HALFLING GHOULS? WHAT WERE YOU THINKING? YOU SHOULD'VE WENT WITH SOMETHING ALIVE— LIKE A TROLL. UNDEAD CREATURES ALWAYS GET STOMPED.
RIBBIT
RIBBIT
RIBBIT
OH
KRSK CHISSSH!
LEAP!
HELLO, KEV. I DID NOT REALIZE THE LICH HAD TURNED YOU INTO ONE OF THOSE STICKY WALL-CLIMBING FROGS.
HE DIDN'T. I LANDED ON A NAIL.

See those nifty magical words spoken by the lich? They're the names of spells from the *Player's Handbook*, disguised by a code of my own creation.

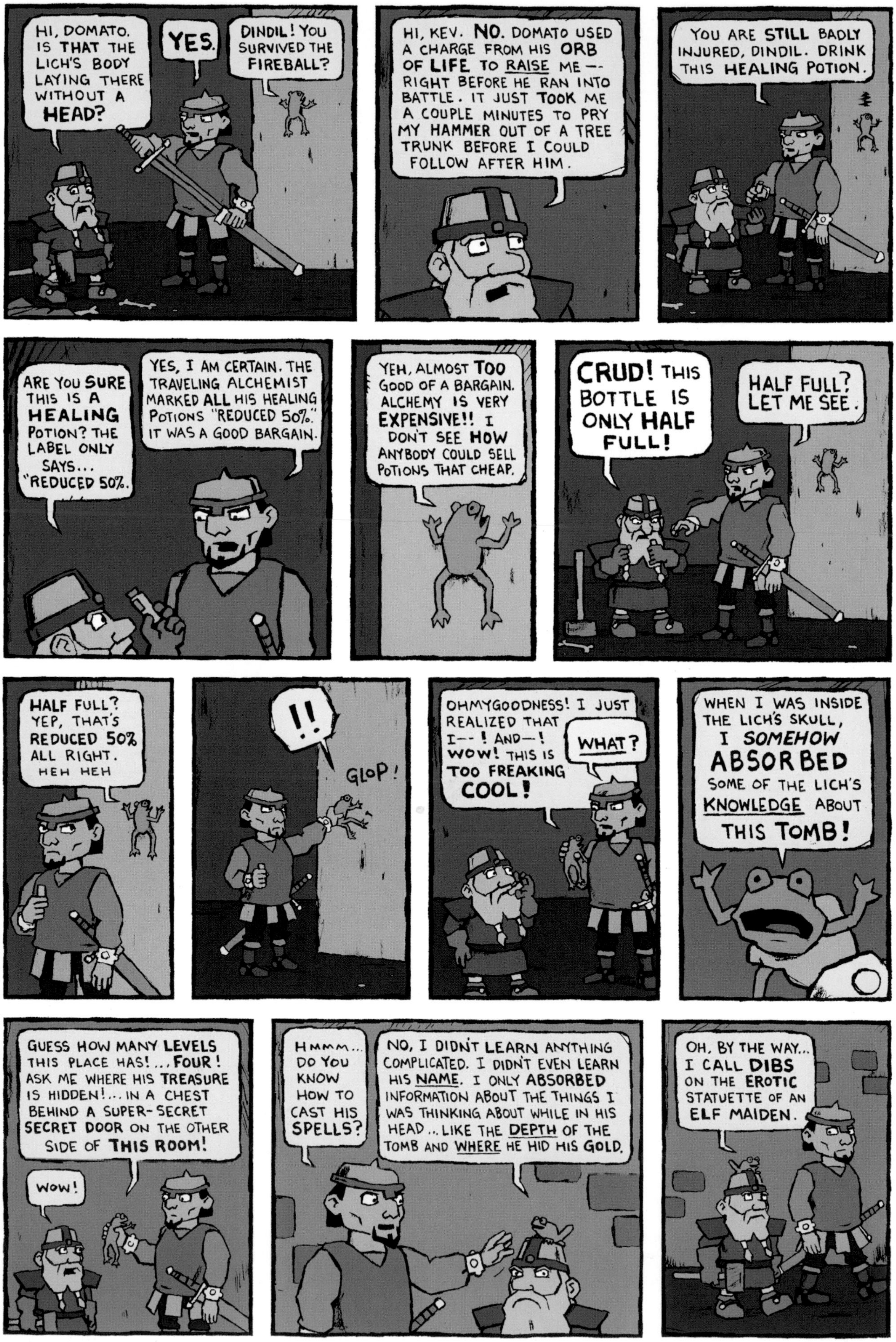
HI, DOMATO. IS THAT THE LICH'S BODY LAYING THERE WITHOUT A HEAD?
YES.
DINDIL! YOU SURVIVED THE FIREBALL?
HI, KEV. NO. DOMATO USED A CHARGE FROM HIS ORB OF LIFE TO RAISE ME -- RIGHT BEFORE HE RAN INTO BATTLE. IT JUST TOOK ME A COUPLE MINUTES TO PRY MY HAMMER OUT OF A TREE TRUNK BEFORE I COULD FOLLOW AFTER HIM.
YOU ARE STILL BADLY INJURED, DINDIL. DRINK THIS HEALING POTION.
ARE YOU SURE THIS IS A HEALING POTION? THE LABEL ONLY SAYS... "REDUCED 50%.
YES, I AM CERTAIN. THE TRAVELING ALCHEMIST MARKED ALL HIS HEALING POTIONS "REDUCED 50%." IT WAS A GOOD BARGAIN.
YEH, ALMOST TOO GOOD OF A BARGAIN. ALCHEMY IS VERY EXPENSIVE!! I DON'T SEE HOW ANYBODY COULD SELL POTIONS THAT CHEAP.
CRUD! THIS BOTTLE IS ONLY HALF FULL!
HALF FULL? LET ME SEE.
HALF FULL? YEP, THAT'S REDUCED 50% ALL RIGHT. HEH HEH
!!
GLOP!
OHMYGOODNESS! I JUST REALIZED THAT I-- ! AND--! WOW! THIS IS TOO FREAKING COOL!
WHAT?
WHEN I WAS INSIDE THE LICH'S SKULL, I SOMEHOW ABSORBED SOME OF THE LICH'S KNOWLEDGE ABOUT THIS TOMB!
GUESS HOW MANY LEVELS THIS PLACE HAS! ... FOUR! ASK ME WHERE HIS TREASURE IS HIDDEN! ... IN A CHEST BEHIND A SUPER-SECRET SECRET DOOR ON THE OTHER SIDE OF THIS ROOM!
WOW!
HMMM... DO YOU KNOW HOW TO CAST HIS SPELLS?
NO, I DIDN'T LEARN ANYTHING COMPLICATED. I DIDN'T EVEN LEARN HIS NAME. I ONLY ABSORBED INFORMATION ABOUT THE THINGS I WAS THINKING ABOUT WHILE IN HIS HEAD... LIKE THE DEPTH OF THE TOMB AND WHERE HE HID HIS GOLD.
OH, BY THE WAY... I CALL DIBS ON THE EROTIC STATUETTE OF AN ELF MAIDEN.

Warning! The last panel is Rated R in your imagination.

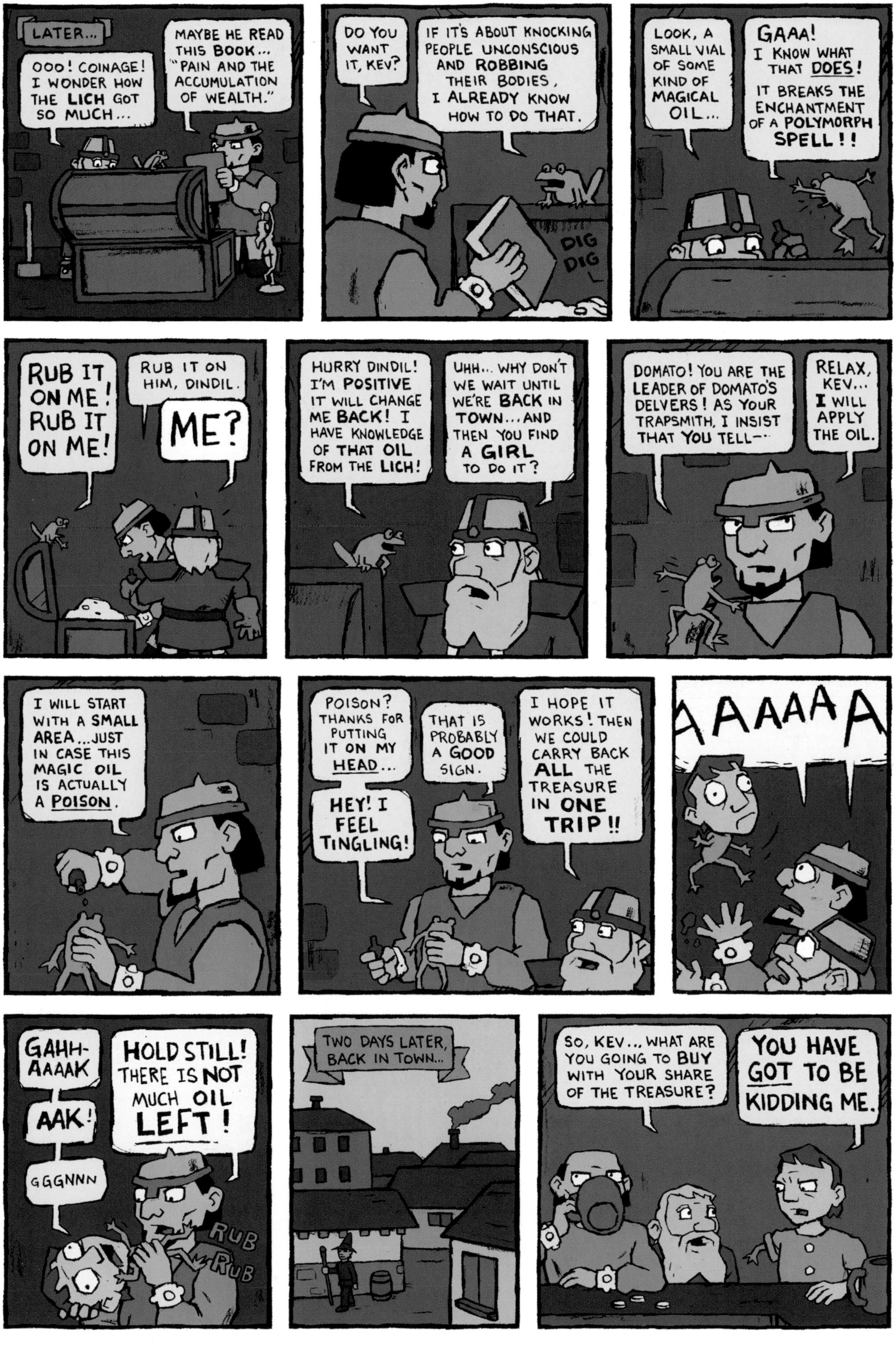
LATER...
OOO! COINAGE! I WONDER HOW THE LICH GOT SO MUCH...
MAYBE HE READ THIS BOOK... "PAIN AND THE ACCUMULATION OF WEALTH."
DO YOU WANT IT, KEV?
IF IT'S ABOUT KNOCKING PEOPLE UNCONSCIOUS AND ROBBING THEIR BODIES, I ALREADY KNOW HOW TO DO THAT.
DIG DIG
LOOK, A SMALL VIAL OF SOME KIND OF MAGICAL OIL...
GAAA! I KNOW WHAT THAT DOES! IT BREAKS THE ENCHANTMENT OF A POLYMORPH SPELL!!
RUB IT ON ME! RUB IT ON ME!
RUB IT ON HIM, DINDIL.
ME?
HURRY DINDIL! I'M POSITIVE IT WILL CHANGE ME BACK! I HAVE KNOWLEDGE OF THAT OIL FROM THE LICH!
UHH... WHY DON'T WE WAIT UNTIL WE'RE BACK IN TOWN... AND THEN YOU FIND A GIRL TO DO IT?
DOMATO! YOU ARE THE LEADER OF DOMATO'S DELVERS! AS YOUR TRAPSMITH, I INSIST THAT YOU TELL--
RELAX, KEV... I WILL APPLY THE OIL.
I WILL START WITH A SMALL AREA... JUST IN CASE THIS MAGIC OIL IS ACTUALLY A POISON.
POISON? THANKS FOR PUTTING IT ON MY HEAD...
THAT IS PROBABLY A GOOD SIGN.
I HOPE IT WORKS! THEN WE COULD CARRY BACK ALL THE TREASURE IN ONE TRIP!!
HEY! I FEEL TINGLING!
AAAAAA
GAHH-AAAAK
AAK!
GGGNNN
HOLD STILL! THERE IS NOT MUCH OIL LEFT!
RUB RUB
TWO DAYS LATER, BACK IN TOWN...
SO, KEV... WHAT ARE YOU GOING TO BUY WITH YOUR SHARE OF THE TREASURE?
YOU HAVE GOT TO BE KIDDING ME.

This and the three previous full-page strips appeared as a special four-page *Zogonia* strip in *Dragon* magazine.

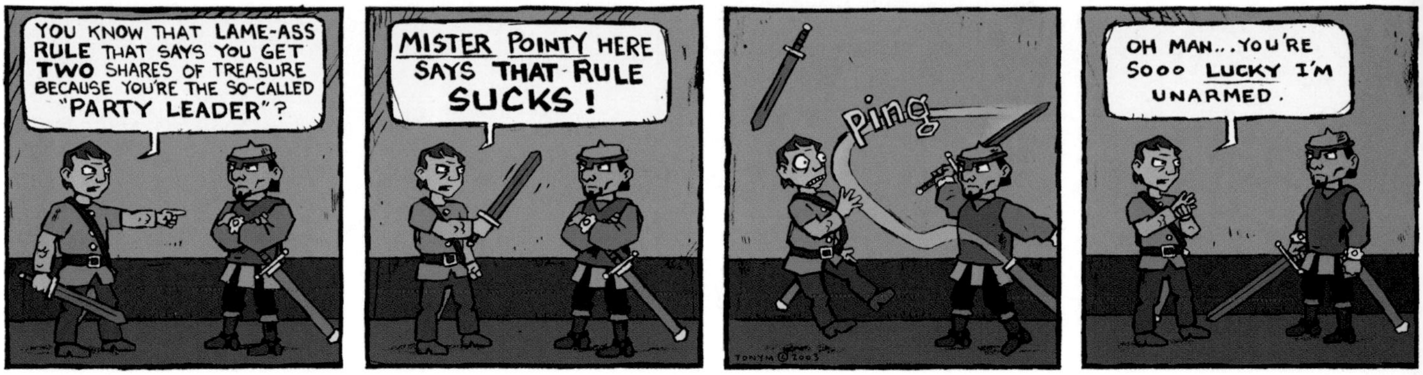
YOU KNOW THAT LAME-ASS RULE THAT SAYS YOU GET TWO SHARES OF TREASURE BECAUSE YOU'RE THE SO-CALLED "PARTY LEADER"?
MISTER POINTY HERE SAYS THAT RULE SUCKS!
Ping
OH MAN... YOU'RE SOOO LUCKY I'M UNARMED.
TONYM © 2003

Yes, Domato gets two shares of treasure. He also spends the extra share on the party, buying whatever he deems useful for the group, such as curative potions, maps to dungeons, charges for his *Orb of Life*, and so forth. It's an efficient system, and less complicated than asking Kev and Dindil to both pitch in money for every group-oriented purchase.

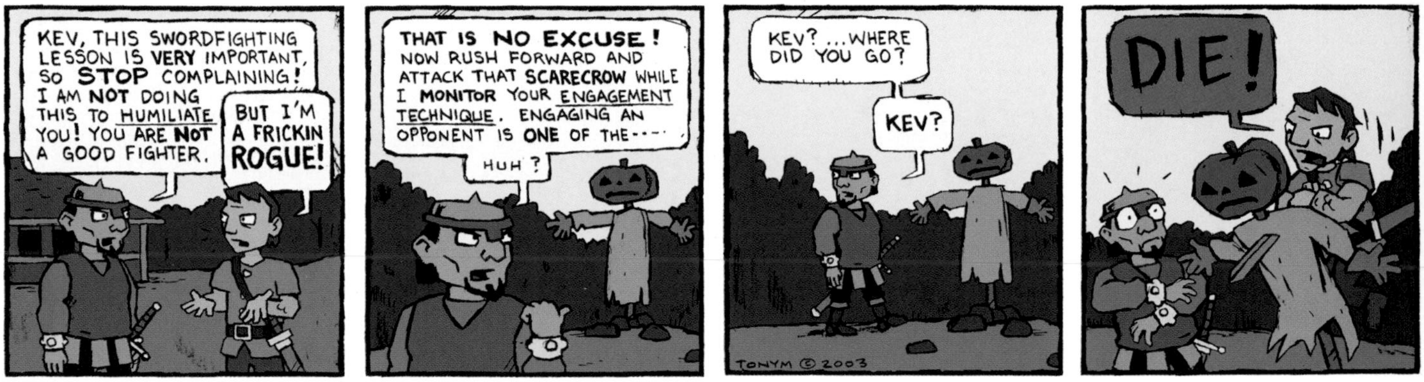
KEV, THIS SWORDFIGHTING LESSON IS VERY IMPORTANT, SO STOP COMPLAINING! I AM NOT DOING THIS TO HUMILIATE YOU! YOU ARE NOT A GOOD FIGHTER.
BUT I'M A FRICKIN ROGUE!
THAT IS NO EXCUSE! NOW RUSH FORWARD AND ATTACK THAT SCARECROW WHILE I MONITOR YOUR ENGAGEMENT TECHNIQUE. ENGAGING AN OPPONENT IS ONE OF THE---
HUH?
KEV? ...WHERE DID YOU GO?
KEV?
TONYM © 2003
DIE!

Critical Hit! Right through the scarecrow's heart! Well, if it had a heart...

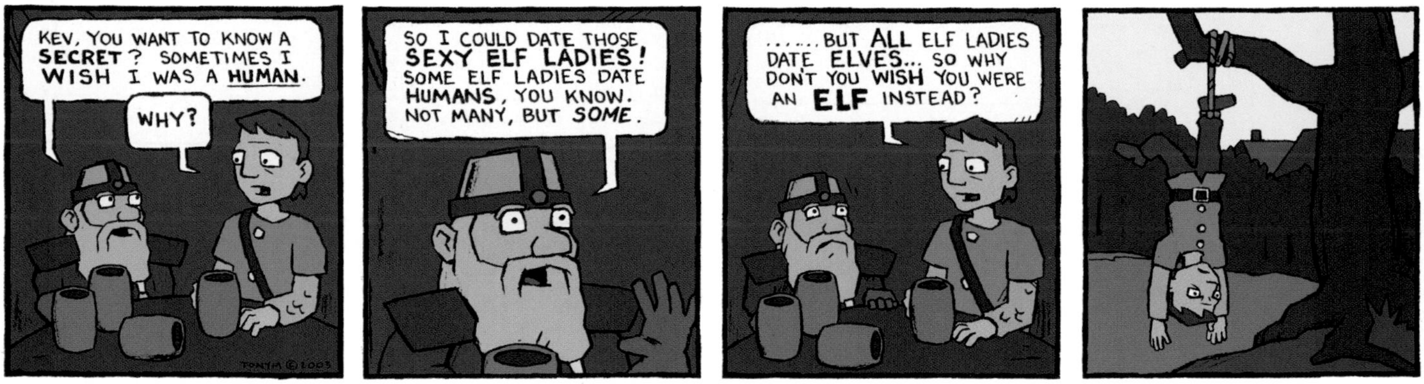
KEV, YOU WANT TO KNOW A SECRET? SOMETIMES I WISH I WAS A HUMAN.
WHY?
TONYM © 2003
SO I COULD DATE THOSE SEXY ELF LADIES! SOME ELF LADIES DATE HUMANS, YOU KNOW. NOT MANY, BUT SOME.
......BUT ALL ELF LADIES DATE ELVES... SO WHY DON'T YOU WISH YOU WERE AN ELF INSTEAD?

Poor Dindil. He loves the elf ladies, but will never kiss one. Or, rather, he'll never kiss a pretty one. If he kisses an elf girl, she'll be one of those hairy, three-legged elves, and will murder him afterward and drink his blood. Poor Dindil.

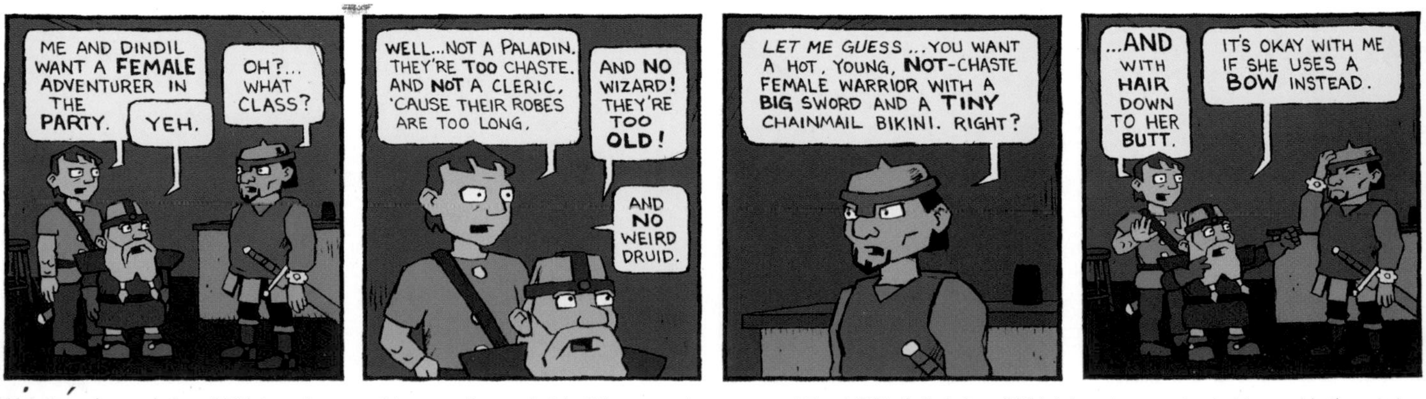
ME AND DINDIL WANT A FEMALE ADVENTURER IN THE PARTY.
YEH.
OH?... WHAT CLASS?
WELL...NOT A PALADIN. THEY'RE TOO CHASTE. AND NOT A CLERIC, 'CAUSE THEIR ROBES ARE TOO LONG.
AND NO WIZARD! THEY'RE TOO OLD!
AND NO WEIRD DRUID.
LET ME GUESS ...YOU WANT A HOT, YOUNG, NOT-CHASTE FEMALE WARRIOR WITH A BIG SWORD AND A TINY CHAINMAIL BIKINI. RIGHT?
...AND WITH HAIR DOWN TO HER BUTT.
IT'S OKAY WITH ME IF SHE USES A BOW INSTEAD.

Many people say chainmail bikinis are inappropriate armor for combat, but those people are wrong. At least 95% of all chainmail bikinis have been enchanted to provide the exact same protection as a full suit of plate armor.

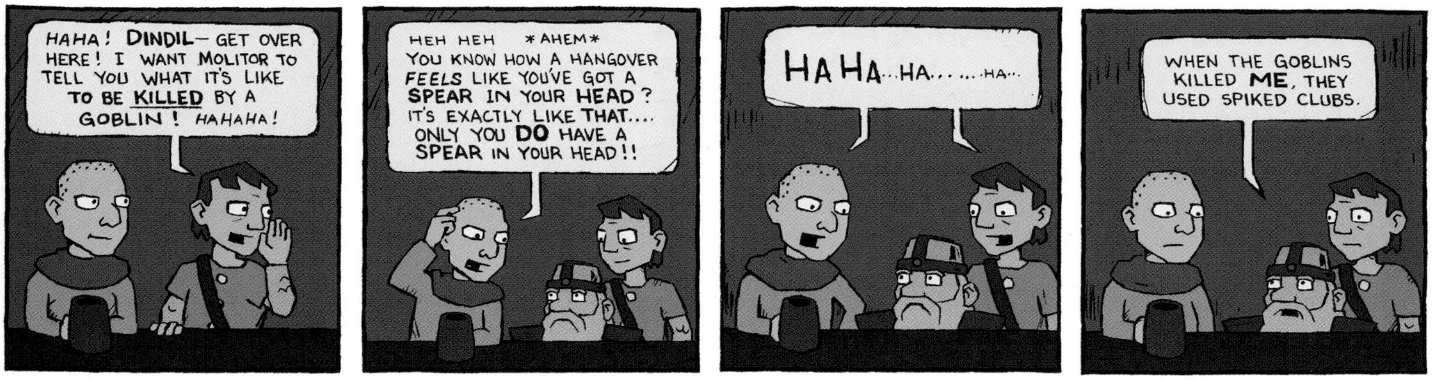
HAHA! DINDIL– GET OVER HERE! I WANT MOLITOR TO TELL YOU WHAT IT'S LIKE TO BE KILLED BY A GOBLIN! HAHAHA!
HEH HEH *AHEM* YOU KNOW HOW A HANGOVER FEELS LIKE YOU'VE GOT A SPEAR IN YOUR HEAD? IT'S EXACTLY LIKE THAT.... ONLY YOU DO HAVE A SPEAR IN YOUR HEAD!!
HAHA...HA.......HA...
WHEN THE GOBLINS KILLED ME, THEY USED SPIKED CLUBS.

Ow. Spiked clubs.

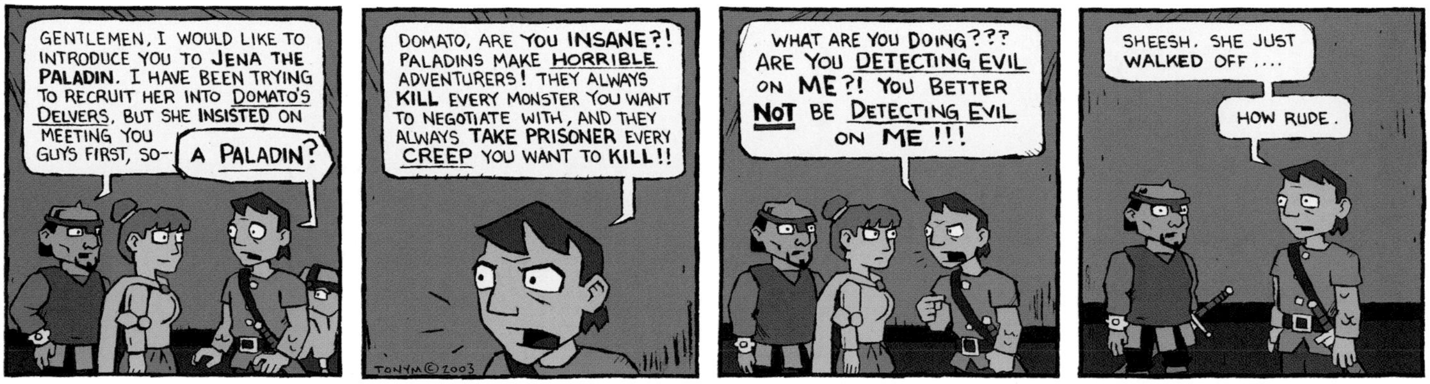
GENTLEMEN, I WOULD LIKE TO INTRODUCE YOU TO JENA THE PALADIN. I HAVE BEEN TRYING TO RECRUIT HER INTO DOMATO'S DELVERS, BUT SHE INSISTED ON MEETING YOU GUYS FIRST, SO–
A PALADIN?
DOMATO, ARE YOU INSANE?! PALADINS MAKE HORRIBLE ADVENTURERS! THEY ALWAYS KILL EVERY MONSTER YOU WANT TO NEGOTIATE WITH, AND THEY ALWAYS TAKE PRISONER EVERY CREEP YOU WANT TO KILL!!
TONYM © 2003
WHAT ARE YOU DOING??? ARE YOU DETECTING EVIL ON ME?! YOU BETTER NOT BE DETECTING EVIL ON ME!!!
SHEESH. SHE JUST WALKED OFF....
HOW RUDE.

This is one of those, "It's funny because it's true" cartoons. Paladins can be a pain. The last paladin I ran would say things like, "Speaking on behalf of my god, I demand that we immediately blah blah blah." Then he'd jiggle his battleaxe to communicate the price of heresy.

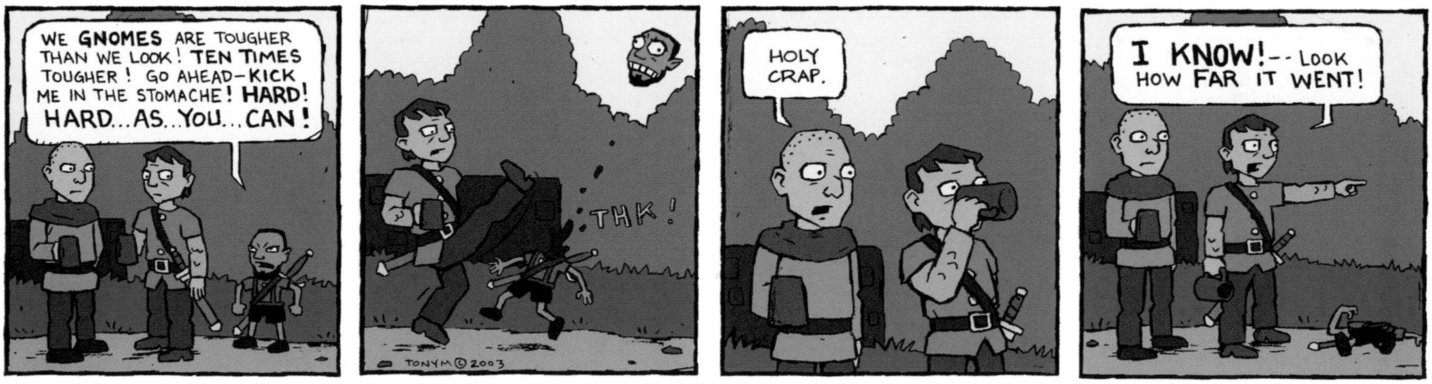
WE GNOMES ARE TOUGHER THAN WE LOOK! TEN TIMES TOUGHER! GO AHEAD–KICK ME IN THE STOMACHE! HARD! HARD...AS...YOU...CAN!
THK!
TONYM © 2003
HOLY CRAP.
I KNOW!-- LOOK HOW FAR IT WENT!

Vorpal shoes? Nope. Just bad aim versus a skinny neck.

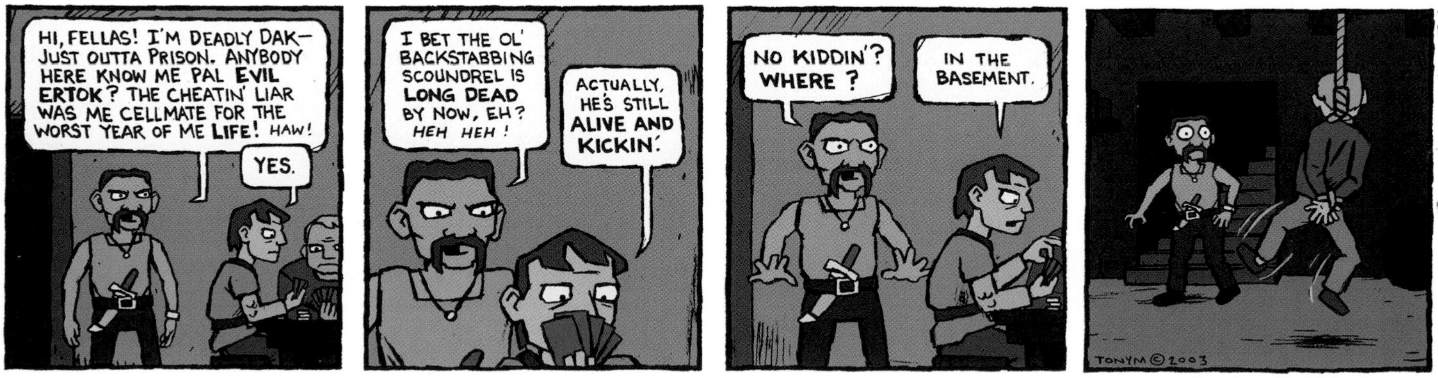
HI, FELLAS! I'M DEADLY DAK– JUST OUTTA PRISON. ANYBODY HERE KNOW ME PAL EVIL ERTOK? THE CHEATIN' LIAR WAS ME CELLMATE FOR THE WORST YEAR OF ME LIFE! HAW!
YES.
I BET THE OL' BACKSTABBING SCOUNDREL IS LONG DEAD BY NOW, EH? HEH HEH!
ACTUALLY, HE'S STILL ALIVE AND KICKIN'.
NO KIDDIN'? WHERE?
IN THE BASEMENT.
TONYM © 2003

If you're wondering what's inside the barrel in the fourth panel, the answer is "rope." In Zogonia, rope is often kept in a barrel. Either that, or it's empty. I forget which. It's been a while since I drew it.

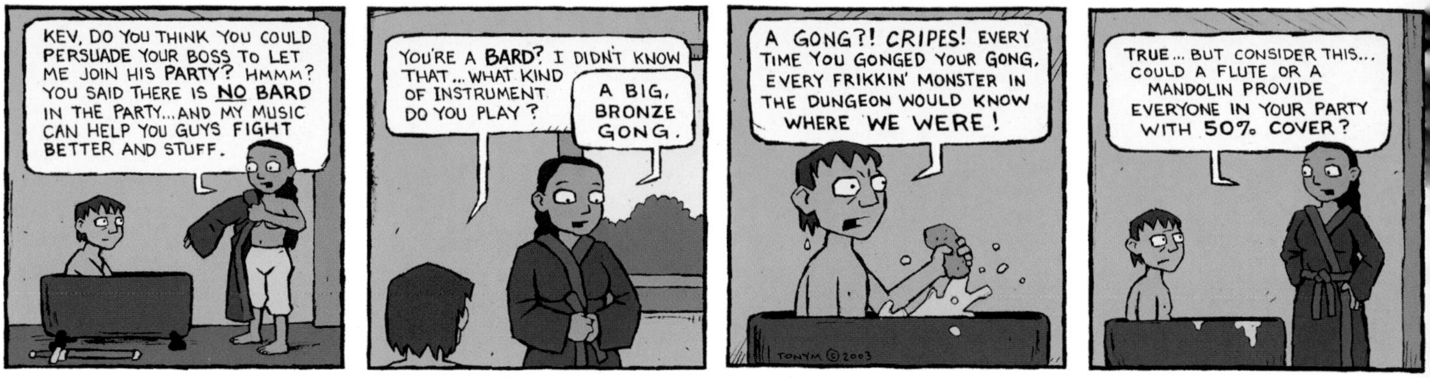

KEV, DO YOU THINK YOU COULD PERSUADE YOUR BOSS TO LET ME JOIN HIS PARTY? HMMM? YOU SAID THERE IS NO BARD IN THE PARTY... AND MY MUSIC CAN HELP YOU GUYS FIGHT BETTER AND STUFF.
YOU'RE A BARD? I DIDN'T KNOW THAT... WHAT KIND OF INSTRUMENT DO YOU PLAY?
A BIG, BRONZE GONG.
A GONG?! CRIPES! EVERY TIME YOU GONGED YOUR GONG, EVERY FRIKKIN' MONSTER IN THE DUNGEON WOULD KNOW WHERE WE WERE!
TRUE... BUT CONSIDER THIS... COULD A FLUTE OR A MANDOLIN PROVIDE EVERYONE IN YOUR PARTY WITH 50% COVER?

Notice how Kev's sword is next to the tub? That's because he recently used it to kill a water elemental in his bathroom. Yes, Kev is bathing in its blood. So to speak.

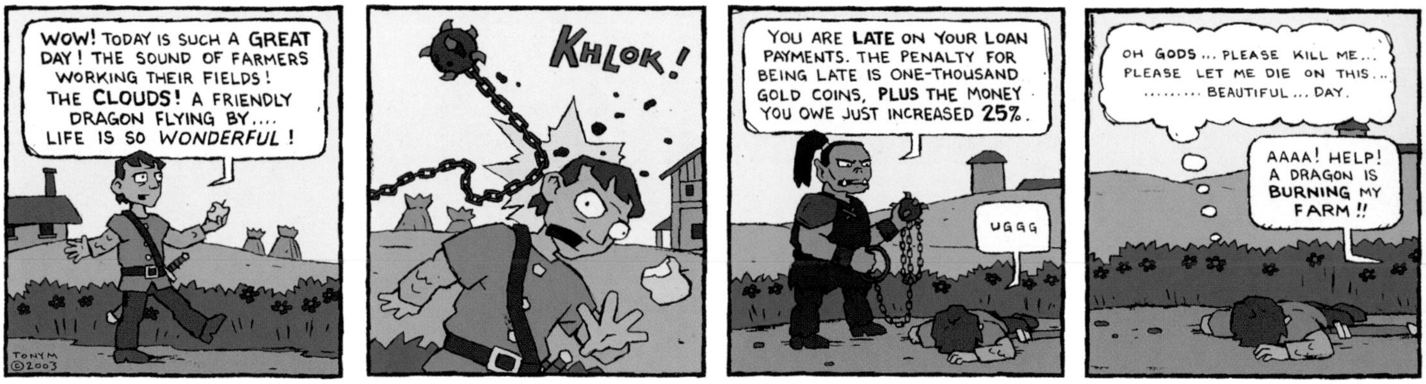

WOW! TODAY IS SUCH A GREAT DAY! THE SOUND OF FARMERS WORKING THEIR FIELDS! THE CLOUDS! A FRIENDLY DRAGON FLYING BY.... LIFE IS SO WONDERFUL!
KHLOK!
YOU ARE LATE ON YOUR LOAN PAYMENTS. THE PENALTY FOR BEING LATE IS ONE-THOUSAND GOLD COINS, PLUS THE MONEY YOU OWE JUST INCREASED 25%.
UGGG
OH GODS... PLEASE KILL ME... PLEASE LET ME DIE ON THIS... .... BEAUTIFUL... DAY.
AAAA! HELP! A DRAGON IS BURNING MY FARM!!

Life is like this cartoon, in a way. One moment everything is fine and dandy, then KHLOK! Spiked ball to the head!

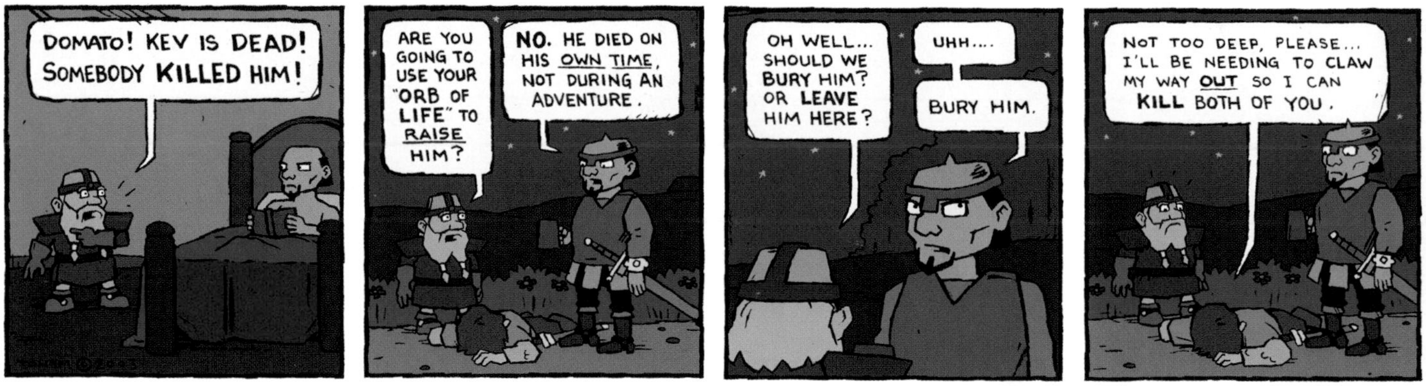

DOMATO! KEV IS DEAD! SOMEBODY KILLED HIM!
ARE YOU GOING TO USE YOUR "ORB OF LIFE" TO RAISE HIM?
NO. HE DIED ON HIS OWN TIME, NOT DURING AN ADVENTURE.
OH WELL... SHOULD WE BURY HIM? OR LEAVE HIM HERE?
UHH....
BURY HIM.
NOT TOO DEEP, PLEASE... I'LL BE NEEDING TO CLAW MY WAY OUT SO I CAN KILL BOTH OF YOU.

Poor Kev. Lying on the ground, with his face in an anthill.

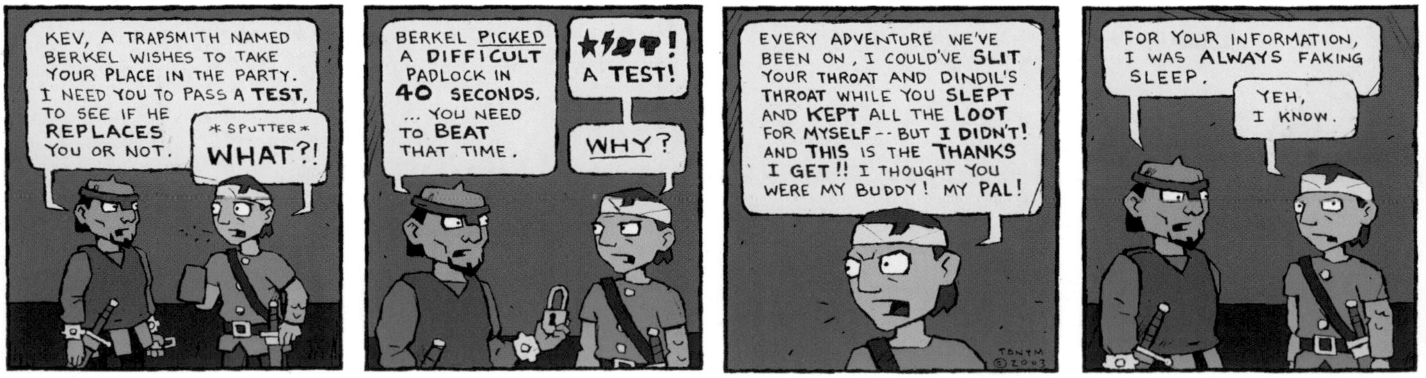

KEV, A TRAPSMITH NAMED BERKEL WISHES TO TAKE YOUR PLACE IN THE PARTY. I NEED YOU TO PASS A TEST, TO SEE IF HE REPLACES YOU OR NOT.
SPUTTER WHAT?!
BERKEL PICKED A DIFFICULT PADLOCK IN 40 SECONDS. ... YOU NEED TO BEAT THAT TIME.
A TEST!
WHY?
EVERY ADVENTURE WE'VE BEEN ON, I COULD'VE SLIT YOUR THROAT AND DINDIL'S THROAT WHILE YOU SLEPT AND KEPT ALL THE LOOT FOR MYSELF -- BUT I DIDN'T! AND THIS IS THE THANKS I GET!! I THOUGHT YOU WERE MY BUDDY! MY PAL!
FOR YOUR INFORMATION, I WAS ALWAYS FAKING SLEEP.
YEH, I KNOW.

No job security for Kev.

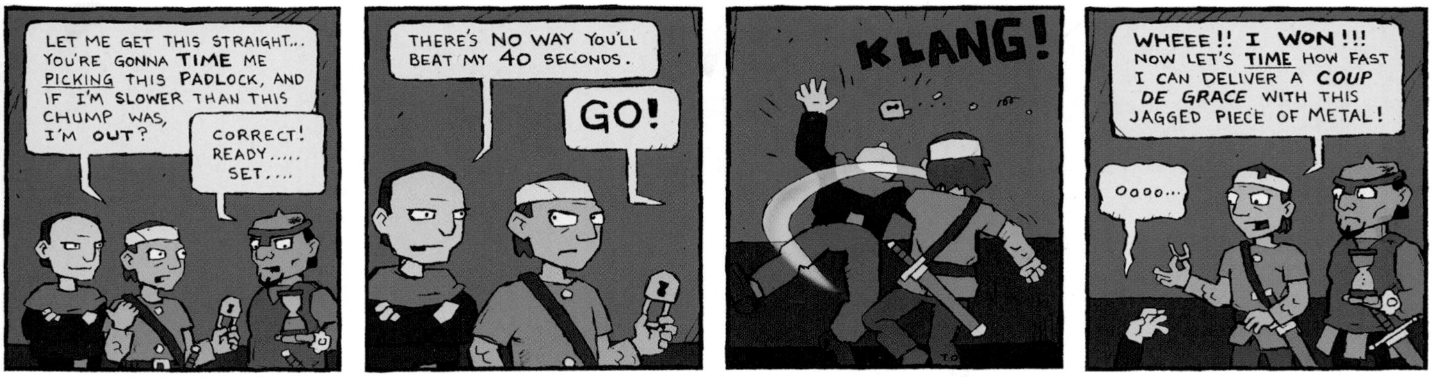
LET ME GET THIS STRAIGHT... YOU'RE GONNA TIME ME PICKING THIS PADLOCK, AND IF I'M SLOWER THAN THIS CHUMP WAS, I'M OUT?
CORRECT! READY..... SET....
THERE'S NO WAY YOU'LL BEAT MY 40 SECONDS.
GO!
KLANG!
WHEEE!! I WON!!! NOW LET'S TIME HOW FAST I CAN DELIVER A COUP DE GRACE WITH THIS JAGGED PIECE OF METAL!
OOOO...

Critical!

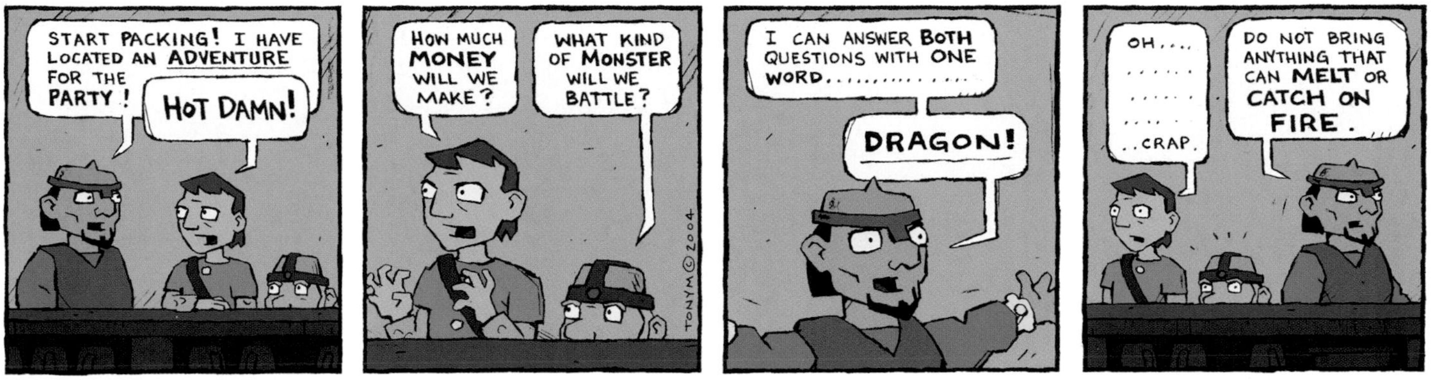
START PACKING! I HAVE LOCATED AN ADVENTURE FOR THE PARTY!
HOT DAMN!
HOW MUCH MONEY WILL WE MAKE?
WHAT KIND OF MONSTER WILL WE BATTLE?
I CAN ANSWER BOTH QUESTIONS WITH ONE WORD..............
DRAGON!
OH.... ....CRAP.
DO NOT BRING ANYTHING THAT CAN MELT OR CATCH ON FIRE.

Domato's Delvers are going after a dragon? A frikkin' dragon? Holy crap.

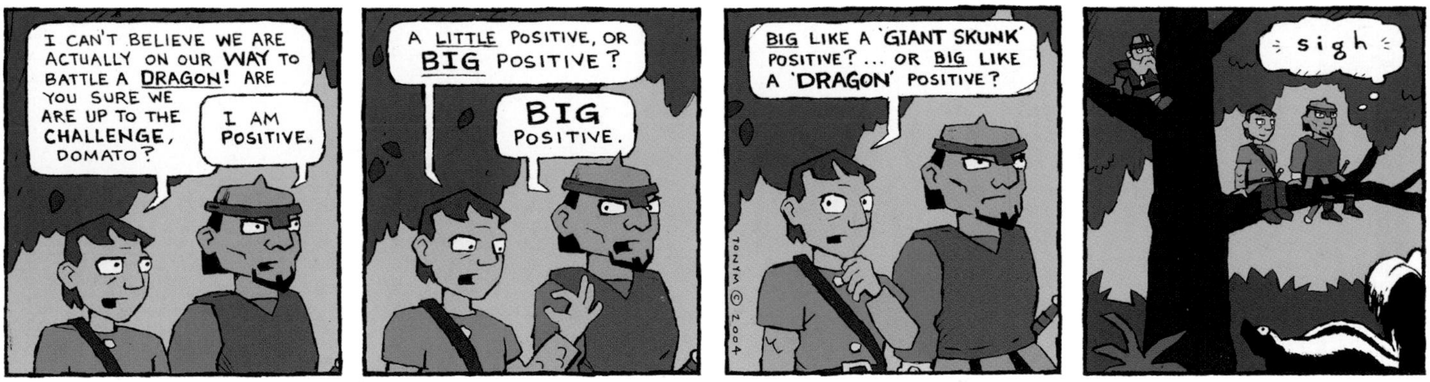
I CAN'T BELIEVE WE ARE ACTUALLY ON OUR WAY TO BATTLE A DRAGON! ARE YOU SURE WE ARE UP TO THE CHALLENGE, DOMATO?
I AM POSITIVE.
A LITTLE POSITIVE, OR BIG POSITIVE?
BIG POSITIVE.
BIG LIKE A 'GIANT SKUNK' POSITIVE?... OR BIG LIKE A 'DRAGON' POSITIVE?
sigh

Regardless of one's skill as a warrior, nobody will risk being sprayed by a giant skunk if there is any other alternative available.

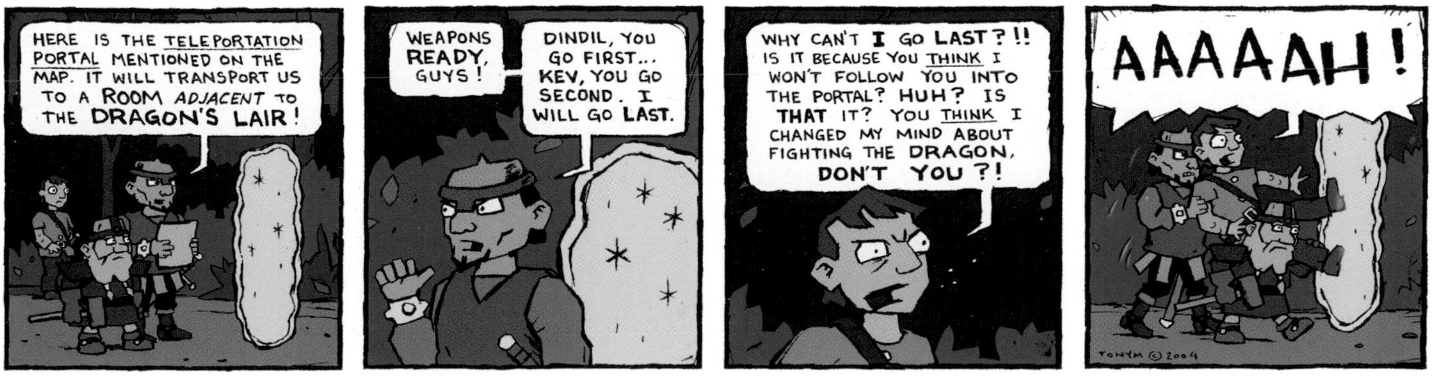
HERE IS THE TELEPORTATION PORTAL MENTIONED ON THE MAP. IT WILL TRANSPORT US TO A ROOM ADJACENT TO THE DRAGON'S LAIR!
WEAPONS READY, GUYS!
DINDIL, YOU GO FIRST... KEV, YOU GO SECOND. I WILL GO LAST.
WHY CAN'T I GO LAST?!! IS IT BECAUSE YOU THINK I WON'T FOLLOW YOU INTO THE PORTAL? HUH? IS THAT IT? YOU THINK I CHANGED MY MIND ABOUT FIGHTING THE DRAGON, DON'T YOU?!
AAAAAH!

Poor Kev. His fellow adventurers have become aware of his knack for self-preservation.

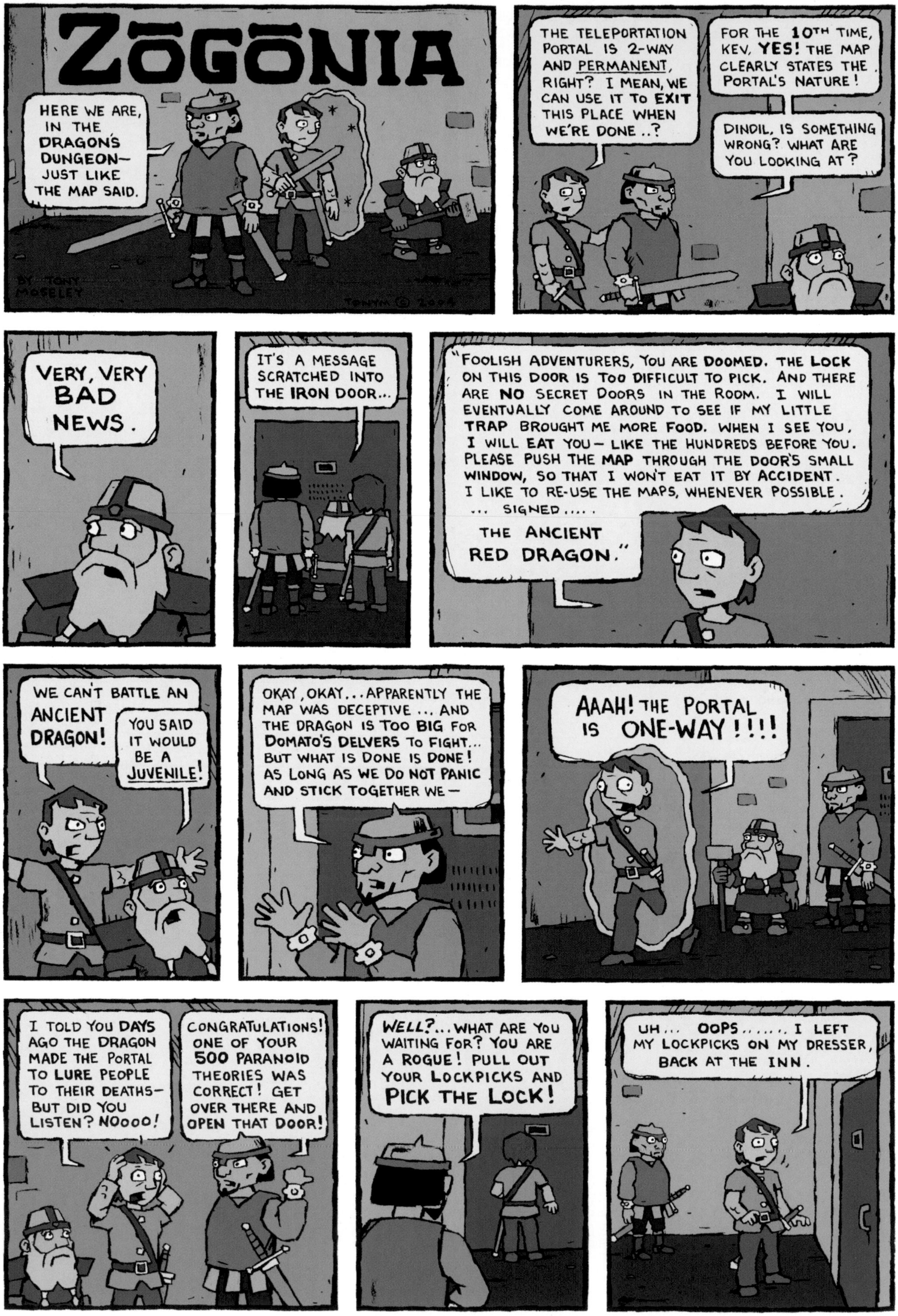
ZŌGŌNIA
HERE WE ARE, IN THE DRAGON'S DUNGEON— JUST LIKE THE MAP SAID.
BY TONY MOSELEY
THE TELEPORTATION PORTAL IS 2-WAY AND PERMANENT, RIGHT? I MEAN, WE CAN USE IT TO EXIT THIS PLACE WHEN WE'RE DONE ..?
FOR THE 10TH TIME, KEV, YES! THE MAP CLEARLY STATES THE PORTAL'S NATURE!
DINDIL, IS SOMETHING WRONG? WHAT ARE YOU LOOKING AT?
VERY, VERY BAD NEWS.
IT'S A MESSAGE SCRATCHED INTO THE IRON DOOR...
"FOOLISH ADVENTURERS, YOU ARE DOOMED. THE LOCK ON THIS DOOR IS TOO DIFFICULT TO PICK. AND THERE ARE NO SECRET DOORS IN THE ROOM. I WILL EVENTUALLY COME AROUND TO SEE IF MY LITTLE TRAP BROUGHT ME MORE FOOD. WHEN I SEE YOU, I WILL EAT YOU— LIKE THE HUNDREDS BEFORE YOU. PLEASE PUSH THE MAP THROUGH THE DOOR'S SMALL WINDOW, SO THAT I WON'T EAT IT BY ACCIDENT. I LIKE TO RE-USE THE MAPS, WHENEVER POSSIBLE. ... SIGNED ..... THE ANCIENT RED DRAGON."
WE CAN'T BATTLE AN ANCIENT DRAGON!
YOU SAID IT WOULD BE A JUVENILE!
OKAY, OKAY... APPARENTLY THE MAP WAS DECEPTIVE ... AND THE DRAGON IS TOO BIG FOR DOMATO'S DELVERS TO FIGHT... BUT WHAT IS DONE IS DONE! AS LONG AS WE DO NOT PANIC AND STICK TOGETHER WE—
AAAH! THE PORTAL IS ONE-WAY!!!!
I TOLD YOU DAYS AGO THE DRAGON MADE THE PORTAL TO LURE PEOPLE TO THEIR DEATHS— BUT DID YOU LISTEN? NOOOO!
CONGRATULATIONS! ONE OF YOUR 500 PARANOID THEORIES WAS CORRECT! GET OVER THERE AND OPEN THAT DOOR!
WELL?... WHAT ARE YOU WAITING FOR? YOU ARE A ROGUE! PULL OUT YOUR LOCKPICKS AND PICK THE LOCK!
UH... OOPS .... I LEFT MY LOCKPICKS ON MY DRESSER, BACK AT THE INN.

It's times like this that Domato probably wishes he had a wizard in the party. Spells can be pretty handy. Oh well. Too late now!

YOU FORGOT Y-Y-YOUR... LOCKPICKS?! *sputter* YOU HAVE DOOMED US ALL!!

IT WASN'T MY FAULT! I WAS IN A HURRY BECAUSE I OVERSLEPT! PLUS I WAS HUNGOVER.

YA WANT ME TO KILL HIM? SAY THE WORD, DOMATO, AND THE THIEF IS MUSH.

MUSH? .... ACTUALLY, DINDIL... THAT IS A GREAT IDEA!

FIRST OF ALL, I'M **NOT** A THIEF! SECOND OF ALL KILLING ME WON'T GET THAT DOOR UNLOCKED! SO FORGET IT!!!

YES IT WILL! LISTEN! OKAY, STEP 1: DINDIL **KILLS** YOU. STEP 2: DINDIL SMASHES YOUR BODY UNTIL IT IS SEPARATED INTO SMALL PIECES — EACH ONE ABOUT **THIS** BIG...

STEP 3: WE PUSH YOUR BODY-CHUNKS **THROUGH** THE SMALL WINDOW IN THE DOOR. STEP 4: I HOLD YOUR LAST PIECE OUTSIDE THE WINDOW... STEP 5: I INVOKE MY **ORB OF LIFE** AND *RAISE* YOU-- OUTSIDE THE **DOOR**!!

STEP 6: YOU GO AND LOCATE THE **KEY** TO THE DOOR... BRING IT HERE, UNLOCK THE DOOR AND WE ESCAPE!

BUT I DON'T WANT TO BE KILLED!!

YOUR **DEATH** IS OUR ONLY CHANCE FOR ESCAPE...

YEH, SO **STOP** BEING SUCH A **WIMP** AND LAY YOUR HEAD ON THE FLOOR... RIGHT **THERE**, SO I CAN SMASH IT.

IT'S AN AWESOME PLAN, I ADMIT IT...BUT LET'S KILL **DINDIL** INSTEAD! HE'S **USED** TO BEING KILLED!

NO, I'M **NOT**!

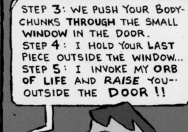

FEH! YOU DIE SO OFTEN, WE OUGHT TO CALL DOMATO'S **ORB OF LIFE** AN **ORB OF DWARF-RAISING**! HE'S NEVER EVEN **USED** IT ON ME BEFORE!

I DIE BECAUSE I'M **BRAVE**!

THE ONLY REASON YOU'VE NEVER DIED IN A FIGHT IS BECAUSE YOU ALWAYS **COWER** IN A SHADOW UNTIL THE FIGHT'S OVER!

HOW **DARE** YOU!!

SKULKING IN THE SHADOWS IS MY STRATEGY!

YEH!! **SURVIVAL** STRATEGY!

BE CAREFUL, GUYS... I ONLY NEED **ONE** DEAD BODY.

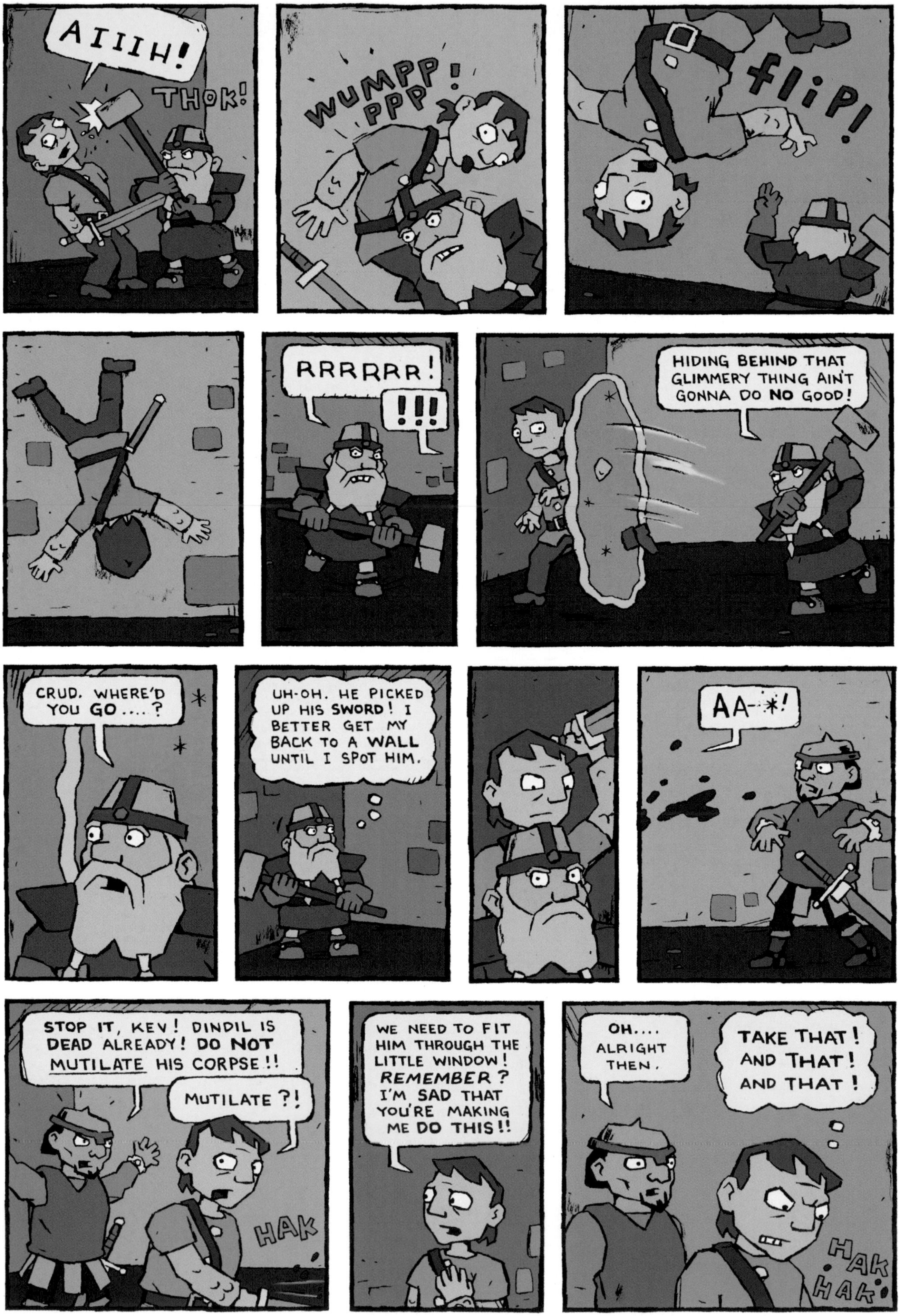
AIIIH!
THOK!
WUMPP PPP!
fliP!
RRRRRR!
!!!
HIDING BEHIND THAT GLIMMERY THING AIN'T GONNA DO NO GOOD!
CRUD. WHERE'D YOU GO....?
UH-OH. HE PICKED UP HIS SWORD! I BETTER GET MY BACK TO A WALL UNTIL I SPOT HIM.
AA-*!
STOP IT, KEV! DINDIL IS DEAD ALREADY! DO NOT MUTILATE HIS CORPSE!!
MUTILATE?!
HAK
WE NEED TO FIT HIM THROUGH THE LITTLE WINDOW! REMEMBER? I'M SAD THAT YOU'RE MAKING ME DO THIS!!
OH.... ALRIGHT THEN.
TAKE THAT! AND THAT! AND THAT!
HAK HAK

Yep, *Zogonia* is not for the squeamish! Not after this page, at least.

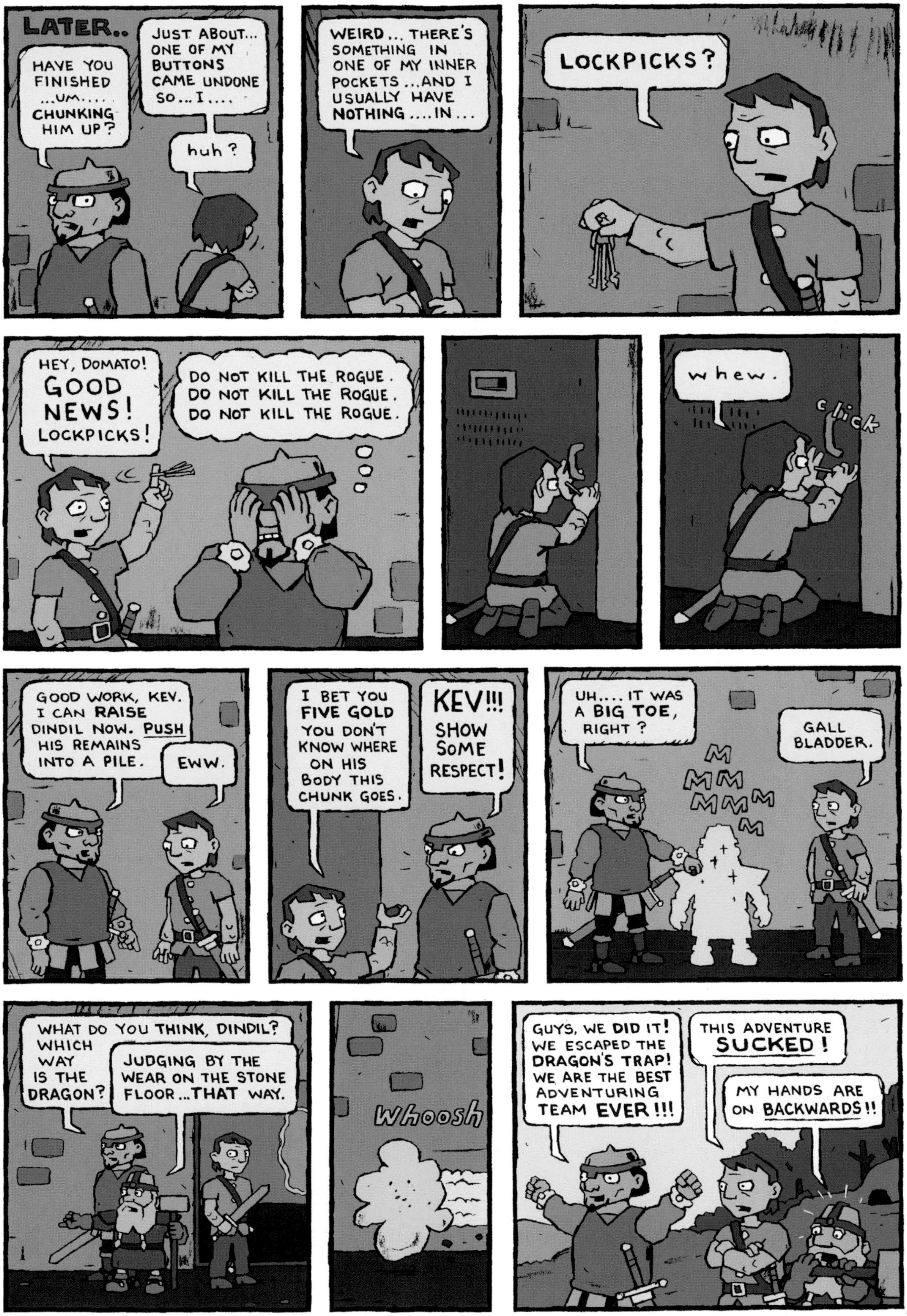
LATER..
HAVE YOU FINISHED ...UM.... CHUNKING HIM UP?
JUST ABOUT... ONE OF MY BUTTONS CAME UNDONE SO... I....
huh?
WEIRD... THERE'S SOMETHING IN ONE OF MY INNER POCKETS ...AND I USUALLY HAVE NOTHING ....IN...
LOCKPICKS?
HEY, DOMATO! GOOD NEWS! LOCKPICKS!
DO NOT KILL THE ROGUE. DO NOT KILL THE ROGUE. DO NOT KILL THE ROGUE.
whew.
click
GOOD WORK, KEV. I CAN RAISE DINDIL NOW. PUSH HIS REMAINS INTO A PILE.
EWW.
I BET YOU FIVE GOLD YOU DON'T KNOW WHERE ON HIS BODY THIS CHUNK GOES.
KEV!!! SHOW SOME RESPECT!
UH.... IT WAS A BIG TOE, RIGHT?
M MM MMMM M
GALL BLADDER.
WHAT DO YOU THINK, DINDIL? WHICH WAY IS THE DRAGON?
JUDGING BY THE WEAR ON THE STONE FLOOR ...THAT WAY.
Whoosh
GUYS, WE DID IT! WE ESCAPED THE DRAGON'S TRAP! WE ARE THE BEST ADVENTURING TEAM EVER!!!
THIS ADVENTURE SUCKED!
MY HANDS ARE ON BACKWARDS!!

All's well that ends with everybody not eaten by a dragon.

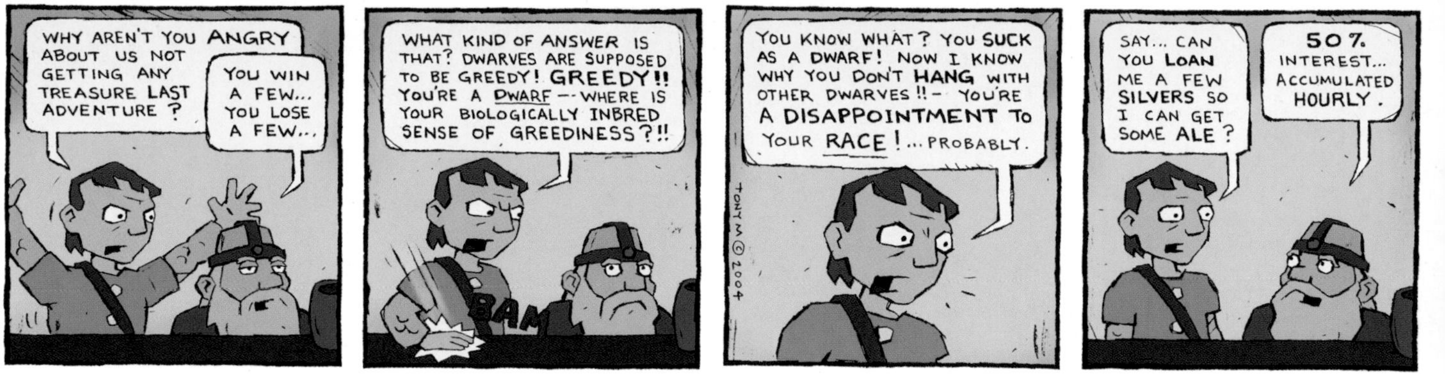
WHY AREN'T YOU ANGRY ABOUT US NOT GETTING ANY TREASURE LAST ADVENTURE ?
YOU WIN A FEW... YOU LOSE A FEW...
WHAT KIND OF ANSWER IS THAT? DWARVES ARE SUPPOSED TO BE GREEDY! GREEDY!! YOU'RE A DWARF -- WHERE IS YOUR BIOLOGICALLY INBRED SENSE OF GREEDINESS?!!
BAM
YOU KNOW WHAT? YOU SUCK AS A DWARF! NOW I KNOW WHY YOU DON'T HANG WITH OTHER DWARVES!! - YOU'RE A DISAPPOINTMENT TO YOUR RACE! ... PROBABLY.
SAY... CAN YOU LOAN ME A FEW SILVERS SO I CAN GET SOME ALE ?
50%. INTEREST... ACCUMULATED HOURLY.

Not getting any treasure at the end of an adventure sucks.

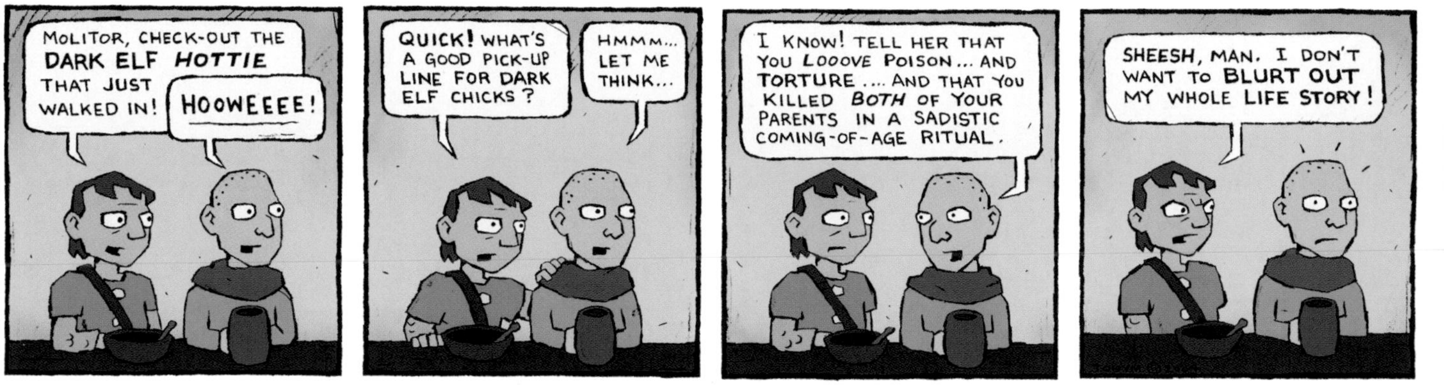
MOLITOR, CHECK-OUT THE DARK ELF HOTTIE THAT JUST WALKED IN!
HOOWEEEE!
QUICK! WHAT'S A GOOD PICK-UP LINE FOR DARK ELF CHICKS ?
HMMM... LET ME THINK...
I KNOW! TELL HER THAT YOU LOOOVE POISON... AND TORTURE .... AND THAT YOU KILLED BOTH OF YOUR PARENTS IN A SADISTIC COMING-OF-AGE RITUAL.
SHEESH, MAN. I DON'T WANT TO BLURT OUT MY WHOLE LIFE STORY!

I was thinking of the Drizzt novels when I made this strip. In those books, the dark elves have extremely dysfunctional families.

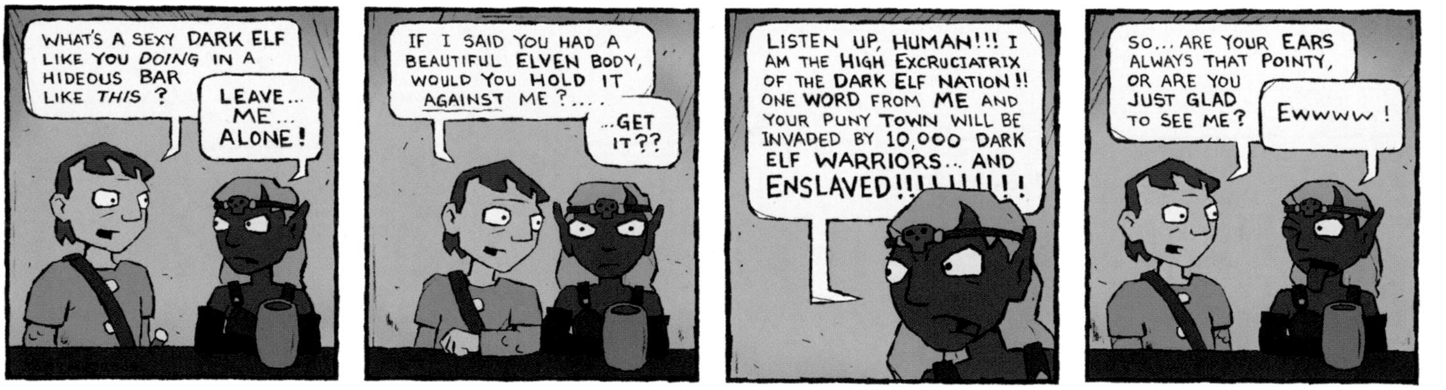
WHAT'S A SEXY DARK ELF LIKE YOU DOING IN A HIDEOUS BAR LIKE THIS ?
LEAVE... ME... ALONE!
IF I SAID YOU HAD A BEAUTIFUL ELVEN BODY, WOULD YOU HOLD IT AGAINST ME ?....
...GET IT??
LISTEN UP, HUMAN!!! I AM THE HIGH EXCRUCIATRIX OF THE DARK ELF NATION!! ONE WORD FROM ME AND YOUR PUNY TOWN WILL BE INVADED BY 10,000 DARK ELF WARRIORS... AND ENSLAVED!!!!!!!!!!!
SO... ARE YOUR EARS ALWAYS THAT POINTY, OR ARE YOU JUST GLAD TO SEE ME?
EWWWW!

Within this bar alone, Kev has started six different wars while trying to pick up women.

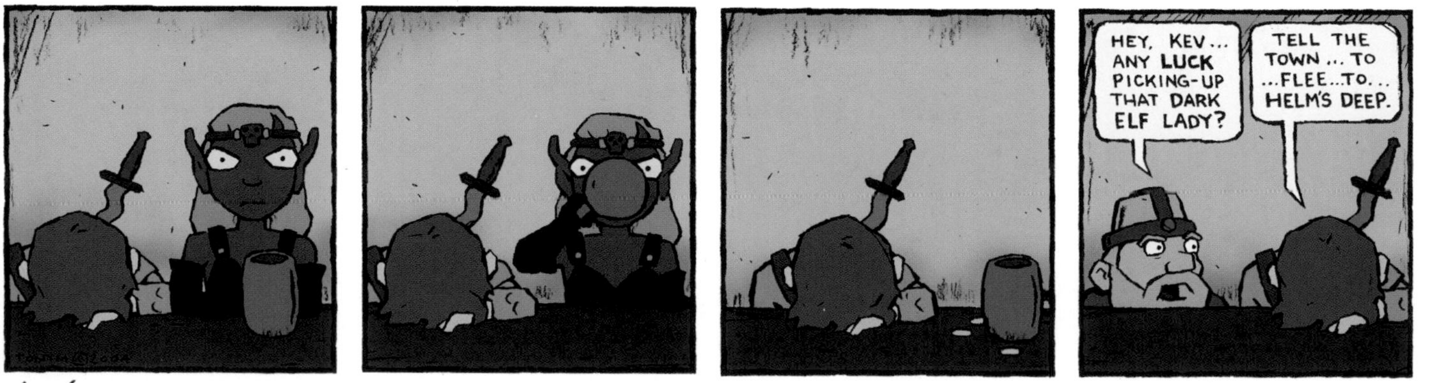
HEY, KEV... ANY LUCK PICKING-UP THAT DARK ELF LADY?
TELL THE TOWN... TO ...FLEE...TO... HELM'S DEEP.

Dang. Kev struck out with the dark elf chick. On the bright side, though, he got himself a fancy dagger for free!

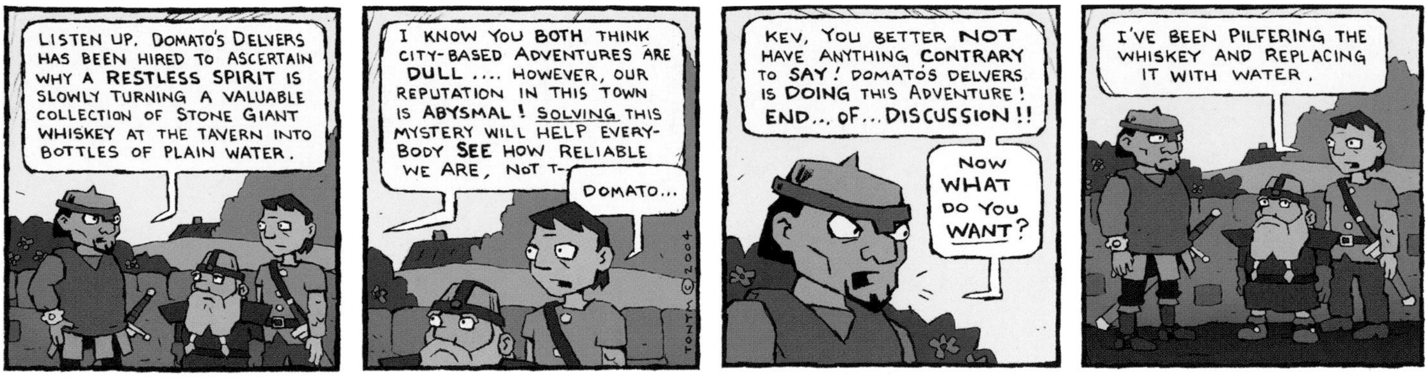
LISTEN UP. DOMATO'S DELVERS HAS BEEN HIRED TO ASCERTAIN WHY A RESTLESS SPIRIT IS SLOWLY TURNING A VALUABLE COLLECTION OF STONE GIANT WHISKEY AT THE TAVERN INTO BOTTLES OF PLAIN WATER.
I KNOW YOU BOTH THINK CITY-BASED ADVENTURES ARE DULL .... HOWEVER, OUR REPUTATION IN THIS TOWN IS ABYSMAL! SOLVING THIS MYSTERY WILL HELP EVERY-BODY SEE HOW RELIABLE WE ARE, NOT T-
DOMATO...
KEV, YOU BETTER NOT HAVE ANYTHING CONTRARY TO SAY! DOMATO'S DELVERS IS DOING THIS ADVENTURE! END... OF... DISCUSSION!!
NOW WHAT DO YOU WANT?
I'VE BEEN PILFERING THE WHISKEY AND REPLACING IT WITH WATER.

See that house in the background? In the basement of that house is a wooden crate containing a healing potion and four gold coins. Yes, my strips are that intricate—even the background houses have cool stuff in them!

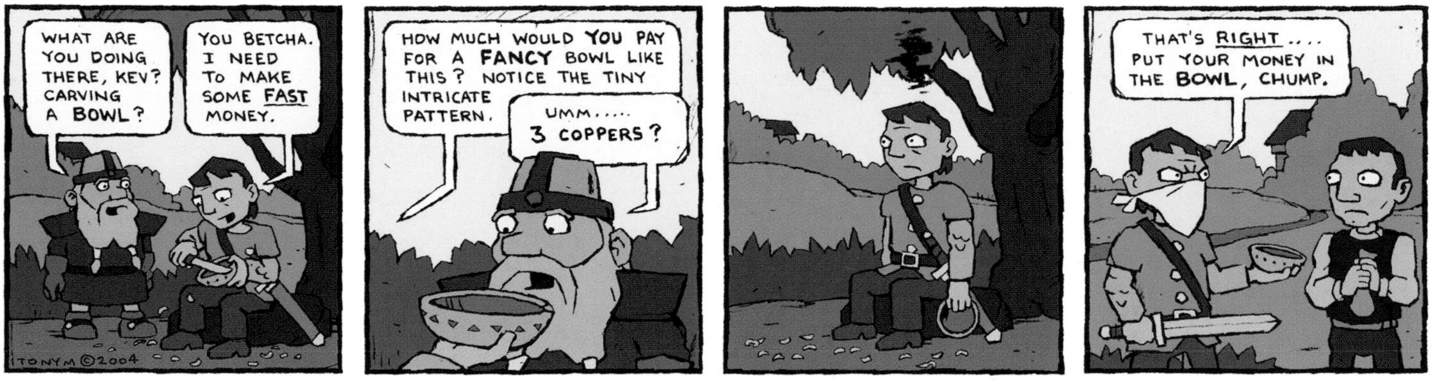
WHAT ARE YOU DOING THERE, KEV? CARVING A BOWL?
YOU BETCHA. I NEED TO MAKE SOME FAST MONEY.
TONYM ©2004
HOW MUCH WOULD YOU PAY FOR A FANCY BOWL LIKE THIS? NOTICE THE TINY INTRICATE PATTERN.
UMM..... 3 COPPERS?
THAT'S RIGHT .... PUT YOUR MONEY IN THE BOWL, CHUMP.

A typical bowl runs about 2 coppers, so 3 coppers is not a terrible price for a bowl... unless you were hoping for 100+ gold, like Kev.

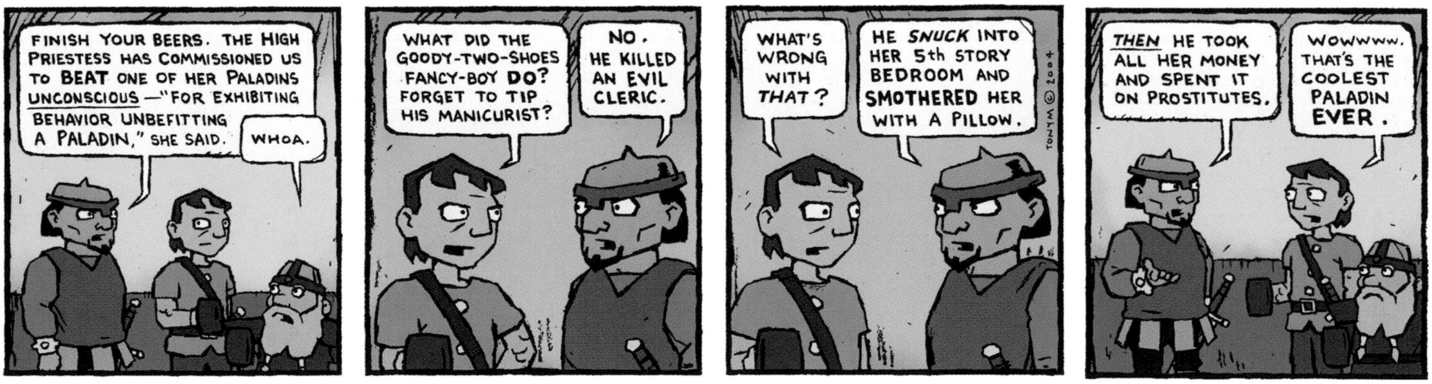
FINISH YOUR BEERS. THE HIGH PRIESTESS HAS COMMISSIONED US TO BEAT ONE OF HER PALADINS UNCONSCIOUS—"FOR EXHIBITING BEHAVIOR UNBEFITTING A PALADIN," SHE SAID.
WHOA.
WHAT DID THE GOODY-TWO-SHOES FANCY-BOY DO? FORGET TO TIP HIS MANICURIST?
NO. HE KILLED AN EVIL CLERIC.
WHAT'S WRONG WITH THAT?
HE SNUCK INTO HER 5th STORY BEDROOM AND SMOTHERED HER WITH A PILLOW.
TONYM © 2004
THEN HE TOOK ALL HER MONEY AND SPENT IT ON PROSTITUTES.
WOWWWW. THAT'S THE COOLEST PALADIN EVER.

Most nights, this paladin lurks in dark alleys, covertly detecting evil on passersby. If somebody pings as evil, he throws a poisoned knife into the offender's back and runs away, laughing.

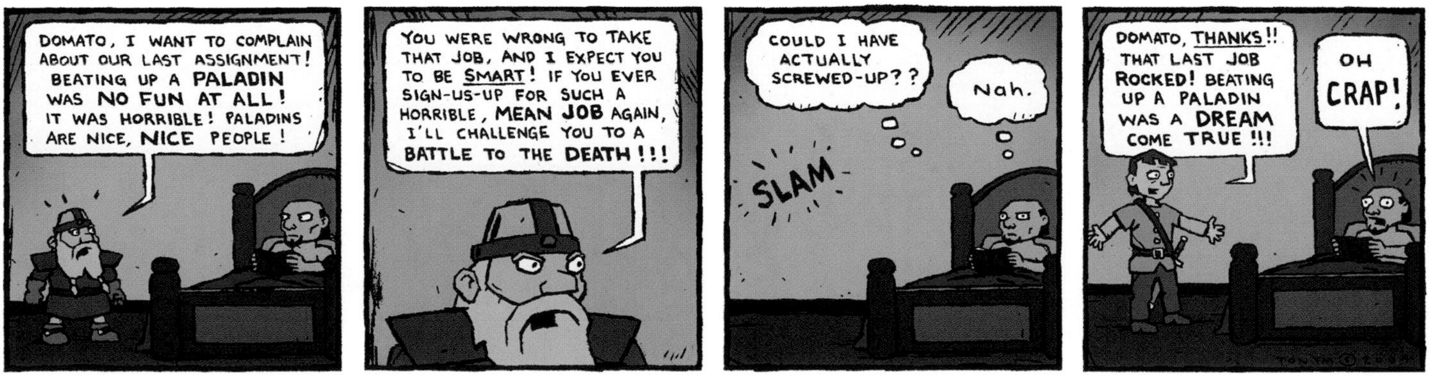
DOMATO, I WANT TO COMPLAIN ABOUT OUR LAST ASSIGNMENT! BEATING UP A PALADIN WAS NO FUN AT ALL! IT WAS HORRIBLE! PALADINS ARE NICE, NICE PEOPLE!
YOU WERE WRONG TO TAKE THAT JOB, AND I EXPECT YOU TO BE SMART! IF YOU EVER SIGN-US-UP FOR SUCH A HORRIBLE, MEAN JOB AGAIN, I'LL CHALLENGE YOU TO A BATTLE TO THE DEATH!!!
COULD I HAVE ACTUALLY SCREWED-UP??
Nah.
SLAM
DOMATO, THANKS!! THAT LAST JOB ROCKED! BEATING UP A PALADIN WAS A DREAM COME TRUE!!!
OH CRAP!

Domato should put a lock on his bedroom door.

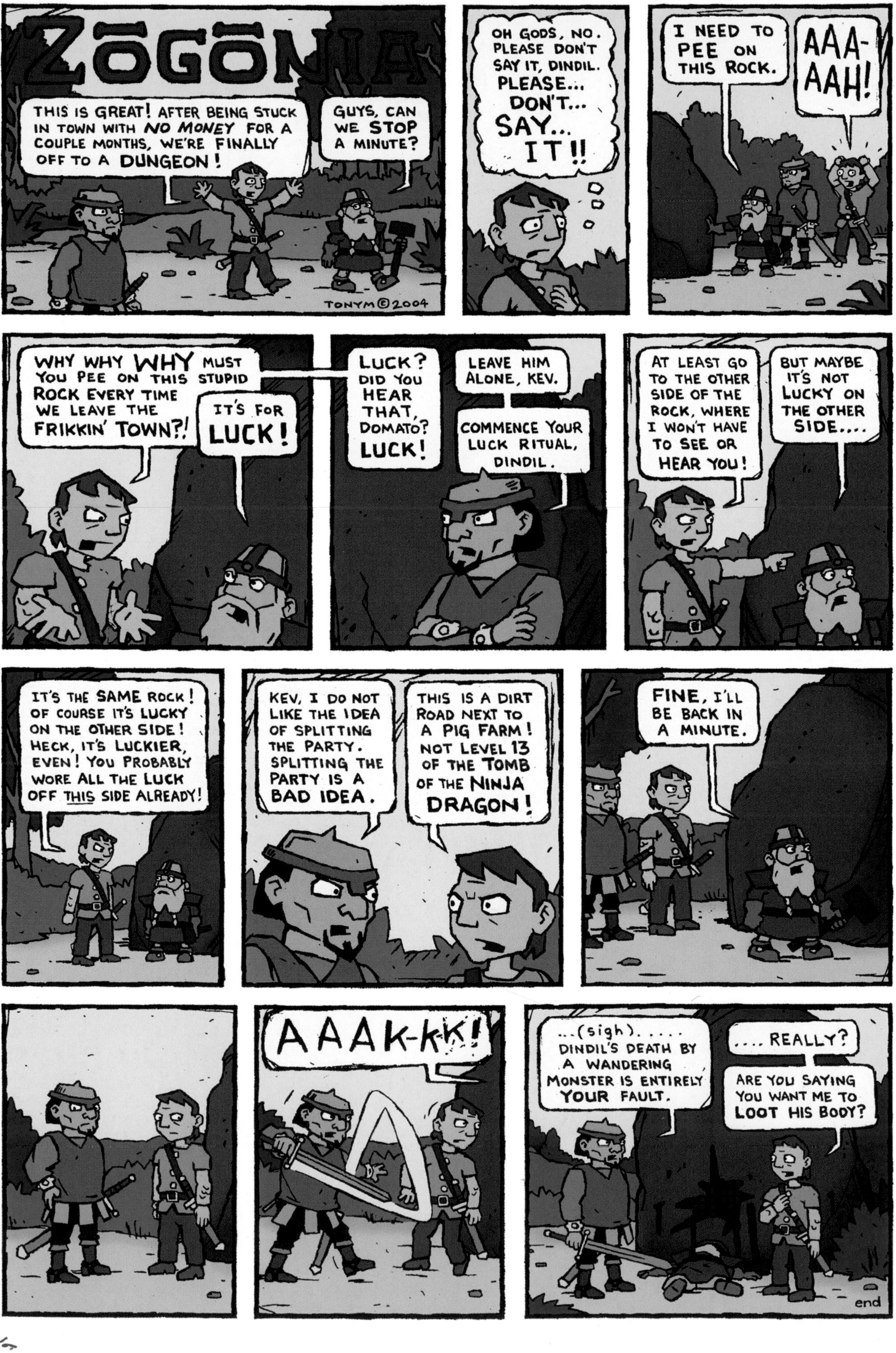
ZŌGŌNIA
THIS IS GREAT! AFTER BEING STUCK IN TOWN WITH NO MONEY FOR A COUPLE MONTHS, WE'RE FINALLY OFF TO A DUNGEON!
GUYS, CAN WE STOP A MINUTE?
TONYM © 2004
OH GODS, NO. PLEASE DON'T SAY IT, DINDIL. PLEASE... DON'T... SAY... IT!!
I NEED TO PEE ON THIS ROCK.
AAA-AAH!
WHY WHY WHY MUST YOU PEE ON THIS STUPID ROCK EVERY TIME WE LEAVE THE FRIKKIN' TOWN?!
IT'S FOR LUCK!
LUCK? DID YOU HEAR THAT, DOMATO? LUCK!
LEAVE HIM ALONE, KEV.
COMMENCE YOUR LUCK RITUAL, DINDIL.
AT LEAST GO TO THE OTHER SIDE OF THE ROCK, WHERE I WON'T HAVE TO SEE OR HEAR YOU!
BUT MAYBE IT'S NOT LUCKY ON THE OTHER SIDE....
IT'S THE SAME ROCK! OF COURSE IT'S LUCKY ON THE OTHER SIDE! HECK, IT'S LUCKIER, EVEN! YOU PROBABLY WORE ALL THE LUCK OFF THIS SIDE ALREADY!
KEV, I DO NOT LIKE THE IDEA OF SPLITTING THE PARTY. SPLITTING THE PARTY IS A BAD IDEA.
THIS IS A DIRT ROAD NEXT TO A PIG FARM! NOT LEVEL 13 OF THE TOMB OF THE NINJA DRAGON!
FINE, I'LL BE BACK IN A MINUTE.
AAAK-KK!
...(sigh)..... DINDIL'S DEATH BY A WANDERING MONSTER IS ENTIRELY YOUR FAULT.
....REALLY?
ARE YOU SAYING YOU WANT ME TO LOOT HIS BODY?
end

In case you're wondering, Dindil was correct about the front side of the rock being lucky. What he didn't realize, however, was that the front side was lucky only because the back side was unlucky. It's like a yin-yang thing, but with a rock.

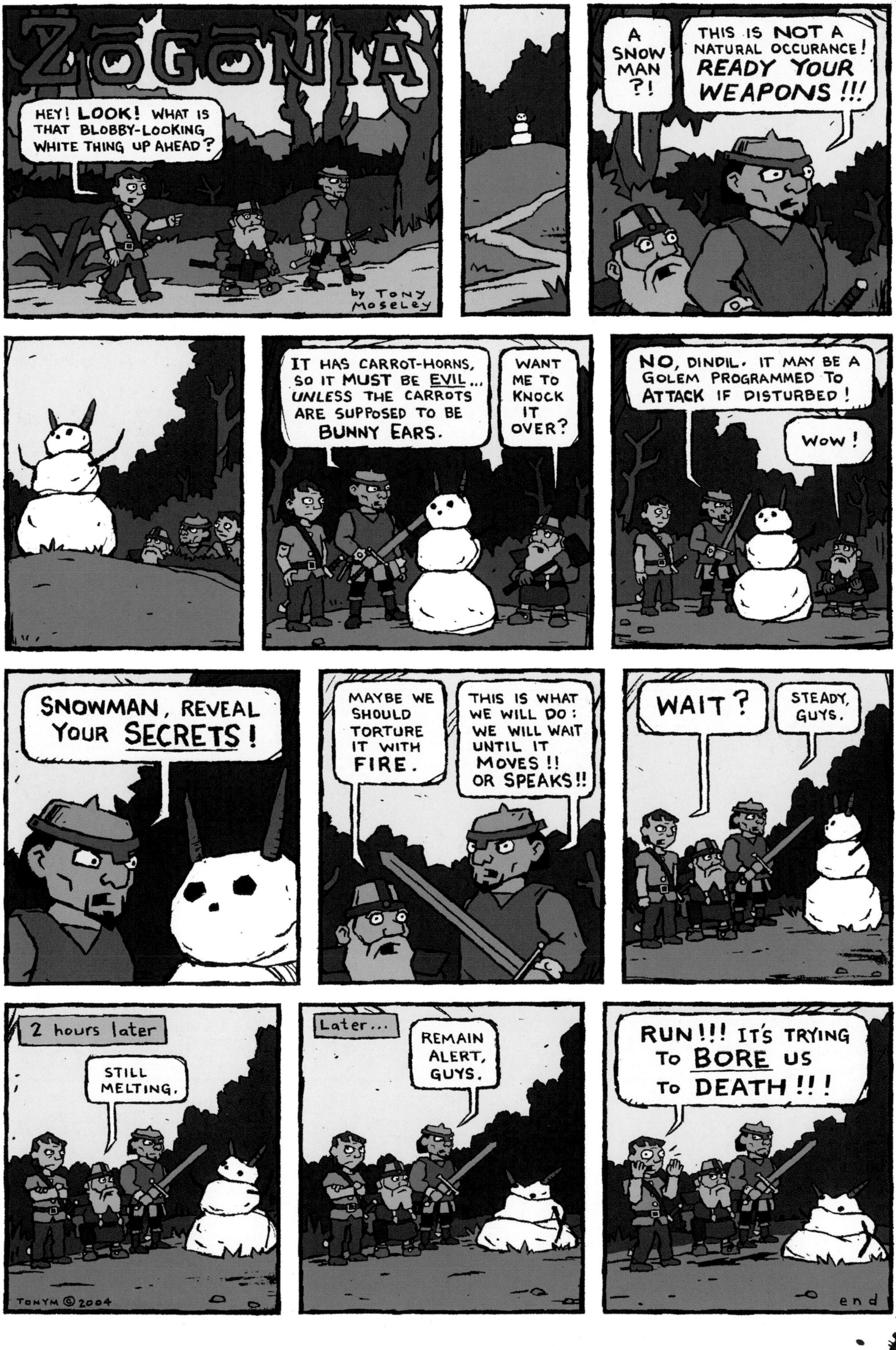
ZOGONIA
HEY! LOOK! WHAT IS THAT BLOBBY-LOOKING WHITE THING UP AHEAD?
by TONY MOSELEY
A SNOW MAN ?!
THIS IS NOT A NATURAL OCCURANCE! READY YOUR WEAPONS!!!
IT HAS CARROT-HORNS, SO IT MUST BE EVIL... UNLESS THE CARROTS ARE SUPPOSED TO BE BUNNY EARS.
WANT ME TO KNOCK IT OVER?
NO, DINDIL. IT MAY BE A GOLEM PROGRAMMED TO ATTACK IF DISTURBED!
WOW!
SNOWMAN, REVEAL YOUR SECRETS!
MAYBE WE SHOULD TORTURE IT WITH FIRE.
THIS IS WHAT WE WILL DO: WE WILL WAIT UNTIL IT MOVES!! OR SPEAKS!!
WAIT?
STEADY, GUYS.
2 hours later
STILL MELTING.
TONYM © 2004
Later...
REMAIN ALERT, GUYS.
RUN!!! IT'S TRYING TO BORE US TO DEATH!!!
end

Why was a snowman on the hill? Why, why, why? It's one of life's great mysteries.

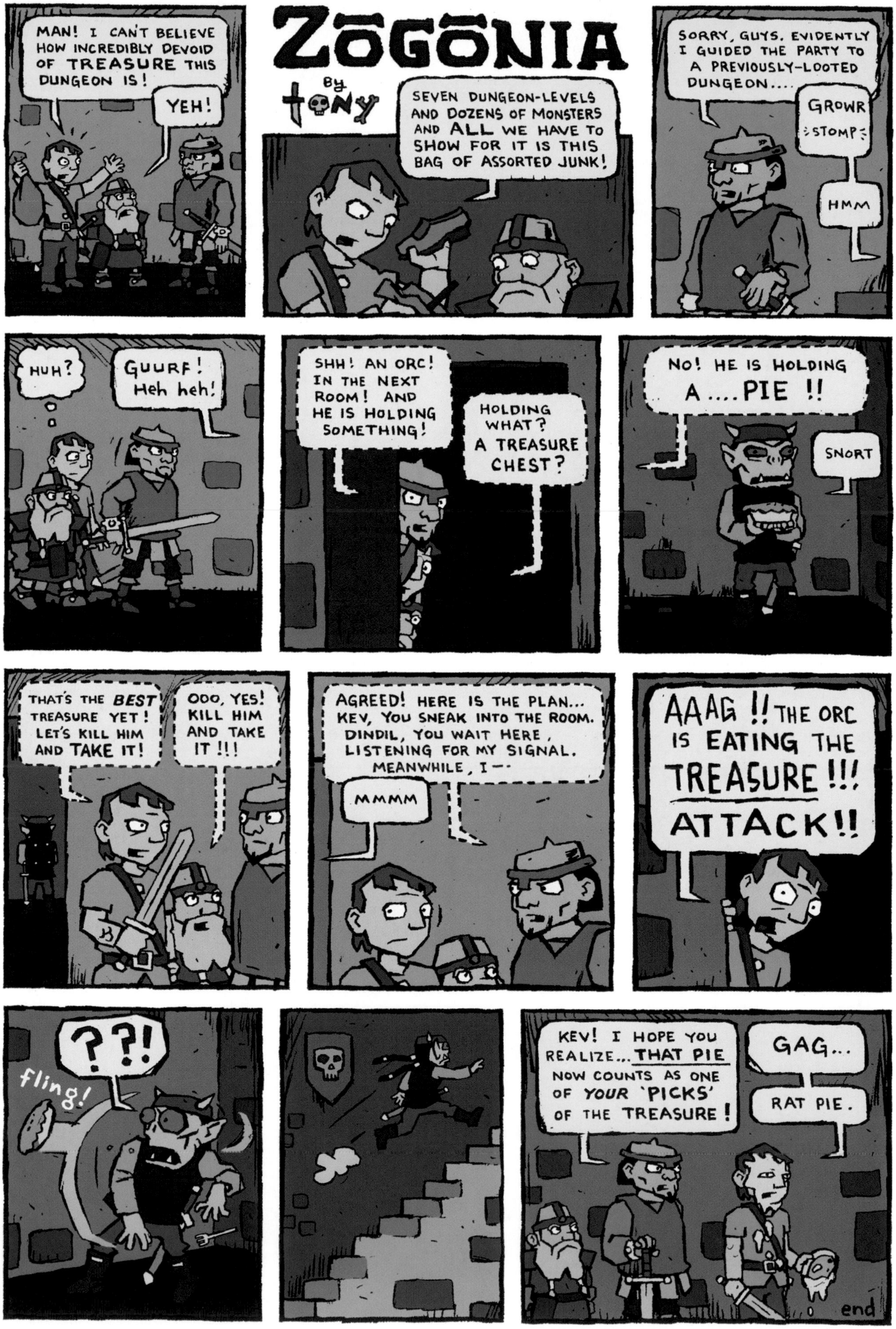

ZOGONIA
By tony
MAN! I CAN'T BELIEVE HOW INCREDIBLY DEVOID OF TREASURE THIS DUNGEON IS!
YEH!
SEVEN DUNGEON-LEVELS AND DOZENS OF MONSTERS AND ALL WE HAVE TO SHOW FOR IT IS THIS BAG OF ASSORTED JUNK!
SORRY, GUYS. EVIDENTLY I GUIDED THE PARTY TO A PREVIOUSLY-LOOTED DUNGEON....
GROWR
STOMP
HMM
HUH?
GUURF! Heh heh!
SHH! AN ORC! IN THE NEXT ROOM! AND HE IS HOLDING SOMETHING!
HOLDING WHAT? A TREASURE CHEST?
NO! HE IS HOLDING A.... PIE !!
SNORT
THAT'S THE BEST TREASURE YET! LET'S KILL HIM AND TAKE IT!
OOO, YES! KILL HIM AND TAKE IT !!!
AGREED! HERE IS THE PLAN... KEV, YOU SNEAK INTO THE ROOM. DINDIL, YOU WAIT HERE, LISTENING FOR MY SIGNAL. MEANWHILE, I--
MMMM
AAAG !! THE ORC IS EATING THE TREASURE !!! ATTACK!!
??!
fling!
KEV! I HOPE YOU REALIZE... THAT PIE NOW COUNTS AS ONE OF YOUR 'PICKS' OF THE TREASURE!
GAG...
RAT PIE.
end

The broken lines around text indicate whispering. Some folks didn't know that.

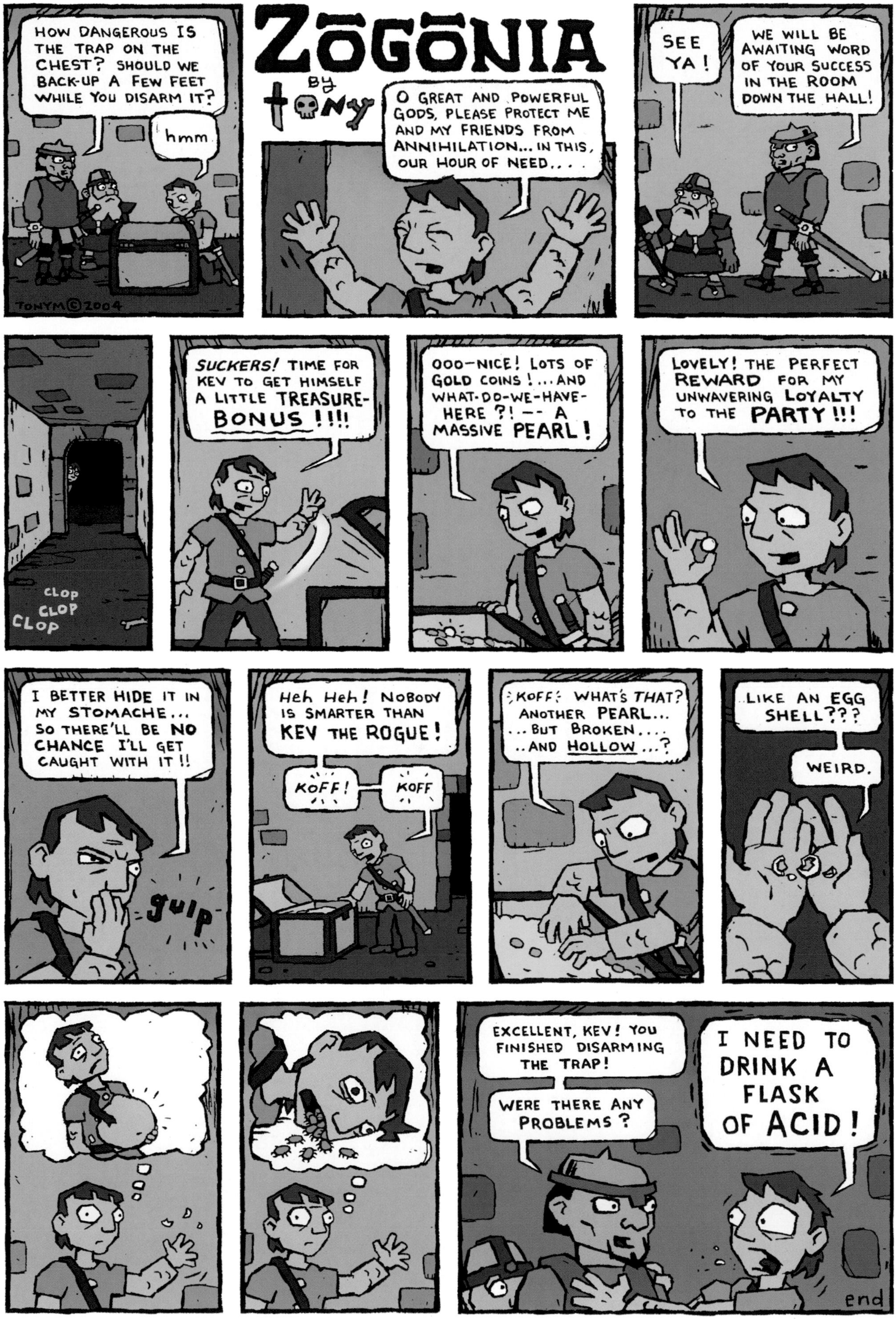
ZOGONIA
BY tony
HOW DANGEROUS IS THE TRAP ON THE CHEST? SHOULD WE BACK-UP A FEW FEET WHILE YOU DISARM IT?
hmm
TONYM©2004
O GREAT AND POWERFUL GODS, PLEASE PROTECT ME AND MY FRIENDS FROM ANNIHILATION... IN THIS, OUR HOUR OF NEED...
SEE YA!
WE WILL BE AWAITING WORD OF YOUR SUCCESS IN THE ROOM DOWN THE HALL!
CLOP CLOP CLOP
SUCKERS! TIME FOR KEV TO GET HIMSELF A LITTLE TREASURE-BONUS!!!!
OOO-NICE! LOTS OF GOLD COINS!... AND WHAT-DO-WE-HAVE-HERE?! -- A MASSIVE PEARL!
LOVELY! THE PERFECT REWARD FOR MY UNWAVERING LOYALTY TO THE PARTY!!!
I BETTER HIDE IT IN MY STOMACHE... SO THERE'LL BE NO CHANCE I'LL GET CAUGHT WITH IT!!
gulp
Heh Heh! NOBODY IS SMARTER THAN KEV THE ROGUE!
KOFF!
KOFF
KOFF WHAT'S THAT? ANOTHER PEARL... ...BUT BROKEN.... ..AND HOLLOW...?
LIKE AN EGG SHELL???
WEIRD.
EXCELLENT, KEV! YOU FINISHED DISARMING THE TRAP!
WERE THERE ANY PROBLEMS?
I NEED TO DRINK A FLASK OF ACID!
end

...and then Domato quickly produced a flask of acid and shoved it into Kev's hands, without even asking any questions. Because that's what pals are for.

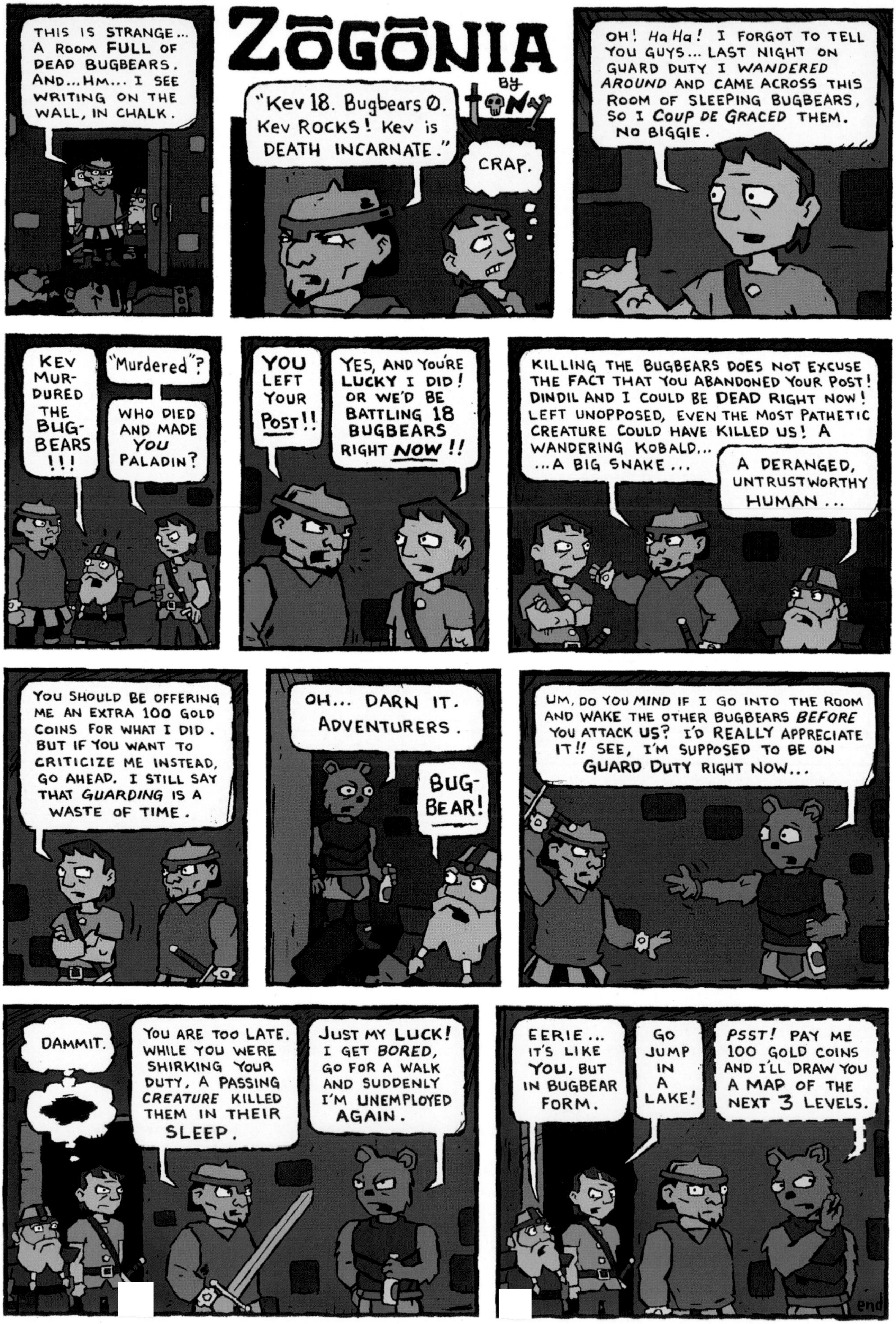
ZŌGŌNIA
BY tony
THIS IS STRANGE... A ROOM FULL OF DEAD BUGBEARS. AND... HM... I SEE WRITING ON THE WALL, IN CHALK.
"Kev 18. Bugbears 0. Kev ROCKS! Kev is DEATH INCARNATE."
CRAP.
OH! Ha Ha! I FORGOT TO TELL YOU GUYS... LAST NIGHT ON GUARD DUTY I WANDERED AROUND AND CAME ACROSS THIS ROOM OF SLEEPING BUGBEARS, SO I COUP DE GRACED THEM. NO BIGGIE.
KEV MURDURED THE BUGBEARS!!!
"Murdered"?
WHO DIED AND MADE YOU PALADIN?
YOU LEFT YOUR POST!!
YES, AND YOU'RE LUCKY I DID! OR WE'D BE BATTLING 18 BUGBEARS RIGHT NOW!!
KILLING THE BUGBEARS DOES NOT EXCUSE THE FACT THAT YOU ABANDONED YOUR POST! DINDIL AND I COULD BE DEAD RIGHT NOW! LEFT UNOPPOSED, EVEN THE MOST PATHETIC CREATURE COULD HAVE KILLED US! A WANDERING KOBALD... ...A BIG SNAKE...
A DERANGED, UNTRUSTWORTHY HUMAN...
YOU SHOULD BE OFFERING ME AN EXTRA 100 GOLD COINS FOR WHAT I DID. BUT IF YOU WANT TO CRITICIZE ME INSTEAD, GO AHEAD. I STILL SAY THAT GUARDING IS A WASTE OF TIME.
OH... DARN IT. ADVENTURERS.
BUG-BEAR!
UM, DO YOU MIND IF I GO INTO THE ROOM AND WAKE THE OTHER BUGBEARS BEFORE YOU ATTACK US? I'D REALLY APPRECIATE IT!! SEE, I'M SUPPOSED TO BE ON GUARD DUTY RIGHT NOW...
DAMMIT.
YOU ARE TOO LATE. WHILE YOU WERE SHIRKING YOUR DUTY, A PASSING CREATURE KILLED THEM IN THEIR SLEEP.
JUST MY LUCK! I GET BORED, GO FOR A WALK AND SUDDENLY I'M UNEMPLOYED AGAIN.
EERIE... IT'S LIKE YOU, BUT IN BUGBEAR FORM.
GO JUMP IN A LAKE!
PSST! PAY ME 100 GOLD COINS AND I'LL DRAW YOU A MAP OF THE NEXT 3 LEVELS.
end

I was sooo tempted to draw antennae on the bugbears... because, ya know, they are called *bug*bears. I should've done it.

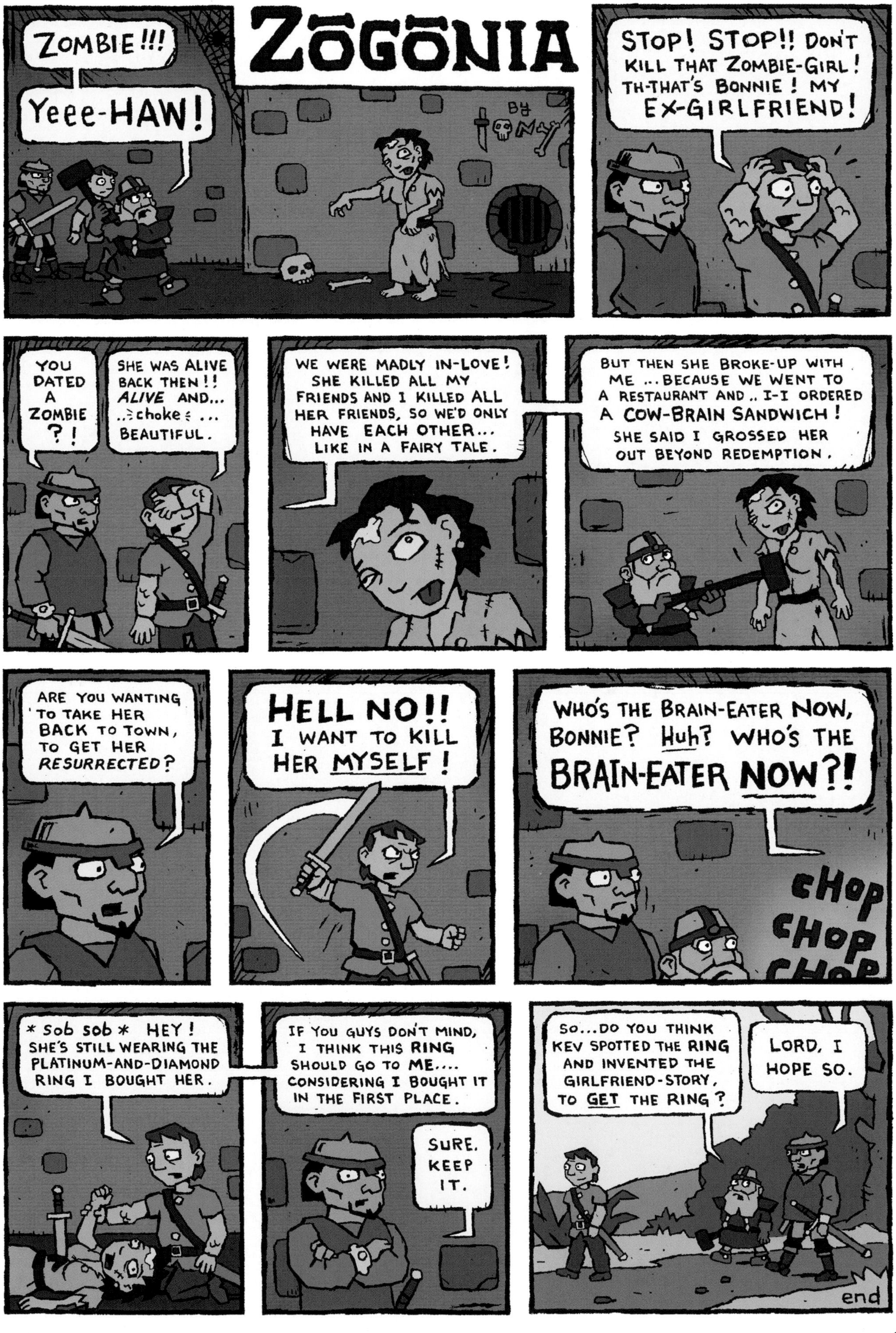
ZŌGŌNIA
By Tony
ZOMBIE!!!
Yeee-HAW!
STOP! STOP!! DON'T KILL THAT ZOMBIE-GIRL! TH-THAT'S BONNIE! MY EX-GIRLFRIEND!
YOU DATED A ZOMBIE ?!
SHE WAS ALIVE BACK THEN!! ALIVE AND... *choke* ... BEAUTIFUL.
WE WERE MADLY IN-LOVE! SHE KILLED ALL MY FRIENDS AND I KILLED ALL HER FRIENDS, SO WE'D ONLY HAVE EACH OTHER... LIKE IN A FAIRY TALE.
BUT THEN SHE BROKE-UP WITH ME ... BECAUSE WE WENT TO A RESTAURANT AND.. I-I ORDERED A COW-BRAIN SANDWICH! SHE SAID I GROSSED HER OUT BEYOND REDEMPTION.
ARE YOU WANTING TO TAKE HER BACK TO TOWN, TO GET HER RESURRECTED?
HELL NO!! I WANT TO KILL HER MYSELF!
WHO'S THE BRAIN-EATER NOW, BONNIE? Huh? WHO'S THE BRAIN-EATER NOW?!
CHOP
CHOP
* sob sob * HEY! SHE'S STILL WEARING THE PLATINUM-AND-DIAMOND RING I BOUGHT HER.
IF YOU GUYS DON'T MIND, I THINK THIS RING SHOULD GO TO ME.... CONSIDERING I BOUGHT IT IN THE FIRST PLACE.
SURE. KEEP IT.
SO...DO YOU THINK KEV SPOTTED THE RING AND INVENTED THE GIRLFRIEND-STORY, TO GET THE RING?
LORD, I HOPE SO.
end

Sorry, Kev. I'm gonna have to side with Bonnie on this one. Cow-brain sandwich? Ewww.

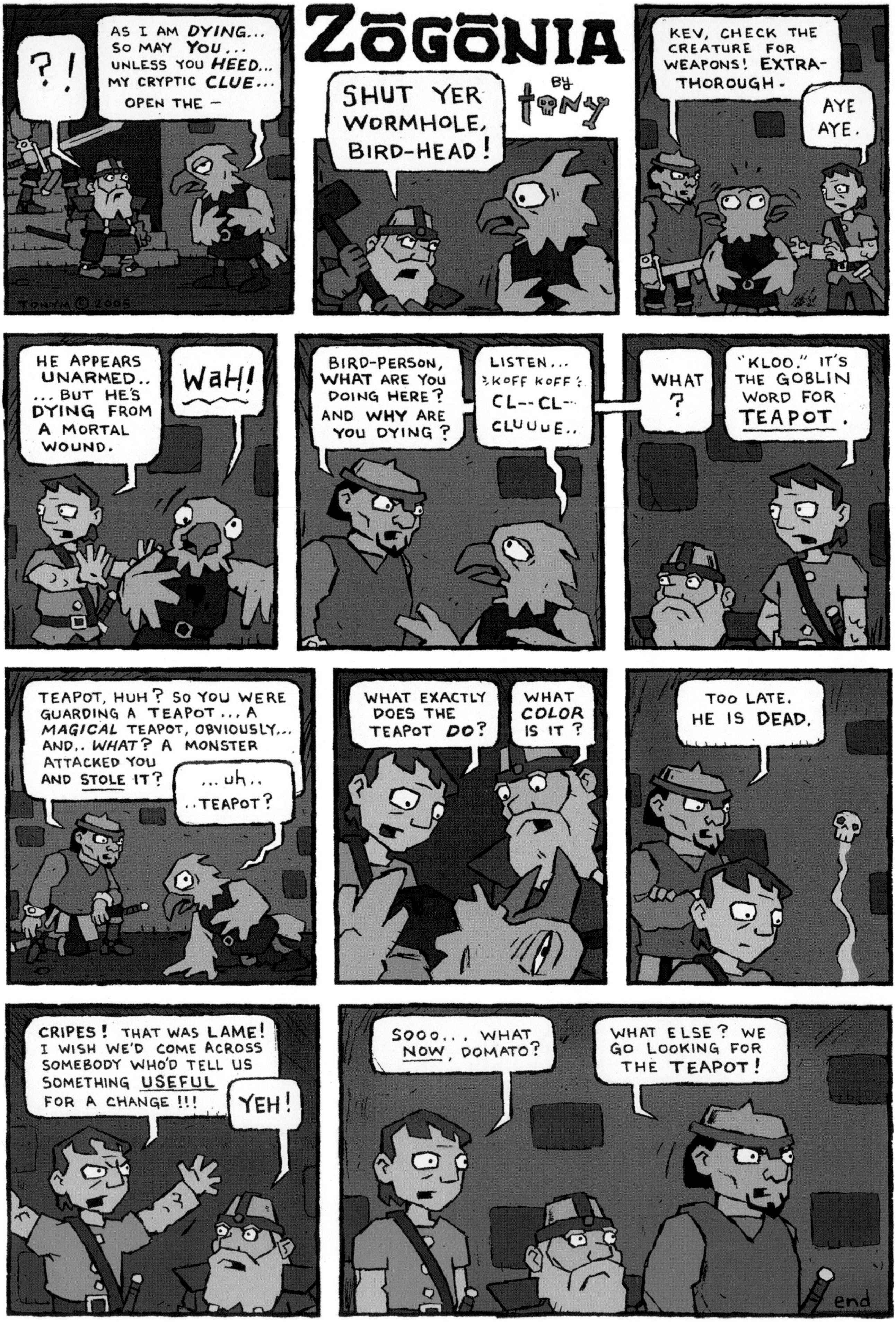
?!
AS I AM DYING... SO MAY YOU... UNLESS YOU HEED... MY CRYPTIC CLUE... OPEN THE –
TONYM © 2005
ZOGONIA
BY TONY
SHUT YER WORMHOLE, BIRD-HEAD!
KEV, CHECK THE CREATURE FOR WEAPONS! EXTRA-THOROUGH.
AYE AYE.
HE APPEARS UNARMED.. ... BUT HE'S DYING FROM A MORTAL WOUND.
WaH!
BIRD-PERSON, WHAT ARE YOU DOING HERE? AND WHY ARE YOU DYING?
LISTEN... KOFF KOFF CL--CL-- CLUUUE..
WHAT?
"KLOO." IT'S THE GOBLIN WORD FOR TEAPOT.
TEAPOT, HUH? SO YOU WERE GUARDING A TEAPOT... A MAGICAL TEAPOT, OBVIOUSLY... AND.. WHAT? A MONSTER ATTACKED YOU AND STOLE IT?
...uh.. ..TEAPOT?
WHAT EXACTLY DOES THE TEAPOT DO?
WHAT COLOR IS IT?
TOO LATE. HE IS DEAD.
CRIPES! THAT WAS LAME! I WISH WE'D COME ACROSS SOMEBODY WHO'D TELL US SOMETHING USEFUL FOR A CHANGE!!!
YEH!
SOOO... WHAT NOW, DOMATO?
WHAT ELSE? WE GO LOOKING FOR THE TEAPOT!
end

Man, wouldn't it be awesome if, when people died for real, a smoky skull floated from their corpse?

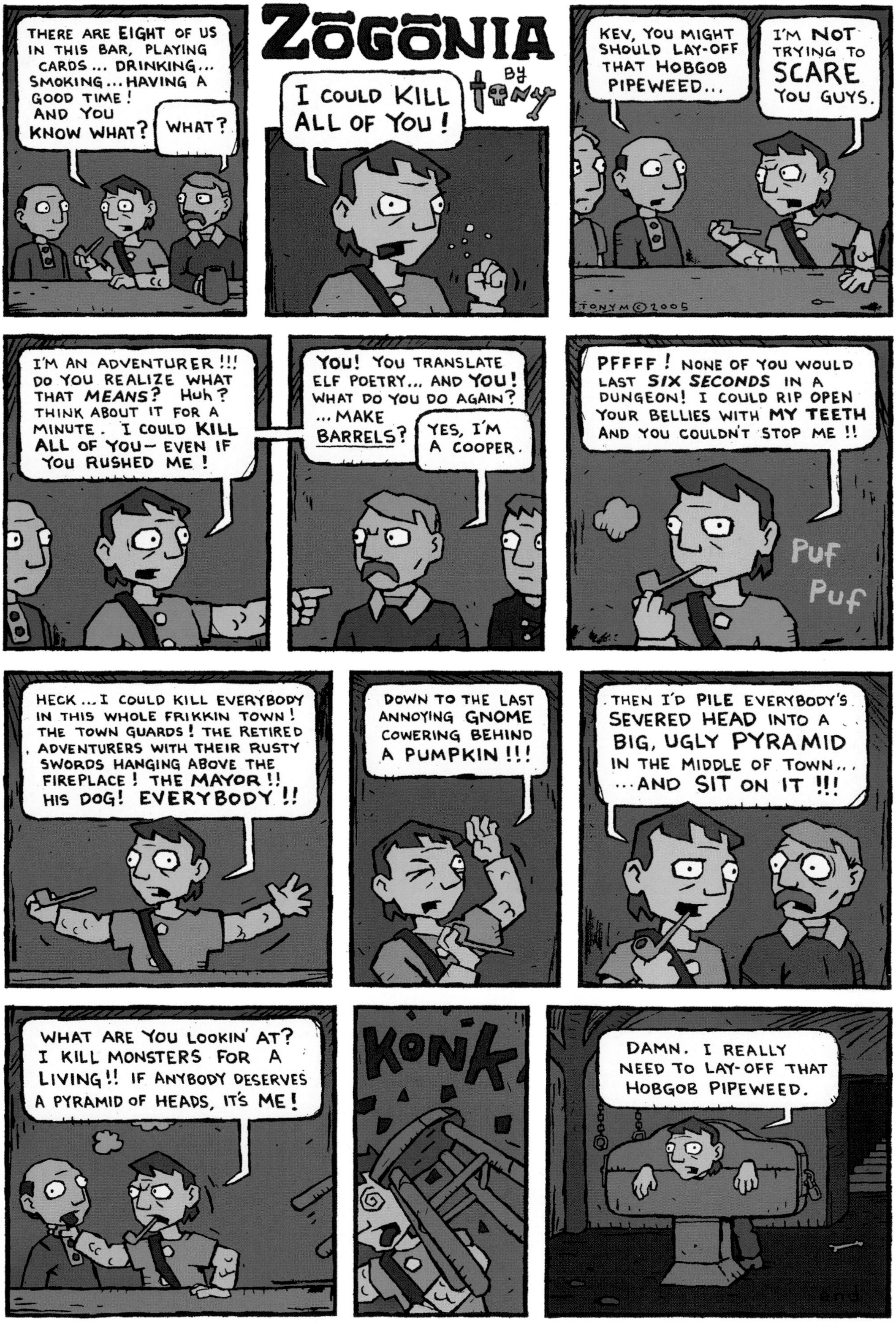
ZŌGŌNIA
BY TONY
THERE ARE EIGHT OF US IN THIS BAR, PLAYING CARDS ... DRINKING... SMOKING... HAVING A GOOD TIME! AND YOU KNOW WHAT?
WHAT?
I COULD KILL ALL OF YOU!
KEV, YOU MIGHT SHOULD LAY-OFF THAT HOBGOB PIPEWEED...
I'M NOT TRYING TO SCARE YOU GUYS.
TONYM©2005
I'M AN ADVENTURER!!! DO YOU REALIZE WHAT THAT MEANS? Huh? THINK ABOUT IT FOR A MINUTE. I COULD KILL ALL OF YOU— EVEN IF YOU RUSHED ME!
YOU! YOU TRANSLATE ELF POETRY... AND YOU! WHAT DO YOU DO AGAIN? ...MAKE BARRELS?
YES, I'M A COOPER.
PFFFF! NONE OF YOU WOULD LAST SIX SECONDS IN A DUNGEON! I COULD RIP OPEN YOUR BELLIES WITH MY TEETH AND YOU COULDN'T STOP ME!!
PUF
PUF
HECK... I COULD KILL EVERYBODY IN THIS WHOLE FRIKKIN TOWN! THE TOWN GUARDS! THE RETIRED ADVENTURERS WITH THEIR RUSTY SWORDS HANGING ABOVE THE FIREPLACE! THE MAYOR!! HIS DOG! EVERYBODY!!
DOWN TO THE LAST ANNOYING GNOME COWERING BEHIND A PUMPKIN!!!
THEN I'D PILE EVERYBODY'S SEVERED HEAD INTO A BIG, UGLY PYRAMID IN THE MIDDLE OF TOWN... ...AND SIT ON IT!!!
WHAT ARE YOU LOOKIN' AT? I KILL MONSTERS FOR A LIVING!! IF ANYBODY DESERVES A PYRAMID OF HEADS, IT'S ME!
KONK
DAMN. I REALLY NEED TO LAY-OFF THAT HOBGOB PIPEWEED.
end

The town in this strip actually has an ordinance against building a pyramid of skulls for any usage resembling or emulating that of a chair, hence the shocked expression of the cooper in panel nine.

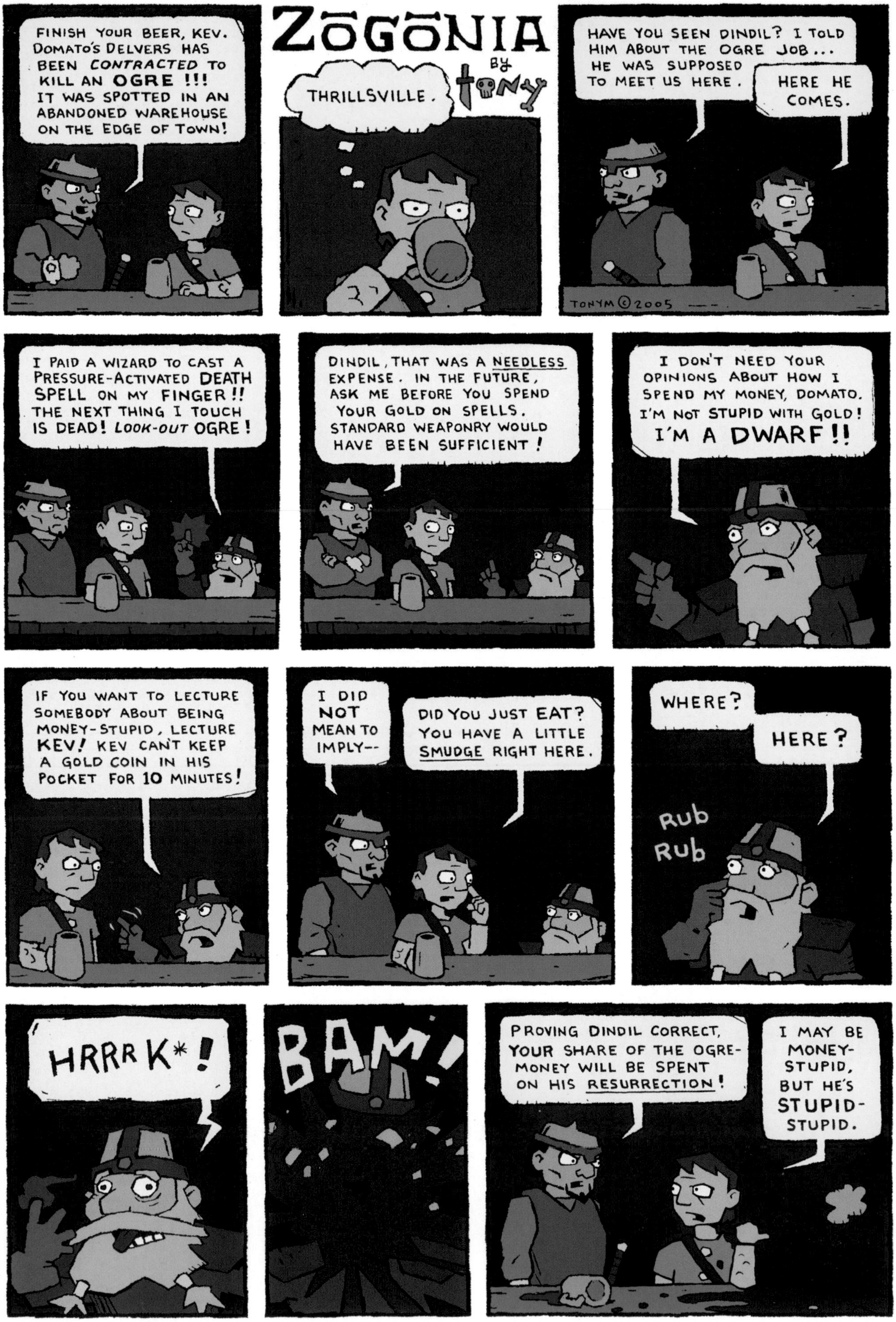
ZOGONIA
BY TONY
FINISH YOUR BEER, KEV. DOMATO'S DELVERS HAS BEEN CONTRACTED TO KILL AN OGRE !!! IT WAS SPOTTED IN AN ABANDONED WAREHOUSE ON THE EDGE OF TOWN!
THRILLSVILLE.
HAVE YOU SEEN DINDIL? I TOLD HIM ABOUT THE OGRE JOB... HE WAS SUPPOSED TO MEET US HERE.
HERE HE COMES.
TONYM © 2005
I PAID A WIZARD TO CAST A PRESSURE-ACTIVATED DEATH SPELL ON MY FINGER!! THE NEXT THING I TOUCH IS DEAD! LOOK-OUT OGRE!
DINDIL, THAT WAS A NEEDLESS EXPENSE. IN THE FUTURE, ASK ME BEFORE YOU SPEND YOUR GOLD ON SPELLS. STANDARD WEAPONRY WOULD HAVE BEEN SUFFICIENT!
I DON'T NEED YOUR OPINIONS ABOUT HOW I SPEND MY MONEY, DOMATO. I'M NOT STUPID WITH GOLD! I'M A DWARF!!
IF YOU WANT TO LECTURE SOMEBODY ABOUT BEING MONEY-STUPID, LECTURE KEV! KEV CAN'T KEEP A GOLD COIN IN HIS POCKET FOR 10 MINUTES!
I DID NOT MEAN TO IMPLY--
DID YOU JUST EAT? YOU HAVE A LITTLE SMUDGE RIGHT HERE.
WHERE?
HERE?
RUB RUB
HRRRK*!
BAM!
PROVING DINDIL CORRECT, YOUR SHARE OF THE OGRE-MONEY WILL BE SPENT ON HIS RESURRECTION!
I MAY BE MONEY-STUPID, BUT HE'S STUPID-STUPID.

You can't see it in the strip, but one of Dindil's bloody skull fragments landed in some guy's bowl of tomato soup on the other side of the bar... and the guy didn't notice! And he's eating the soup right now! Hahaha.

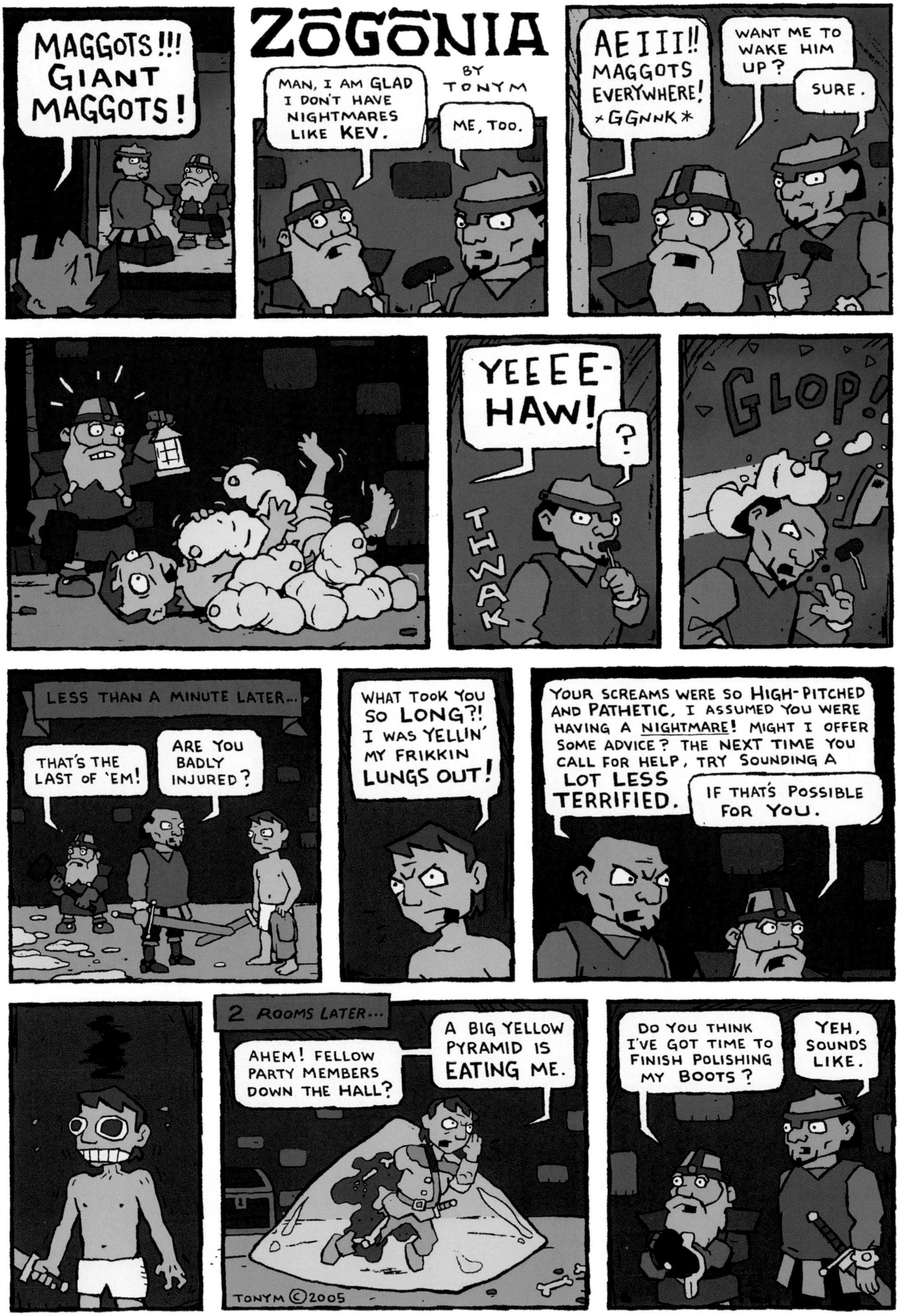
ZŌGŌNIA
BY TONYM
MAGGOTS!!! GIANT MAGGOTS!
MAN, I AM GLAD I DON'T HAVE NIGHTMARES LIKE KEV.
ME, TOO.
AEIII!! MAGGOTS EVERYWHERE! *GGNNK*
WANT ME TO WAKE HIM UP?
SURE.
YEEEE-HAW!
?
THWAK
GLOP!
LESS THAN A MINUTE LATER...
THAT'S THE LAST OF 'EM!
ARE YOU BADLY INJURED?
WHAT TOOK YOU SO LONG?! I WAS YELLIN' MY FRIKKIN LUNGS OUT!
YOUR SCREAMS WERE SO HIGH-PITCHED AND PATHETIC, I ASSUMED YOU WERE HAVING A NIGHTMARE! MIGHT I OFFER SOME ADVICE? THE NEXT TIME YOU CALL FOR HELP, TRY SOUNDING A LOT LESS TERRIFIED.
IF THAT'S POSSIBLE FOR YOU.
2 ROOMS LATER...
AHEM! FELLOW PARTY MEMBERS DOWN THE HALL?
A BIG YELLOW PYRAMID IS EATING ME.
TONYM ©2005
DO YOU THINK I'VE GOT TIME TO FINISH POLISHING MY BOOTS?
YEH, SOUNDS LIKE.

In the first half of this strip, Domato is gnawing on a zogon sausage. A zogon sausage is so healthy that a person's body utilizes the whole thing, down to the last sausage molecule. Absolutely no waste is left to excrete.

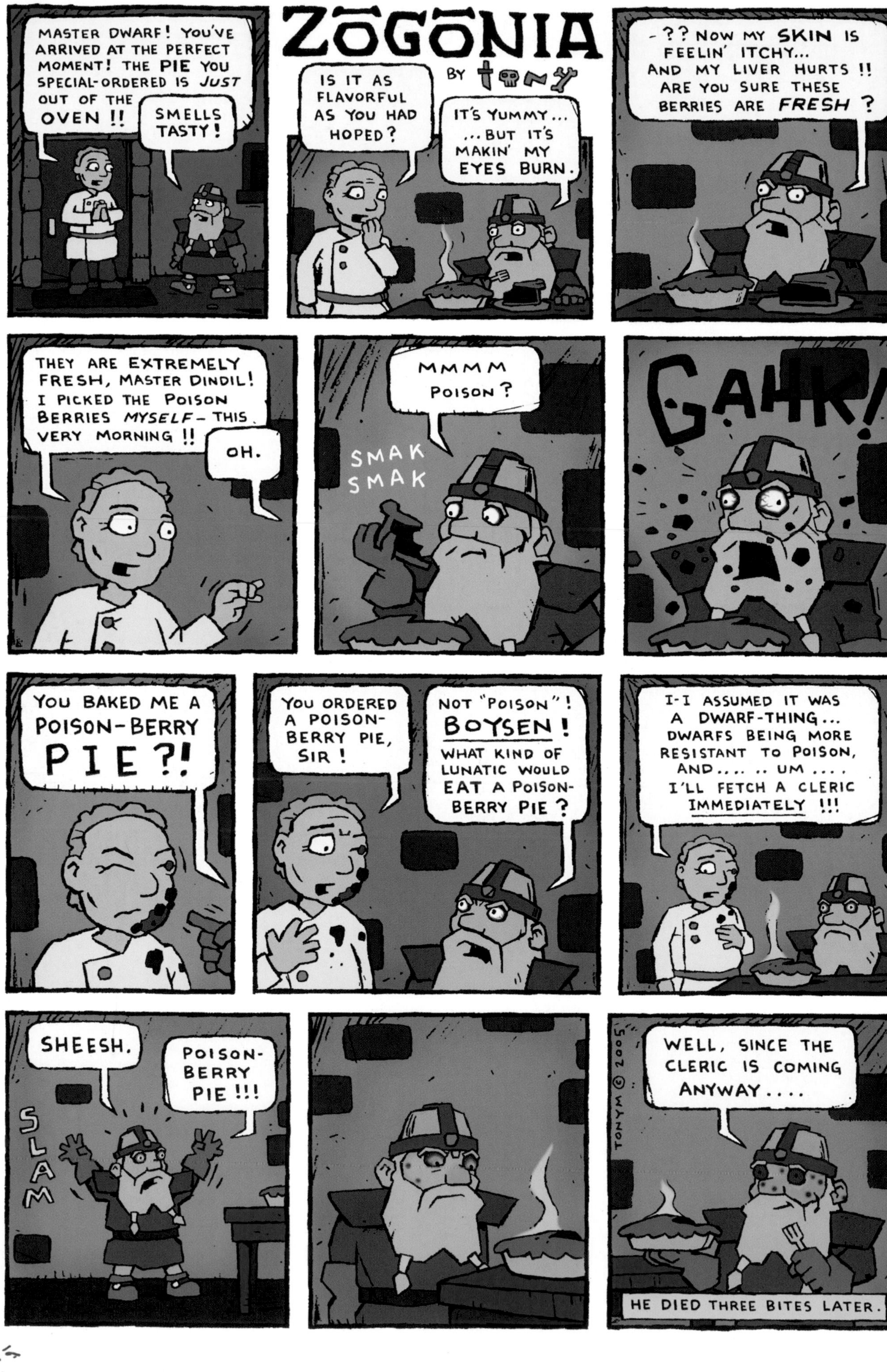
ZOGONIA
BY tony
MASTER DWARF! YOU'VE ARRIVED AT THE PERFECT MOMENT! THE PIE YOU SPECIAL-ORDERED IS JUST OUT OF THE OVEN !!
SMELLS TASTY!
IS IT AS FLAVORFUL AS YOU HAD HOPED?
IT'S YUMMY... ...BUT IT'S MAKIN' MY EYES BURN.
-?? NOW MY SKIN IS FEELIN' ITCHY... AND MY LIVER HURTS !! ARE YOU SURE THESE BERRIES ARE FRESH ?
THEY ARE EXTREMELY FRESH, MASTER DINDIL! I PICKED THE POISON BERRIES MYSELF – THIS VERY MORNING !!
OH.
MMMM POISON?
SMAK SMAK
GAHR!
YOU BAKED ME A POISON-BERRY PIE ?!
YOU ORDERED A POISON-BERRY PIE, SIR!
NOT "POISON"! BOYSEN! WHAT KIND OF LUNATIC WOULD EAT A POISON-BERRY PIE?
I-I ASSUMED IT WAS A DWARF-THING... DWARFS BEING MORE RESISTANT TO POISON, AND...... UM.... I'LL FETCH A CLERIC IMMEDIATELY !!!
SHEESH.
POISON-BERRY PIE !!!
SLAM
TONYM © 2005
WELL, SINCE THE CLERIC IS COMING ANYWAY....
HE DIED THREE BITES LATER.

Too bad the chef didn't sprinkle cinnamon on top. Cinnamon was the antidote.

ZOGONIA
by T.M.

Panel 1: A DARK ELF SLAVE-GETTER! EEEEEEEE!!

TONYM © 2005

Panel 2: SAVE ME! — HOW MUCH MONEY YOU GOT?

Panel 3: HIYA... I'M JUST PASSIN' THROUGH HERE AND HAVE A QUESTION.... HAVE ANY DEVILS BEEN ROAMING AROUND, LIKE THEY'RE SEARCHING FOR SOMEBODY?

Panel 4: HMM... NOT THAT I RECALL. — WHY? — I GOTTA TAKE THIS CHAOS BATTERY TO A DRAGON, AND AN EVIL PRIESTESS' DEVIL-MINIONS ARE TRYING TO FIND ME AND STEAL IT.

Panel 5: EXCUSE ME, WHAT'S A BATTERY?

Panel 6: YOU KNOW... A KIND OF ANACHRONISM.

Panel 7: THAT THING MUST BE WORTH 10,000 GOLD!!! PERHAPS EVEN MORE THAN I OWE THE DICEHALL!

Panel 8: DIE, SLAVER! — SLAVER? I'M ON THE SURFACE 15 MINUTES, AND ALREADY SOME YOKEL IS PROFILING ME! — SHING

Panel 9: WHA—?!. — EEP EEP EEP — ZZZ

Panel 10: ★⚡☠✳! I'VE BEEN GNOMED!

Panel 11: KILL ME!! YOU CAN'T LEAVE ME LIKE THIS! PLEASE! — AND GET GNOME BLOOD ON MY SWORD? EWW.

Panel 12: SOB... SOB... MY LIFE IS HELL. — WHOA! DARK ELF!! YOU FORGOT YOUR SLAVE!!

Notice how Kev's sword turned into a screwdriver when he was gnomed? Even worse, the gold coins in Kev's back pocket turned into marshmallows!

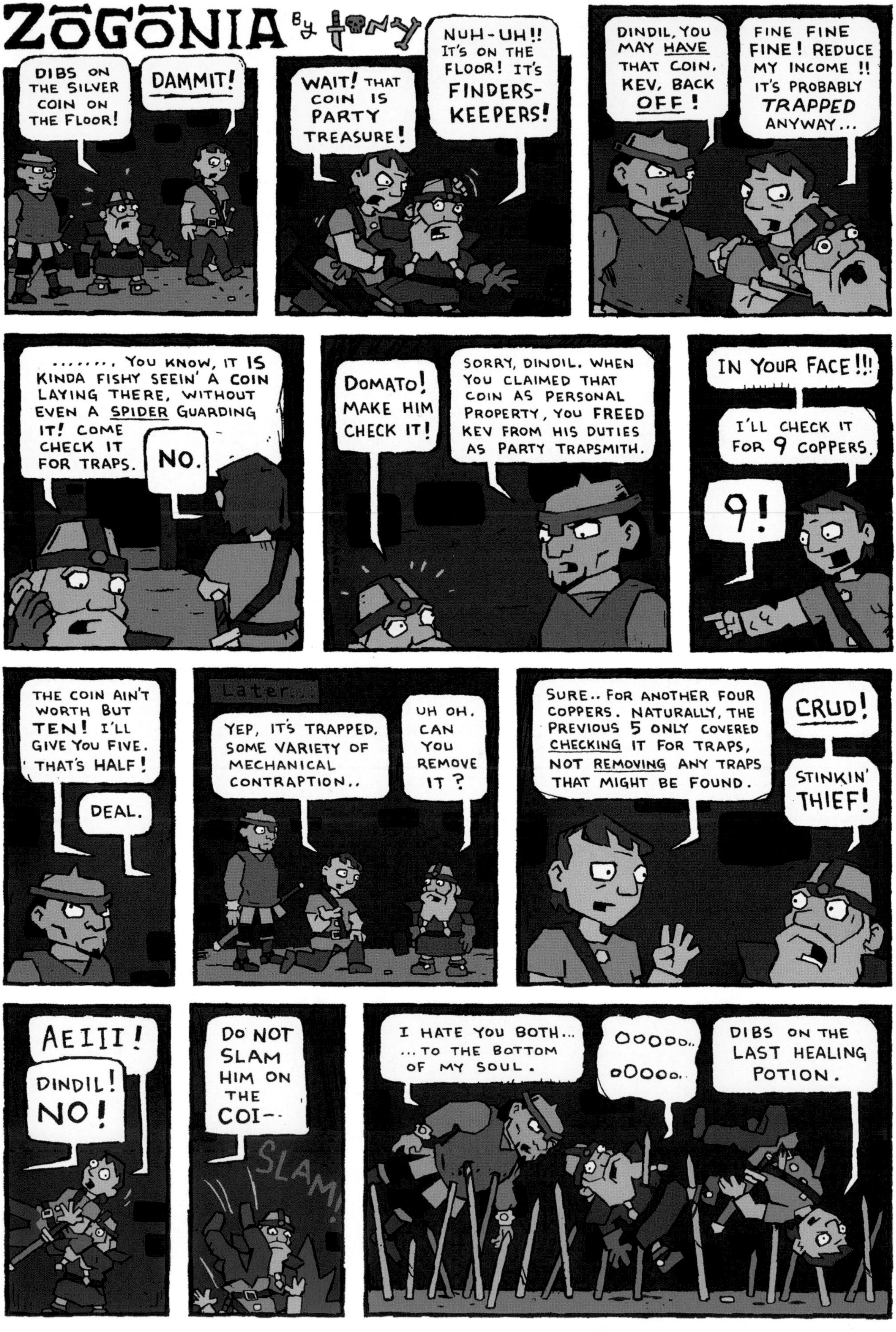
ZŌGŌNIA By Tony
DIBS ON THE SILVER COIN ON THE FLOOR!
DAMMIT!
WAIT! THAT COIN IS PARTY TREASURE!
NUH-UH!! IT'S ON THE FLOOR! IT'S FINDERS-KEEPERS!
DINDIL, YOU MAY HAVE THAT COIN, KEV, BACK OFF!
FINE FINE FINE! REDUCE MY INCOME!! IT'S PROBABLY TRAPPED ANYWAY...
......., YOU KNOW, IT IS KINDA FISHY SEEIN' A COIN LAYING THERE, WITHOUT EVEN A SPIDER GUARDING IT! COME CHECK IT FOR TRAPS.
NO.
DOMATO! MAKE HIM CHECK IT!
SORRY, DINDIL. WHEN YOU CLAIMED THAT COIN AS PERSONAL PROPERTY, YOU FREED KEV FROM HIS DUTIES AS PARTY TRAPSMITH.
IN YOUR FACE!!!
I'LL CHECK IT FOR 9 COPPERS.
9!
THE COIN AIN'T WORTH BUT TEN! I'LL GIVE YOU FIVE. THAT'S HALF!
DEAL.
Later...
YEP, IT'S TRAPPED, SOME VARIETY OF MECHANICAL CONTRAPTION..
UH OH. CAN YOU REMOVE IT?
SURE.. FOR ANOTHER FOUR COPPERS. NATURALLY, THE PREVIOUS 5 ONLY COVERED CHECKING IT FOR TRAPS, NOT REMOVING ANY TRAPS THAT MIGHT BE FOUND.
CRUD!
STINKIN' THIEF!
AEIII!
DINDIL! NO!
DO NOT SLAM HIM ON THE COI--
SLAM!
I HATE YOU BOTH... ...TO THE BOTTOM OF MY SOUL.
OOOOo.. oOOOo..
DIBS ON THE LAST HEALING POTION.

Actually, there was a spider guarding the coin five minutes earlier, but it was eaten by a wandering centipede.

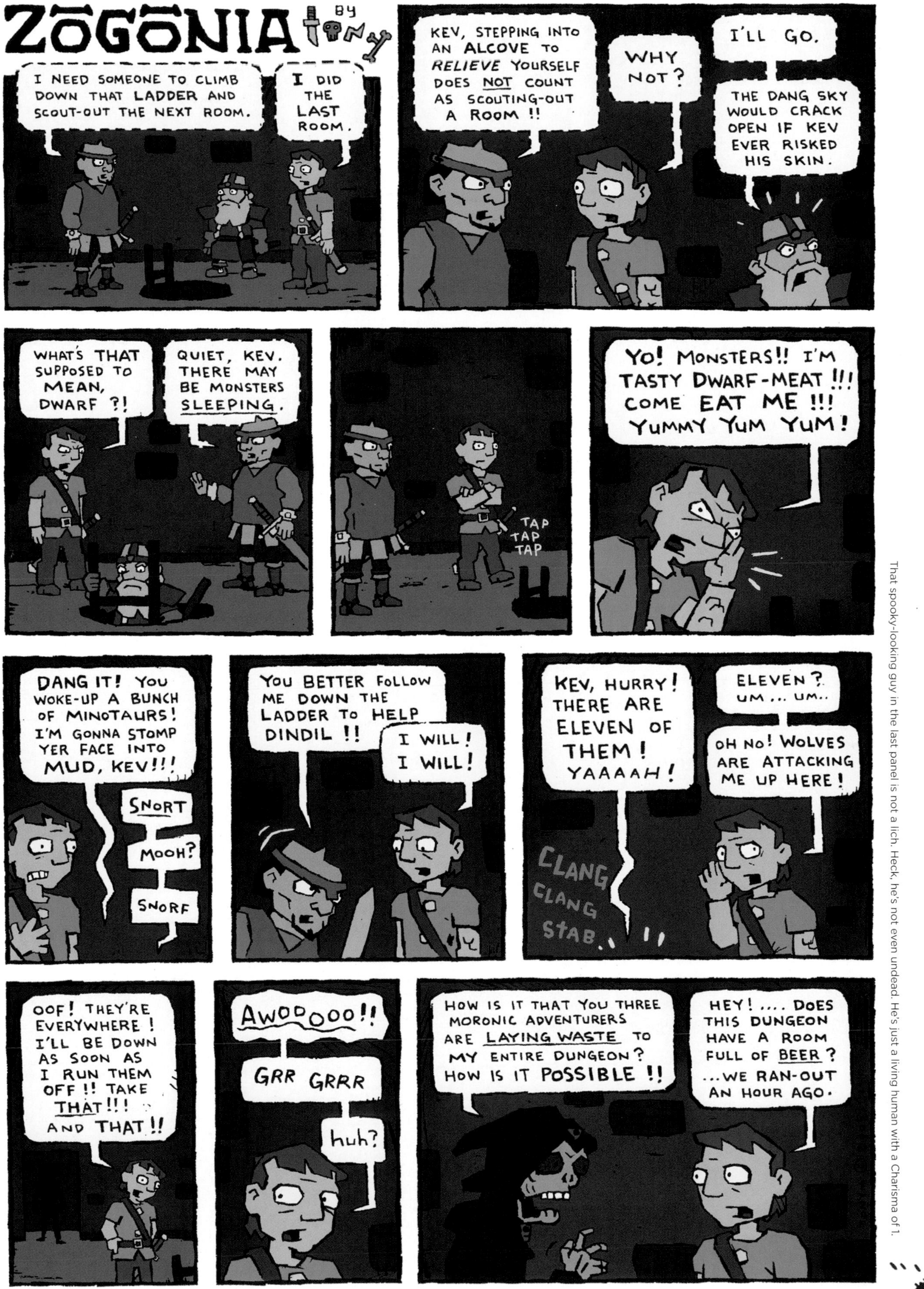
ZOGONIA
BY Tony
I NEED SOMEONE TO CLIMB DOWN THAT LADDER AND SCOUT-OUT THE NEXT ROOM.
I DID THE LAST ROOM.
KEV, STEPPING INTO AN ALCOVE TO RELIEVE YOURSELF DOES NOT COUNT AS SCOUTING-OUT A ROOM !!
WHY NOT?
I'LL GO.
THE DANG SKY WOULD CRACK OPEN IF KEV EVER RISKED HIS SKIN.
WHAT'S THAT SUPPOSED TO MEAN, DWARF ?!
QUIET, KEV. THERE MAY BE MONSTERS SLEEPING.
TAP TAP TAP
YO! MONSTERS!! I'M TASTY DWARF-MEAT !!! COME EAT ME !!! YUMMY YUM YUM!
DANG IT! YOU WOKE-UP A BUNCH OF MINOTAURS! I'M GONNA STOMP YER FACE INTO MUD, KEV!!!
SNORT
MOOH?
SNORF
YOU BETTER FOLLOW ME DOWN THE LADDER TO HELP DINDIL !!
I WILL! I WILL!
KEV, HURRY! THERE ARE ELEVEN OF THEM! YAAAAH!
CLANG CLANG STAB
ELEVEN? UM... UM..
OH NO! WOLVES ARE ATTACKING ME UP HERE!
OOF! THEY'RE EVERYWHERE! I'LL BE DOWN AS SOON AS I RUN THEM OFF!! TAKE THAT!!! AND THAT!!
AWOOOOO!!
GRR GRRR
huh?
HOW IS IT THAT YOU THREE MORONIC ADVENTURERS ARE LAYING WASTE TO MY ENTIRE DUNGEON? HOW IS IT POSSIBLE !!
HEY! .... DOES THIS DUNGEON HAVE A ROOM FULL OF BEER? ...WE RAN-OUT AN HOUR AGO.

That spooky-looking guy in the last panel is not a lich. Heck, he's not even undead. He's just a living human with a Charisma of 1.

ZŌGŌNIA
BY T.M.
THIS BIRD FLEW ONTO MY HAND THIS MORNING! IS THAT NOT AMAZING?! I HAVE DECLARED IT OUR NEW MASCOT!
A BIRD!
IT'S PROBABLY A WIZARD'S FAMILIAR. WE SHOULD KILL IT IMMEDIATELY.
DO NOT DISRESPECT THE MASCOT WITH FALSE ACCUSATIONS, KEV. NOW GO AND DIG UP A WORM FOR ITS MEAL.
DIG?! DINDIL IS THE DWARF, NOT ME!
STUPID IDIOT BIRD. RUINING MY LIFE. MAKING ME USE A SHOVEL....
HEY, I DUG AND DUG, BUT THERE ARE NO WORMS OUT HERE.
THEN YOU DIDN'T DIG DEEP ENOUGH. IT AIN'T RAINED IN A WHILE, SO THE WORMS ARE DEEP WHERE THE MOIST DIRT IS.
STUPID IDIOT DWARF, KNOWING WHERE THE WORMS GO, RUINING MY LIFE....
CRIPES! STILL NO WORMS. I WONDER HOW MUCH DEEPER I SHOULD DIG?
WHY'S THE GROUND MOVING?
DINDIL, GO SEE WHAT KEV IS YELLING ABOUT.
HE PROBABLY FOUND A WORM AND IS SCARED TO TOUCH IT.
AAA
...AND THAT IS HOW KEV MANAGED TO KILL MY BIRD AND DESTROY 40% OF THE TOWN....AND YOU KNOW WHAT? HE DOES NOT CARE.
WA HA HA HA HA!!
TONYM © 2005

Don't feel sad about the death of the bird. That bird was an evil bird. The world is a much better place with that bird dead!

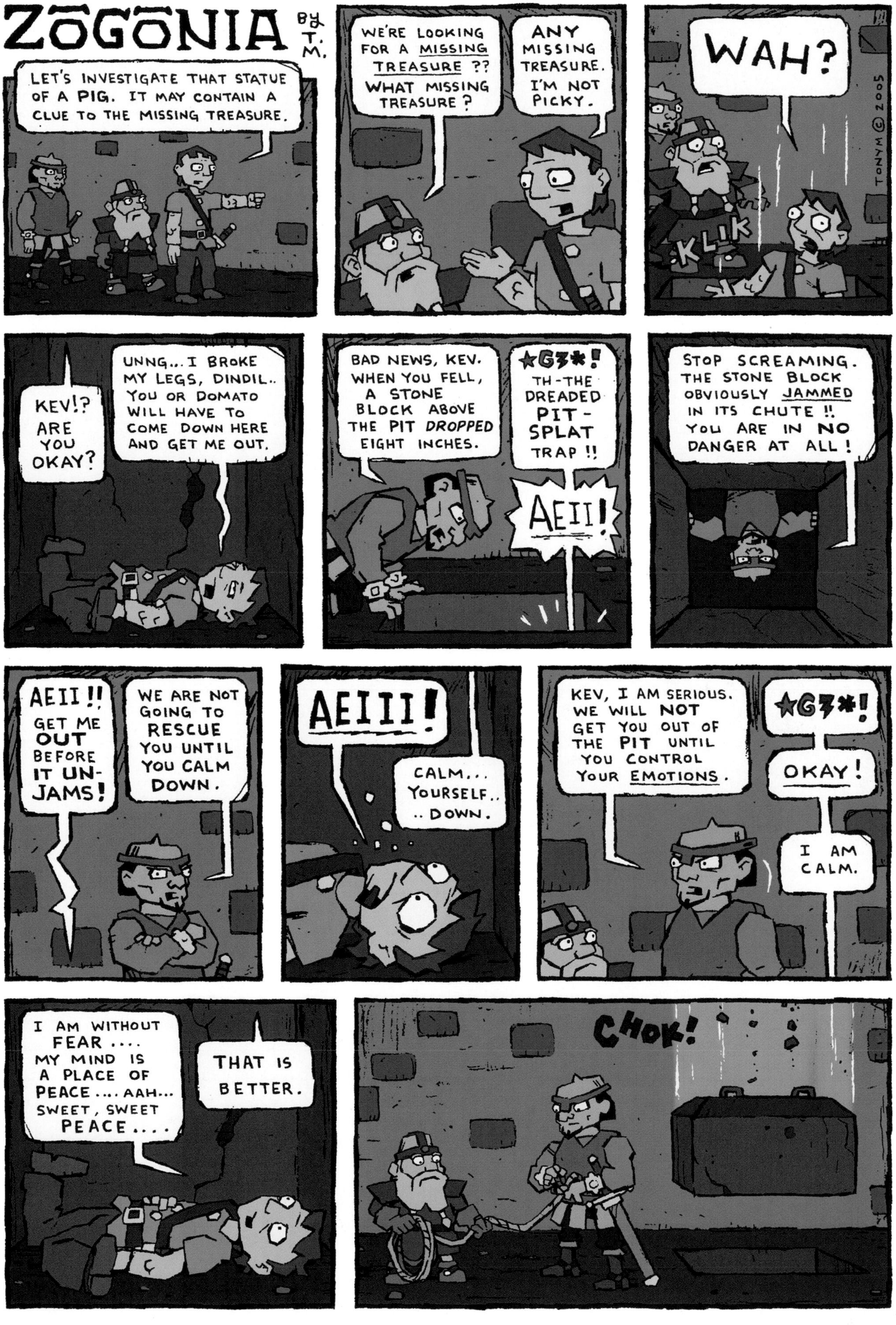

ZOGONIA BY T. M.
LET'S INVESTIGATE THAT STATUE OF A PIG. IT MAY CONTAIN A CLUE TO THE MISSING TREASURE.
WE'RE LOOKING FOR A MISSING TREASURE ?? WHAT MISSING TREASURE ?
ANY MISSING TREASURE. I'M NOT PICKY.
WAH?
KLIK
TONYM © 2005
KEV!? ARE YOU OKAY?
UNNG... I BROKE MY LEGS, DINDIL.. YOU OR DOMATO WILL HAVE TO COME DOWN HERE AND GET ME OUT.
BAD NEWS, KEV. WHEN YOU FELL, A STONE BLOCK ABOVE THE PIT DROPPED EIGHT INCHES.
★G3*! TH-THE DREADED PIT-SPLAT TRAP !!
AEII!
STOP SCREAMING. THE STONE BLOCK OBVIOUSLY JAMMED IN ITS CHUTE !!. YOU ARE IN NO DANGER AT ALL !
AEII !! GET ME OUT BEFORE IT UN-JAMS!
WE ARE NOT GOING TO RESCUE YOU UNTIL YOU CALM DOWN.
AEIII!
CALM... YOURSELF.. ..DOWN.
KEV, I AM SERIOUS. WE WILL NOT GET YOU OUT OF THE PIT UNTIL YOU CONTROL YOUR EMOTIONS.
★G3*!
OKAY!
I AM CALM.
I AM WITHOUT FEAR.... MY MIND IS A PLACE OF PEACE.... AAH... SWEET, SWEET PEACE....
THAT IS BETTER.
CHOK!

Kev is dead!

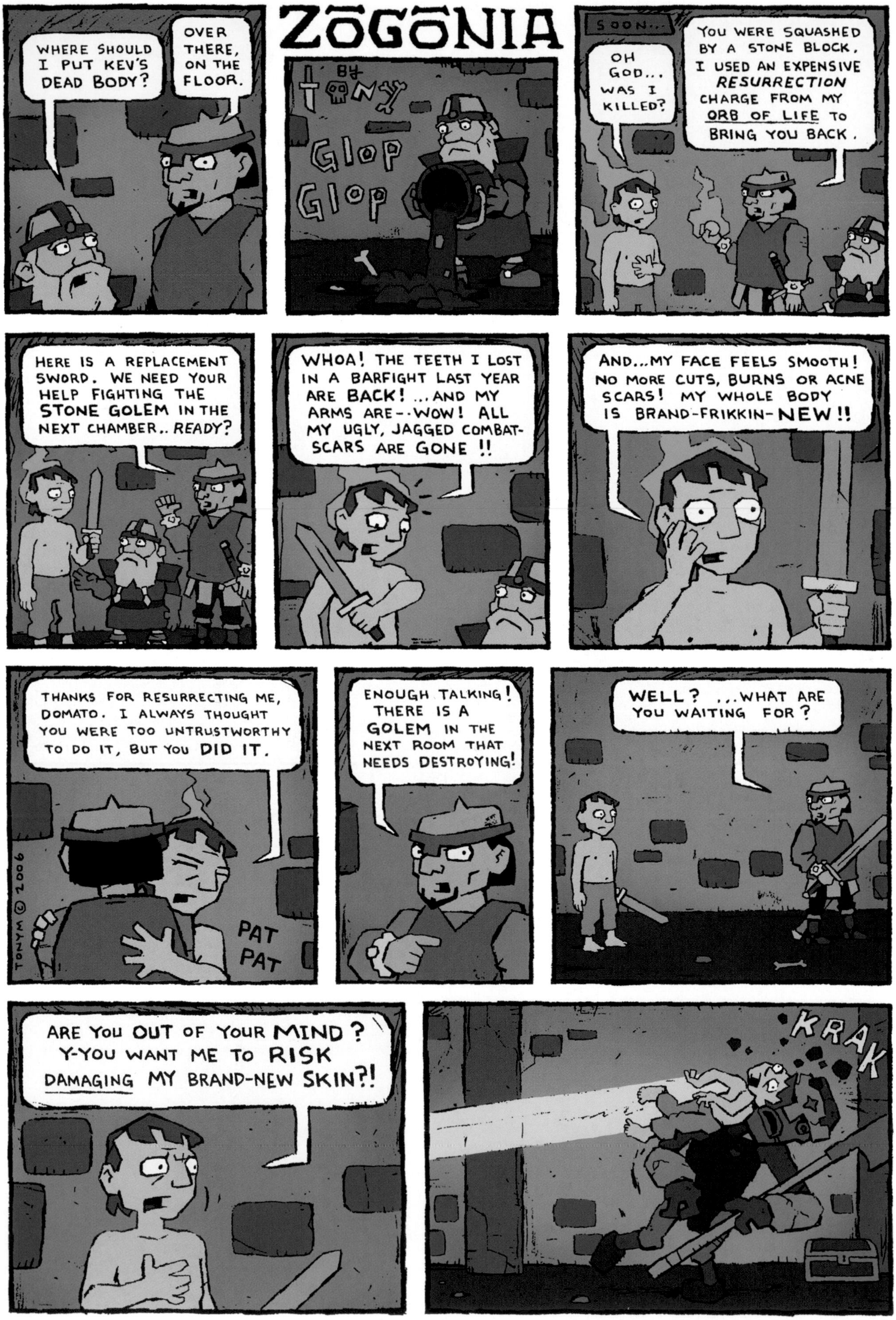
ZŌGŌNIA
BY TONY
WHERE SHOULD I PUT KEV'S DEAD BODY?
OVER THERE, ON THE FLOOR.
Glop Glop
SOON...
OH GOD... WAS I KILLED?
YOU WERE SQUASHED BY A STONE BLOCK. I USED AN EXPENSIVE RESURRECTION CHARGE FROM MY ORB OF LIFE TO BRING YOU BACK.
HERE IS A REPLACEMENT SWORD. WE NEED YOUR HELP FIGHTING THE STONE GOLEM IN THE NEXT CHAMBER.. READY?
WHOA! THE TEETH I LOST IN A BARFIGHT LAST YEAR ARE BACK! ...AND MY ARMS ARE--WOW! ALL MY UGLY, JAGGED COMBAT-SCARS ARE GONE !!
AND...MY FACE FEELS SMOOTH! NO MORE CUTS, BURNS OR ACNE SCARS! MY WHOLE BODY IS BRAND-FRIKKIN-NEW !!
THANKS FOR RESURRECTING ME, DOMATO. I ALWAYS THOUGHT YOU WERE TOO UNTRUSTWORTHY TO DO IT, BUT YOU DID IT.
TONYM © 2006
PAT PAT
ENOUGH TALKING! THERE IS A GOLEM IN THE NEXT ROOM THAT NEEDS DESTROYING!
WELL? ...WHAT ARE YOU WAITING FOR?
ARE YOU OUT OF YOUR MIND? Y-YOU WANT ME TO RISK DAMAGING MY BRAND-NEW SKIN?!
KRAK

In Zogonia, some wealthy people kill themselves every year for the purpose of being resurrected into a newer body. A few of these people even frequent special resorts where they are killed in strange, sensual ways; for example, being pelted to death with grapes or drowned in an enormous pool filled with raw oysters and tadpoles.

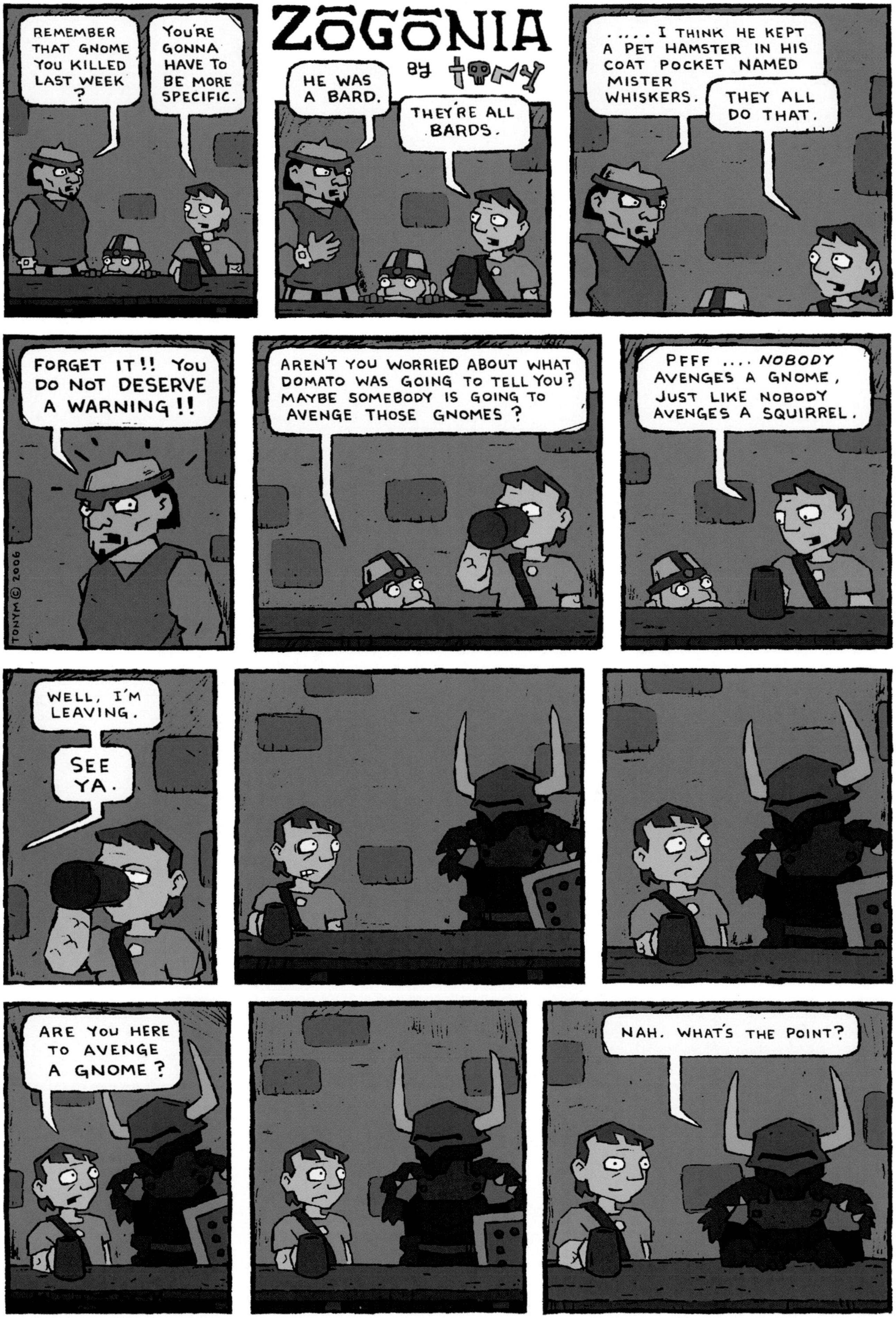
ZOGONIA
BY TONY
REMEMBER THAT GNOME YOU KILLED LAST WEEK?
YOU'RE GONNA HAVE TO BE MORE SPECIFIC.
HE WAS A BARD.
THEY'RE ALL BARDS.
..... I THINK HE KEPT A PET HAMSTER IN HIS COAT POCKET NAMED MISTER WHISKERS.
THEY ALL DO THAT.
FORGET IT!! YOU DO NOT DESERVE A WARNING!!
TONYM © 2006
AREN'T YOU WORRIED ABOUT WHAT DOMATO WAS GOING TO TELL YOU? MAYBE SOMEBODY IS GOING TO AVENGE THOSE GNOMES?
PFFF .... NOBODY AVENGES A GNOME, JUST LIKE NOBODY AVENGES A SQUIRREL.
WELL, I'M LEAVING.
SEE YA.
ARE YOU HERE TO AVENGE A GNOME?
NAH. WHAT'S THE POINT?

Did you know that in Zogonia, seeing a dead gnome on the side of the road is considered good luck? Strange, but true!

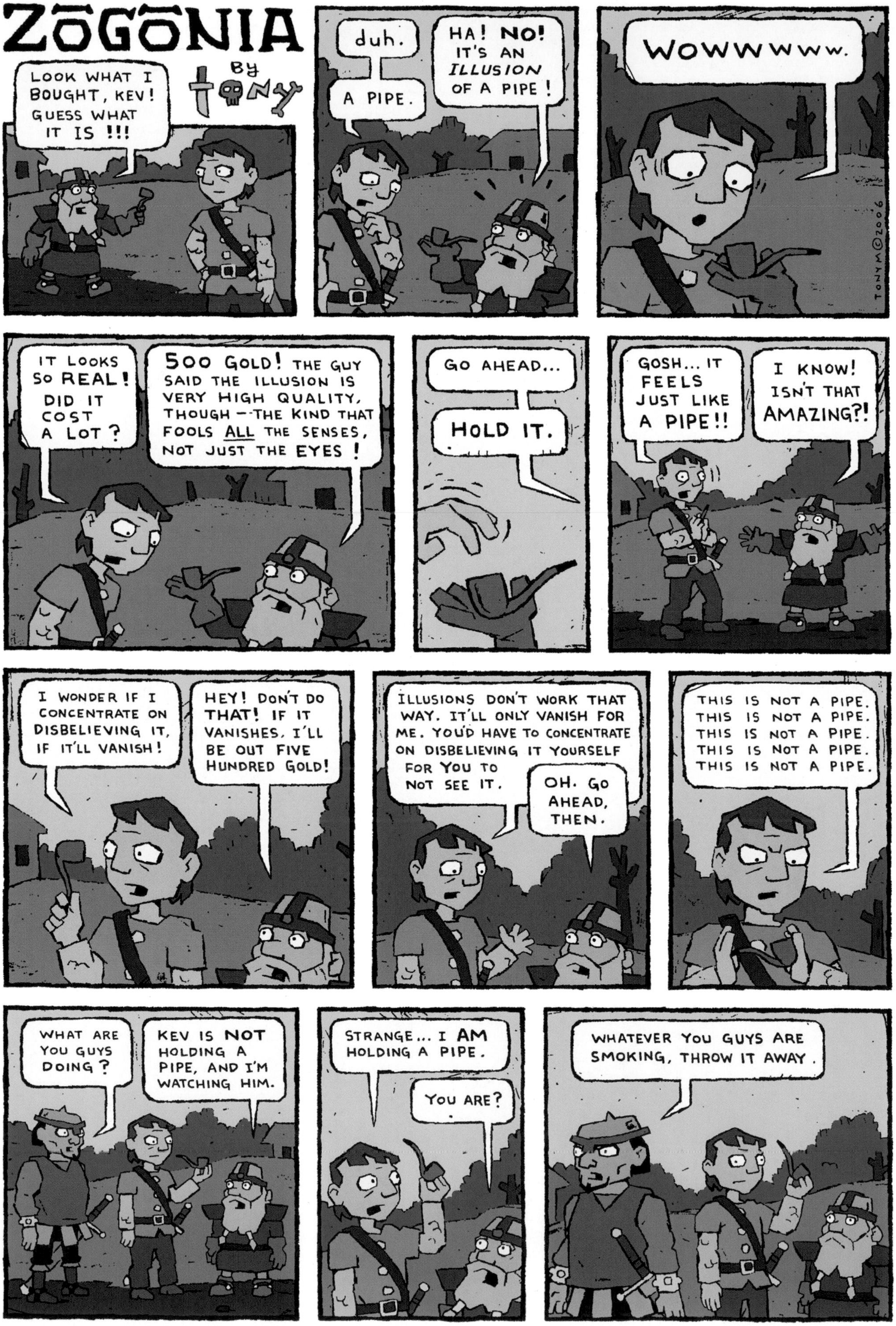
ZŌGŌNIA
By tony
LOOK WHAT I BOUGHT, KEV! GUESS WHAT IT IS !!!
duh.
A PIPE.
HA! NO! IT'S AN ILLUSION OF A PIPE!
WOWWWWW.
TONYM©2006
IT LOOKS SO REAL! DID IT COST A LOT?
500 GOLD! THE GUY SAID THE ILLUSION IS VERY HIGH QUALITY, THOUGH -- THE KIND THAT FOOLS ALL THE SENSES, NOT JUST THE EYES!
GO AHEAD...
HOLD IT.
GOSH... IT FEELS JUST LIKE A PIPE!!
I KNOW! ISN'T THAT AMAZING?!
I WONDER IF I CONCENTRATE ON DISBELIEVING IT, IF IT'LL VANISH!
HEY! DON'T DO THAT! IF IT VANISHES, I'LL BE OUT FIVE HUNDRED GOLD!
ILLUSIONS DON'T WORK THAT WAY. IT'LL ONLY VANISH FOR ME. YOU'D HAVE TO CONCENTRATE ON DISBELIEVING IT YOURSELF FOR YOU TO NOT SEE IT.
OH. GO AHEAD, THEN.
THIS IS NOT A PIPE. THIS IS NOT A PIPE. THIS IS NOT A PIPE. THIS IS NOT A PIPE. THIS IS NOT A PIPE.
WHAT ARE YOU GUYS DOING?
KEV IS NOT HOLDING A PIPE, AND I'M WATCHING HIM.
STRANGE... I AM HOLDING A PIPE.
YOU ARE?
WHATEVER YOU GUYS ARE SMOKING, THROW IT AWAY.

This strip was inspired by Magritte's painting, *Ceci n'est pas une pipe.*

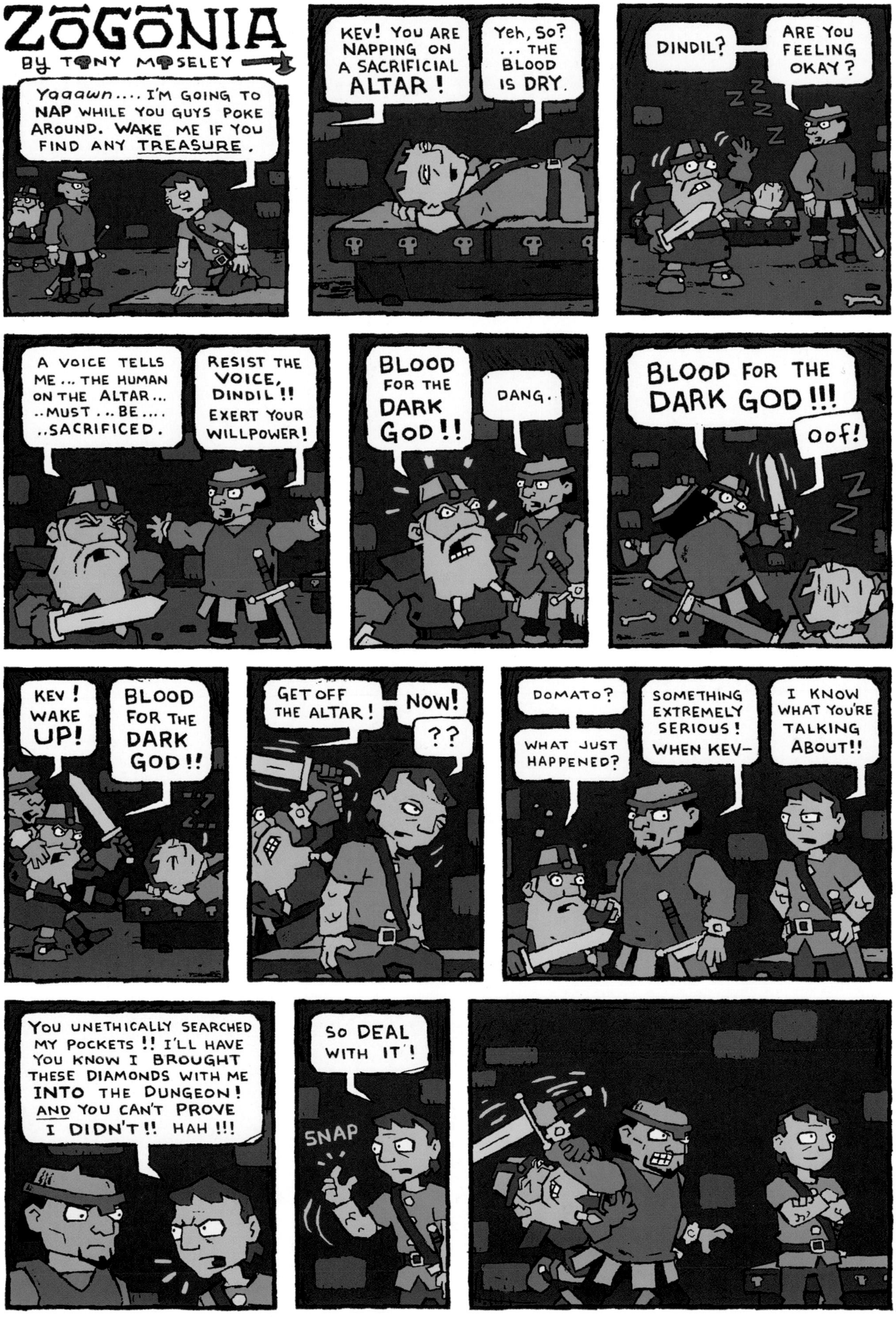
ZOGONIA
BY TONY MOSELEY
Yaaawn.... I'M GOING TO NAP WHILE YOU GUYS POKE AROUND. WAKE ME IF YOU FIND ANY TREASURE.
KEV! YOU ARE NAPPING ON A SACRIFICIAL ALTAR!
Yeh, So? ... THE BLOOD IS DRY.
DINDIL?
ARE YOU FEELING OKAY?
Z Z Z
A VOICE TELLS ME... THE HUMAN ON THE ALTAR... ..MUST... BE.... ..SACRIFICED.
RESIST THE VOICE, DINDIL!! EXERT YOUR WILLPOWER!
BLOOD FOR THE DARK GOD!!
DANG.
BLOOD FOR THE DARK GOD!!!
Oof!
Z Z
KEV! WAKE UP!
BLOOD FOR THE DARK GOD!!
GET OFF THE ALTAR!
NOW!
??
DOMATO?
WHAT JUST HAPPENED?
SOMETHING EXTREMELY SERIOUS! WHEN KEV-
I KNOW WHAT YOU'RE TALKING ABOUT!!
YOU UNETHICALLY SEARCHED MY POCKETS!! I'LL HAVE YOU KNOW I BROUGHT THESE DIAMONDS WITH ME INTO THE DUNGEON! AND YOU CAN'T PROVE I DIDN'T!! HAH!!!
So DEAL WITH IT!
SNAP

This strip was *not* inspired by Magritte's painting, *Ceci n'est pas une pipe*.

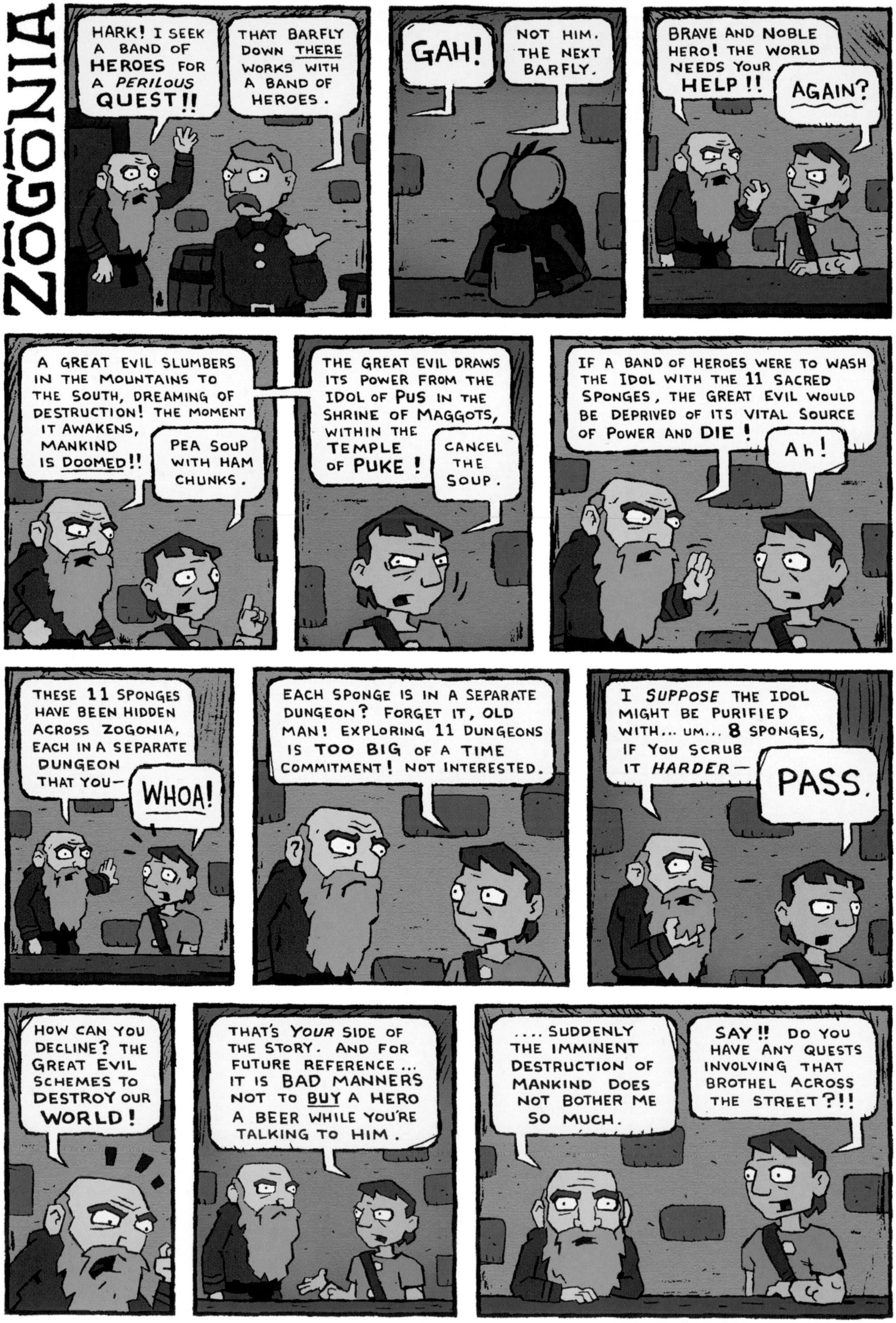
ZOGONIA
HARK! I SEEK A BAND OF HEROES FOR A PERILOUS QUEST!!
THAT BARFLY DOWN THERE WORKS WITH A BAND OF HEROES.
GAH!
NOT HIM. THE NEXT BARFLY.
BRAVE AND NOBLE HERO! THE WORLD NEEDS YOUR HELP!!
AGAIN?
A GREAT EVIL SLUMBERS IN THE MOUNTAINS TO THE SOUTH, DREAMING OF DESTRUCTION! THE MOMENT IT AWAKENS, MANKIND IS DOOMED!!
PEA SOUP WITH HAM CHUNKS.
THE GREAT EVIL DRAWS ITS POWER FROM THE IDOL OF PUS IN THE SHRINE OF MAGGOTS, WITHIN THE TEMPLE OF PUKE!
CANCEL THE SOUP.
IF A BAND OF HEROES WERE TO WASH THE IDOL WITH THE 11 SACRED SPONGES, THE GREAT EVIL WOULD BE DEPRIVED OF ITS VITAL SOURCE OF POWER AND DIE!
Ah!
THESE 11 SPONGES HAVE BEEN HIDDEN ACROSS ZOGONIA, EACH IN A SEPARATE DUNGEON THAT YOU—
WHOA!
EACH SPONGE IS IN A SEPARATE DUNGEON? FORGET IT, OLD MAN! EXPLORING 11 DUNGEONS IS TOO BIG OF A TIME COMMITMENT! NOT INTERESTED.
I SUPPOSE THE IDOL MIGHT BE PURIFIED WITH... UM... 8 SPONGES, IF YOU SCRUB IT HARDER—
PASS.
HOW CAN YOU DECLINE? THE GREAT EVIL SCHEMES TO DESTROY OUR WORLD!
THAT'S YOUR SIDE OF THE STORY. AND FOR FUTURE REFERENCE... IT IS BAD MANNERS NOT TO BUY A HERO A BEER WHILE YOU'RE TALKING TO HIM.
.... SUDDENLY THE IMMINENT DESTRUCTION OF MANKIND DOES NOT BOTHER ME SO MUCH.
SAY!! DO YOU HAVE ANY QUESTS INVOLVING THAT BROTHEL ACROSS THE STREET?!!

The old man should've talked to the disgusting barfly in panel two. That barfly was a 19th-level paladin. It doesn't pay to jump to conclusions in Zogonia.

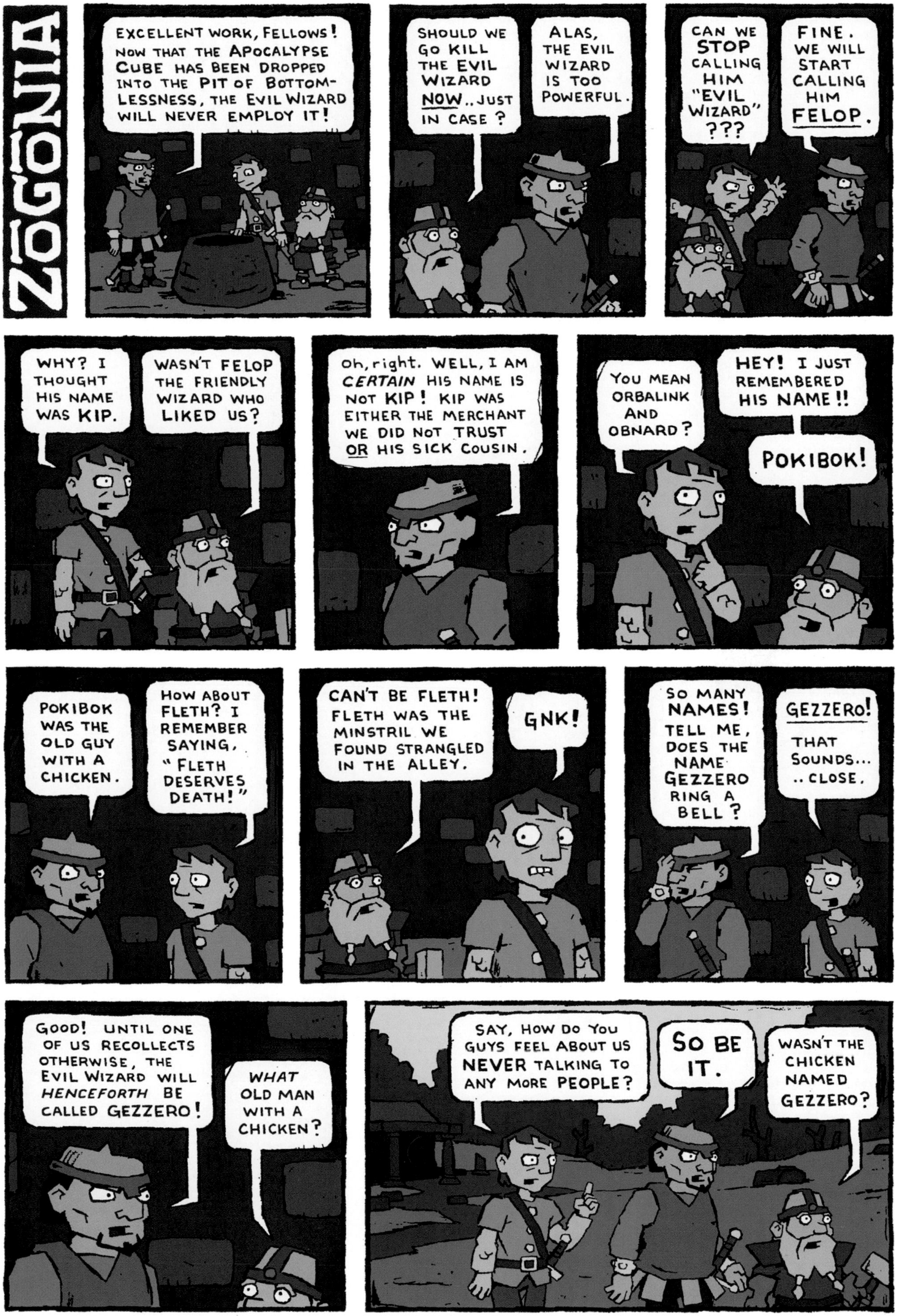
ZOGONIA
EXCELLENT WORK, FELLOWS! NOW THAT THE APOCALYPSE CUBE HAS BEEN DROPPED INTO THE PIT OF BOTTOMLESSNESS, THE EVIL WIZARD WILL NEVER EMPLOY IT!
SHOULD WE GO KILL THE EVIL WIZARD NOW.. JUST IN CASE?
ALAS, THE EVIL WIZARD IS TOO POWERFUL.
CAN WE STOP CALLING HIM "EVIL WIZARD" ???
FINE. WE WILL START CALLING HIM FELOP.
WHY? I THOUGHT HIS NAME WAS KIP.
WASN'T FELOP THE FRIENDLY WIZARD WHO LIKED US?
Oh, right. WELL, I AM CERTAIN HIS NAME IS NOT KIP! KIP WAS EITHER THE MERCHANT WE DID NOT TRUST OR HIS SICK COUSIN.
YOU MEAN ORBALINK AND OBNARD?
HEY! I JUST REMEMBERED HIS NAME!!
POKIBOK!
POKIBOK WAS THE OLD GUY WITH A CHICKEN.
HOW ABOUT FLETH? I REMEMBER SAYING, "FLETH DESERVES DEATH!"
CAN'T BE FLETH! FLETH WAS THE MINSTRIL WE FOUND STRANGLED IN THE ALLEY.
GNK!
SO MANY NAMES! TELL ME, DOES THE NAME GEZZERO RING A BELL?
GEZZERO! THAT SOUNDS... .. CLOSE.
GOOD! UNTIL ONE OF US RECOLLECTS OTHERWISE, THE EVIL WIZARD WILL HENCEFORTH BE CALLED GEZZERO!
WHAT OLD MAN WITH A CHICKEN?
SAY, HOW DO YOU GUYS FEEL ABOUT US NEVER TALKING TO ANY MORE PEOPLE?
SO BE IT.
WASN'T THE CHICKEN NAMED GEZZERO?

Want to drive your GM nuts? Keep a detailed record of the names and professions of his NPCs. Then one day hand him a quiz, where he has to match the names to the professions by connecting them with lines. Whee!

ZOGONIA

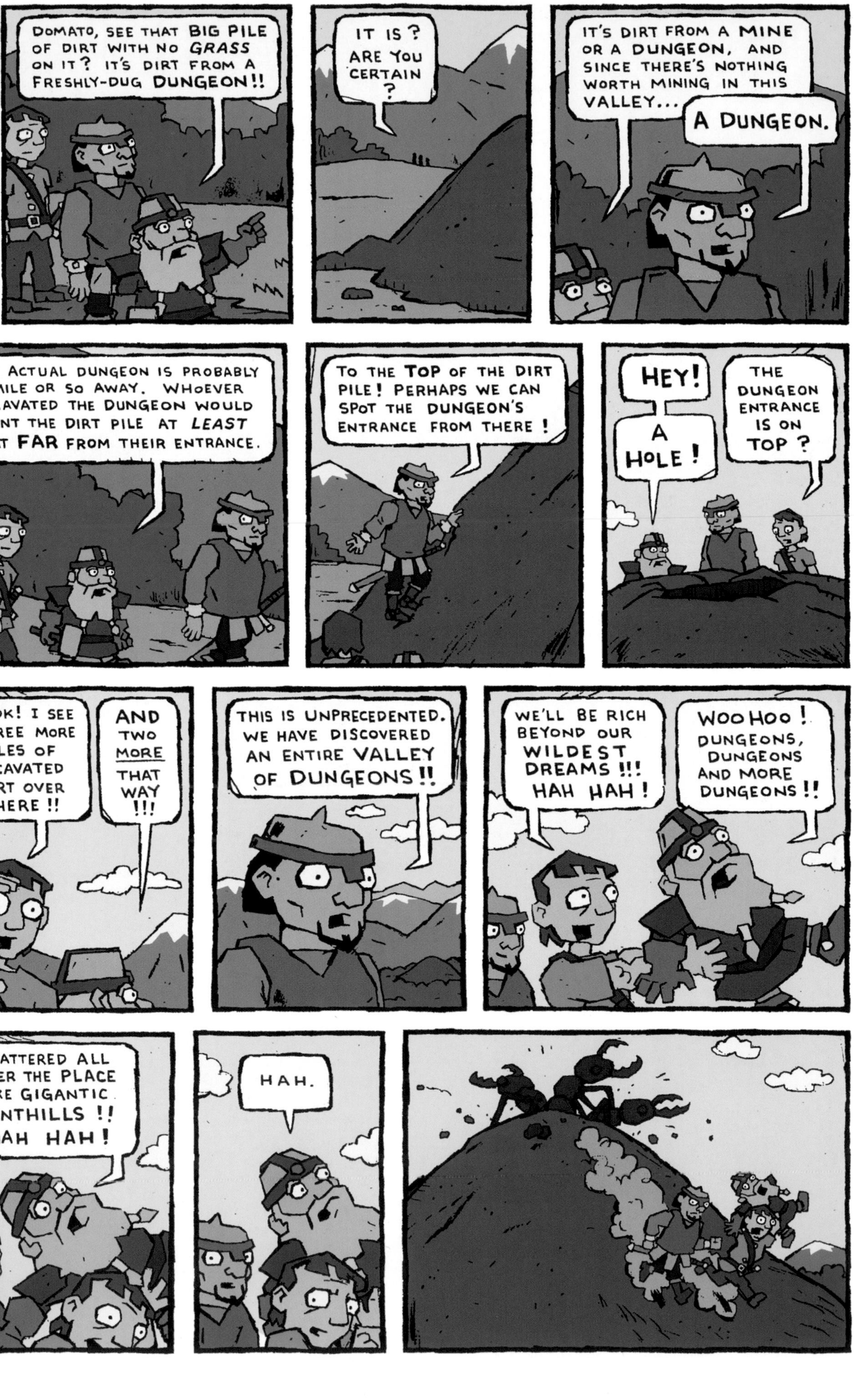

DOMATO, SEE THAT BIG PILE OF DIRT WITH NO GRASS ON IT? IT'S DIRT FROM A FRESHLY-DUG DUNGEON!!
IT IS? ARE YOU CERTAIN?
IT'S DIRT FROM A MINE OR A DUNGEON, AND SINCE THERE'S NOTHING WORTH MINING IN THIS VALLEY...
A DUNGEON.
THE ACTUAL DUNGEON IS PROBABLY A MILE OR SO AWAY. WHOEVER EXCAVATED THE DUNGEON WOULD WANT THE DIRT PILE AT LEAST THAT FAR FROM THEIR ENTRANCE.
TO THE TOP OF THE DIRT PILE! PERHAPS WE CAN SPOT THE DUNGEON'S ENTRANCE FROM THERE!
HEY!
A HOLE!
THE DUNGEON ENTRANCE IS ON TOP?
LOOK! I SEE THREE MORE PILES OF EXCAVATED DIRT OVER THERE!!
AND TWO MORE THAT WAY!!!
THIS IS UNPRECEDENTED. WE HAVE DISCOVERED AN ENTIRE VALLEY OF DUNGEONS!!
WE'LL BE RICH BEYOND OUR WILDEST DREAMS!!! HAH HAH!
WOOHOO! DUNGEONS, DUNGEONS AND MORE DUNGEONS!!
SCATTERED ALL OVER THE PLACE LIKE GIGANTIC ANTHILLS!! HAH HAH!
HAH.

Seriously, when a dungeon is excavated, where does all the dirt and rock go?

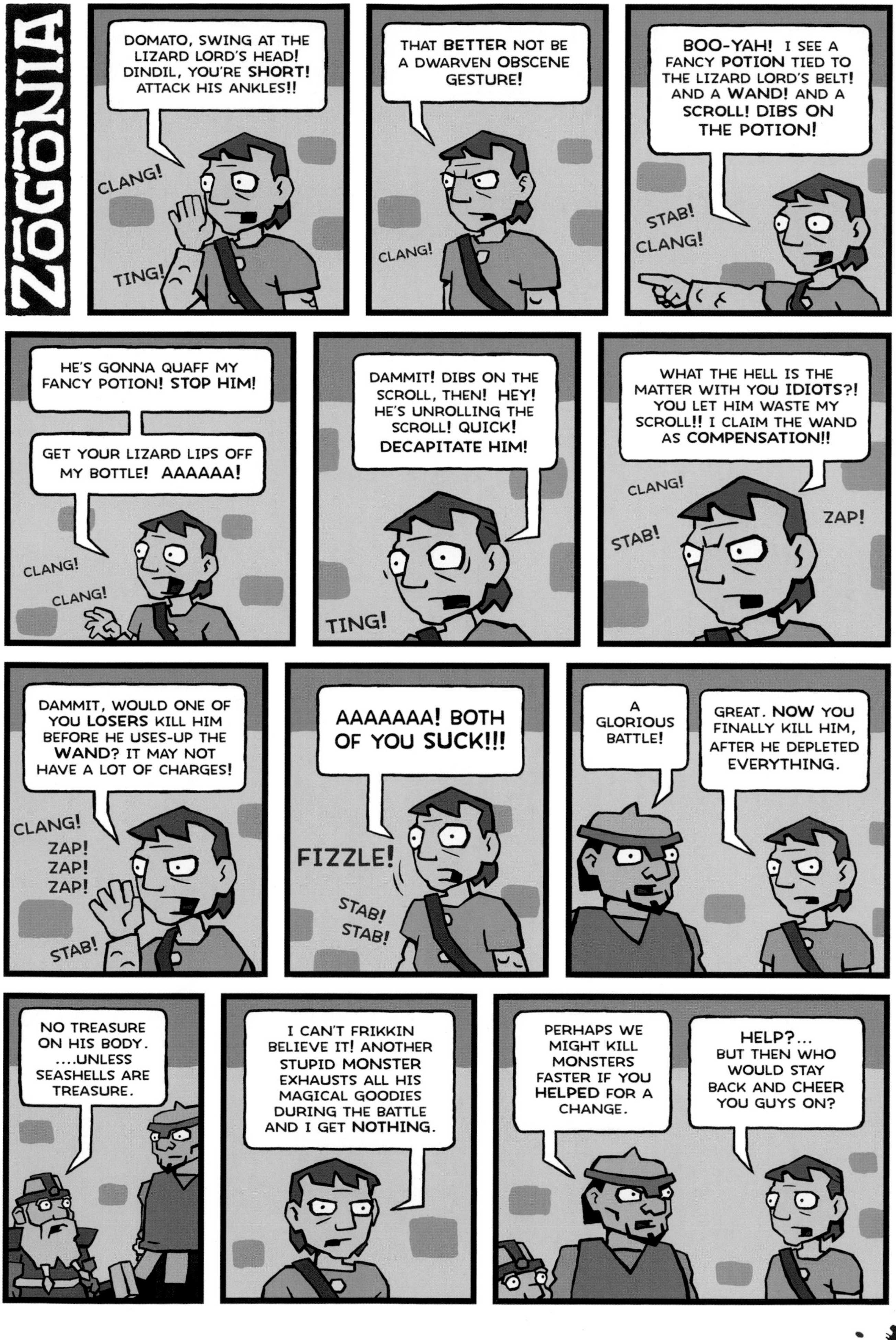
ZOGONIA
DOMATO, SWING AT THE LIZARD LORD'S HEAD! DINDIL, YOU'RE SHORT! ATTACK HIS ANKLES!!
CLANG!
TING!
THAT BETTER NOT BE A DWARVEN OBSCENE GESTURE!
CLANG!
BOO-YAH! I SEE A FANCY POTION TIED TO THE LIZARD LORD'S BELT! AND A WAND! AND A SCROLL! DIBS ON THE POTION!
STAB!
CLANG!
HE'S GONNA QUAFF MY FANCY POTION! STOP HIM!
GET YOUR LIZARD LIPS OFF MY BOTTLE! AAAAAA!
CLANG!
CLANG!
DAMMIT! DIBS ON THE SCROLL, THEN! HEY! HE'S UNROLLING THE SCROLL! QUICK! DECAPITATE HIM!
TING!
WHAT THE HELL IS THE MATTER WITH YOU IDIOTS?! YOU LET HIM WASTE MY SCROLL!! I CLAIM THE WAND AS COMPENSATION!!
CLANG!
STAB!
ZAP!
DAMMIT, WOULD ONE OF YOU LOSERS KILL HIM BEFORE HE USES-UP THE WAND? IT MAY NOT HAVE A LOT OF CHARGES!
CLANG!
ZAP!
ZAP!
ZAP!
STAB!
AAAAAAA! BOTH OF YOU SUCK!!!
FIZZLE!
STAB!
STAB!
A GLORIOUS BATTLE!
GREAT. NOW YOU FINALLY KILL HIM, AFTER HE DEPLETED EVERYTHING.
NO TREASURE ON HIS BODY. ....UNLESS SEASHELLS ARE TREASURE.
I CAN'T FRIKKIN BELIEVE IT! ANOTHER STUPID MONSTER EXHAUSTS ALL HIS MAGICAL GOODIES DURING THE BATTLE AND I GET NOTHING.
PERHAPS WE MIGHT KILL MONSTERS FASTER IF YOU HELPED FOR A CHANGE.
HELP?... BUT THEN WHO WOULD STAY BACK AND CHEER YOU GUYS ON?

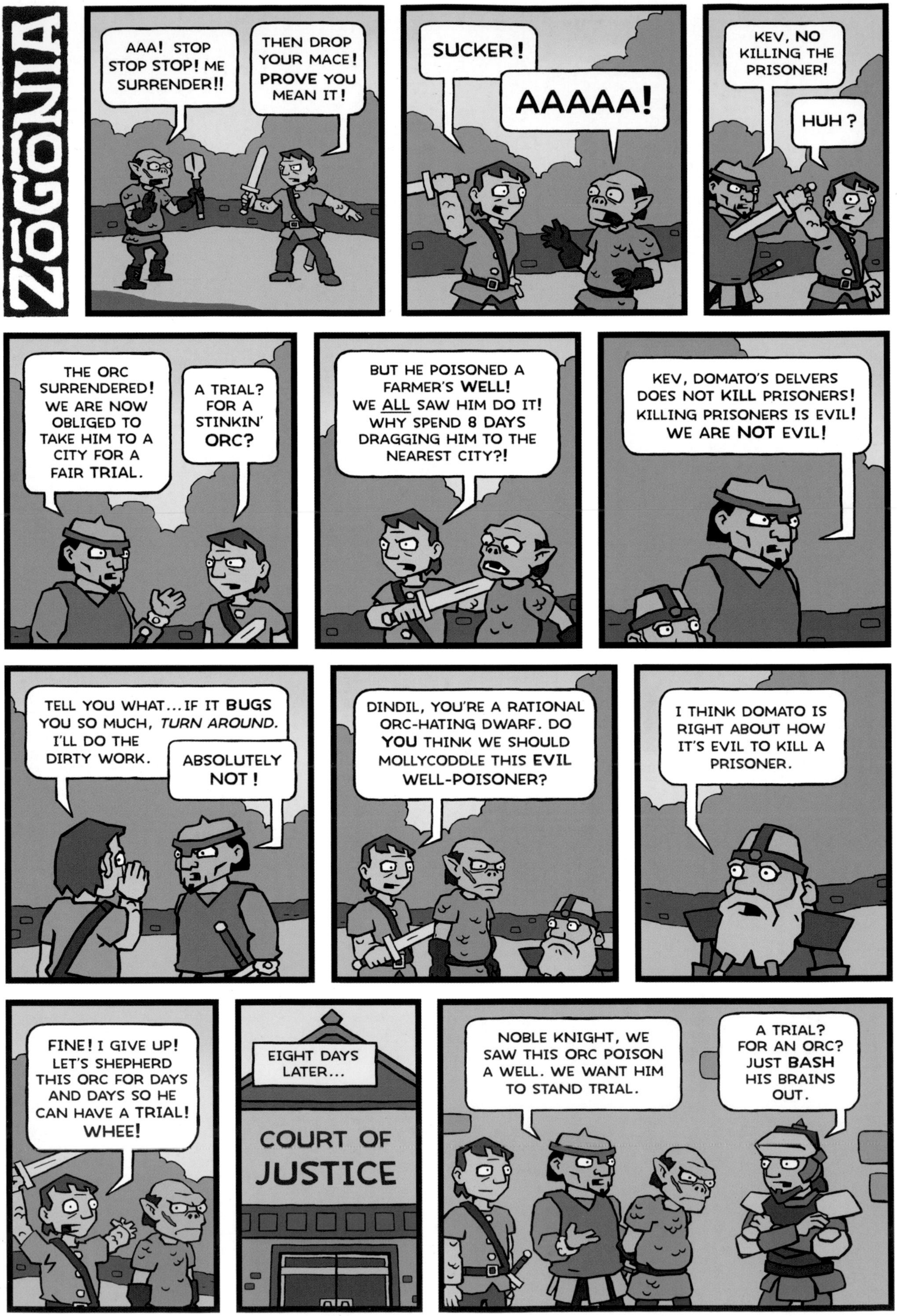
ZOGONIA
AAA! STOP STOP STOP! ME SURRENDER!!
THEN DROP YOUR MACE! PROVE YOU MEAN IT!
SUCKER!
AAAAA!
KEV, NO KILLING THE PRISONER!
HUH?
THE ORC SURRENDERED! WE ARE NOW OBLIGED TO TAKE HIM TO A CITY FOR A FAIR TRIAL.
A TRIAL? FOR A STINKIN' ORC?
BUT HE POISONED A FARMER'S WELL! WE ALL SAW HIM DO IT! WHY SPEND 8 DAYS DRAGGING HIM TO THE NEAREST CITY?!
KEV, DOMATO'S DELVERS DOES NOT KILL PRISONERS! KILLING PRISONERS IS EVIL! WE ARE NOT EVIL!
TELL YOU WHAT... IF IT BUGS YOU SO MUCH, TURN AROUND. I'LL DO THE DIRTY WORK.
ABSOLUTELY NOT!
DINDIL, YOU'RE A RATIONAL ORC-HATING DWARF. DO YOU THINK WE SHOULD MOLLYCODDLE THIS EVIL WELL-POISONER?
I THINK DOMATO IS RIGHT ABOUT HOW IT'S EVIL TO KILL A PRISONER.
FINE! I GIVE UP! LET'S SHEPHERD THIS ORC FOR DAYS AND DAYS SO HE CAN HAVE A TRIAL! WHEE!
EIGHT DAYS LATER...
COURT OF JUSTICE
NOBLE KNIGHT, WE SAW THIS ORC POISON A WELL. WE WANT HIM TO STAND TRIAL.
A TRIAL? FOR AN ORC? JUST BASH HIS BRAINS OUT.

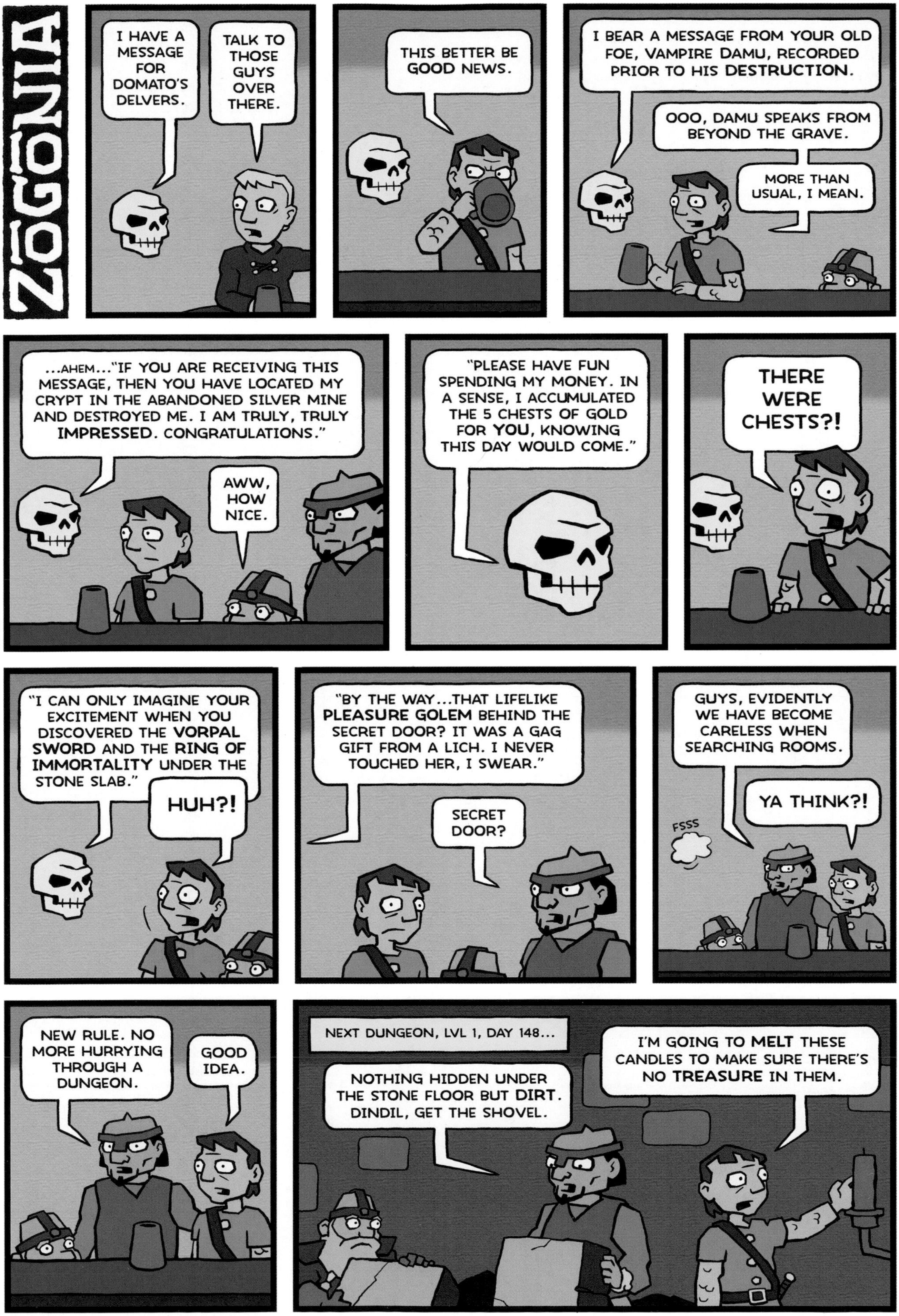
ZOGONIA
I HAVE A MESSAGE FOR DOMATO'S DELVERS.
TALK TO THOSE GUYS OVER THERE.
THIS BETTER BE GOOD NEWS.
I BEAR A MESSAGE FROM YOUR OLD FOE, VAMPIRE DAMU, RECORDED PRIOR TO HIS DESTRUCTION.
OOO, DAMU SPEAKS FROM BEYOND THE GRAVE.
MORE THAN USUAL, I MEAN.
...AHEM..."IF YOU ARE RECEIVING THIS MESSAGE, THEN YOU HAVE LOCATED MY CRYPT IN THE ABANDONED SILVER MINE AND DESTROYED ME. I AM TRULY, TRULY IMPRESSED. CONGRATULATIONS."
AWW, HOW NICE.
"PLEASE HAVE FUN SPENDING MY MONEY. IN A SENSE, I ACCUMULATED THE 5 CHESTS OF GOLD FOR YOU, KNOWING THIS DAY WOULD COME."
THERE WERE CHESTS?!
"I CAN ONLY IMAGINE YOUR EXCITEMENT WHEN YOU DISCOVERED THE VORPAL SWORD AND THE RING OF IMMORTALITY UNDER THE STONE SLAB."
HUH?!
"BY THE WAY...THAT LIFELIKE PLEASURE GOLEM BEHIND THE SECRET DOOR? IT WAS A GAG GIFT FROM A LICH. I NEVER TOUCHED HER, I SWEAR."
SECRET DOOR?
GUYS, EVIDENTLY WE HAVE BECOME CARELESS WHEN SEARCHING ROOMS.
YA THINK?!
FSSS
NEW RULE. NO MORE HURRYING THROUGH A DUNGEON.
GOOD IDEA.
NEXT DUNGEON, LVL 1, DAY 148...
NOTHING HIDDEN UNDER THE STONE FLOOR BUT DIRT. DINDIL, GET THE SHOVEL.
I'M GOING TO MELT THESE CANDLES TO MAKE SURE THERE'S NO TREASURE IN THEM.

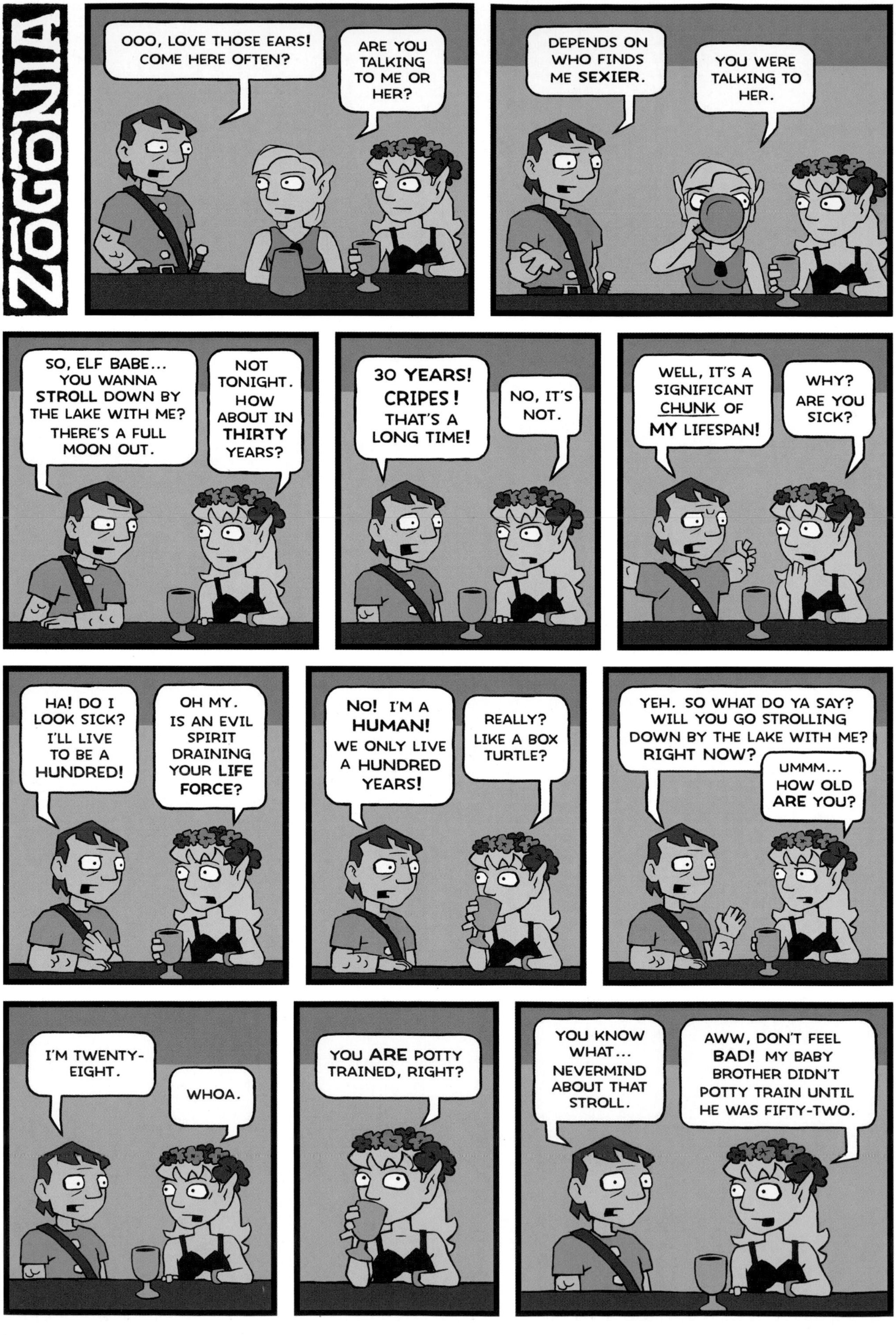
ZOGONIA
OOO, LOVE THOSE EARS! COME HERE OFTEN?
ARE YOU TALKING TO ME OR HER?
DEPENDS ON WHO FINDS ME SEXIER.
YOU WERE TALKING TO HER.
SO, ELF BABE... YOU WANNA STROLL DOWN BY THE LAKE WITH ME? THERE'S A FULL MOON OUT.
NOT TONIGHT. HOW ABOUT IN THIRTY YEARS?
30 YEARS! CRIPES! THAT'S A LONG TIME!
NO, IT'S NOT.
WELL, IT'S A SIGNIFICANT CHUNK OF MY LIFESPAN!
WHY? ARE YOU SICK?
HA! DO I LOOK SICK? I'LL LIVE TO BE A HUNDRED!
OH MY. IS AN EVIL SPIRIT DRAINING YOUR LIFE FORCE?
NO! I'M A HUMAN! WE ONLY LIVE A HUNDRED YEARS!
REALLY? LIKE A BOX TURTLE?
YEH. SO WHAT DO YA SAY? WILL YOU GO STROLLING DOWN BY THE LAKE WITH ME? RIGHT NOW?
UMMM... HOW OLD ARE YOU?
I'M TWENTY-EIGHT.
WHOA.
YOU ARE POTTY TRAINED, RIGHT?
YOU KNOW WHAT... NEVERMIND ABOUT THAT STROLL.
AWW, DON'T FEEL BAD! MY BABY BROTHER DIDN'T POTTY TRAIN UNTIL HE WAS FIFTY-TWO.

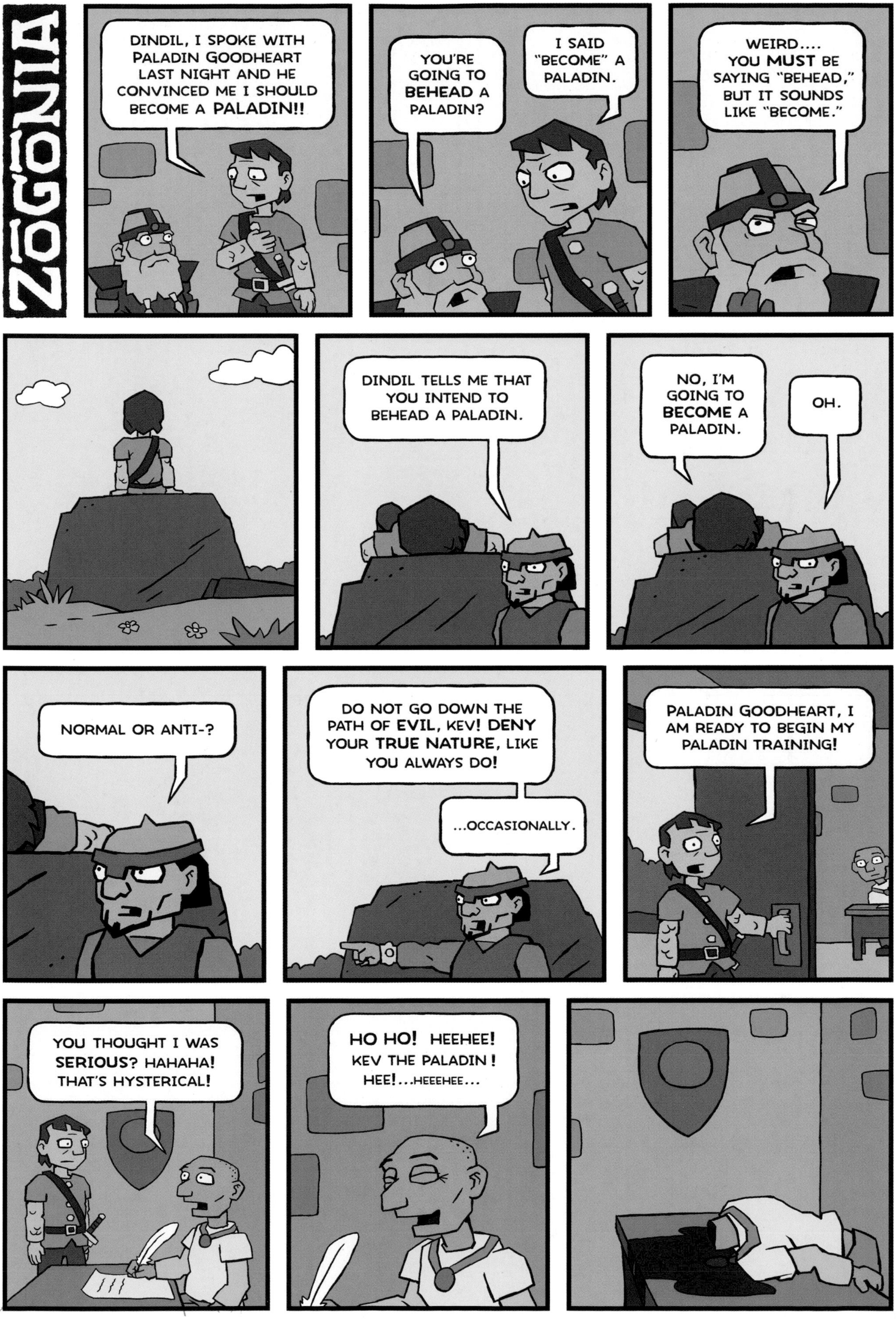
ZOGONIA
DINDIL, I SPOKE WITH PALADIN GOODHEART LAST NIGHT AND HE CONVINCED ME I SHOULD BECOME A PALADIN!!
YOU'RE GOING TO BEHEAD A PALADIN?
I SAID "BECOME" A PALADIN.
WEIRD.... YOU MUST BE SAYING "BEHEAD," BUT IT SOUNDS LIKE "BECOME."
DINDIL TELLS ME THAT YOU INTEND TO BEHEAD A PALADIN.
NO, I'M GOING TO BECOME A PALADIN.
OH.
NORMAL OR ANTI-?
DO NOT GO DOWN THE PATH OF EVIL, KEV! DENY YOUR TRUE NATURE, LIKE YOU ALWAYS DO!
...OCCASIONALLY.
PALADIN GOODHEART, I AM READY TO BEGIN MY PALADIN TRAINING!
YOU THOUGHT I WAS SERIOUS? HAHAHA! THAT'S HYSTERICAL!
HO HO! HEEHEE! KEV THE PALADIN! HEE!...HEEEHEE...

ZOGONIA

WANNA SEE A **TUNNELING BRAINBEETLE**? DON'T WORRY, IT'S DEAD.

DO NOT SPEAK TO ME.

I THOUGHT YOU **DARK ELF** CHICKS LIKED THIS SORT OF THING-- **OW!** WHAT THE HELL?

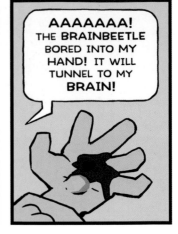

AAAAAAA! THE **BRAINBEETLE** BORED INTO MY **HAND!** IT WILL TUNNEL TO MY **BRAIN!**

TAKE THIS KNIFE! QUICK! CUT OFF MY HAND! DO IT! AAAA! **TOO LATE!** IT'S IN MY FOREARM! SAW OFF MY ARM AT THE ELBOW! **NOW!!**

WHY AREN'T YOU DOING **SOMETHING,** LADY?! SNAP OUT OF IT! CRAP! IT'S IN MY UPPER ARM! IT'S TUNNELING THROUGH MY BICEP! CUT OFF MY WHOLE ARM! NOW! NOW! NOW!

THE PAIN! ONLY SECONDS LEFT! DIE, BEETLE! **DIE!**

STAB!

ACKKLICKK! IT'S IN MY **CHEST**...GOING **UP!** IT'S IN **MY NECK!** MY... AGGCKG!

HACKKK!

HURRRGHGH!

AKGHKK!!

WOW, I COUGHED IT UP. LUCKY ME.

THANKS FOR *WATCHING* ME **ALMOST** **DIE,** YOU COLD-HEARTED, SOULLESS, PSYCHOTIC ABOMINATION!

YOUR SUFFERING HAS ARROUSED MY **LUST,** HUMAN.

54

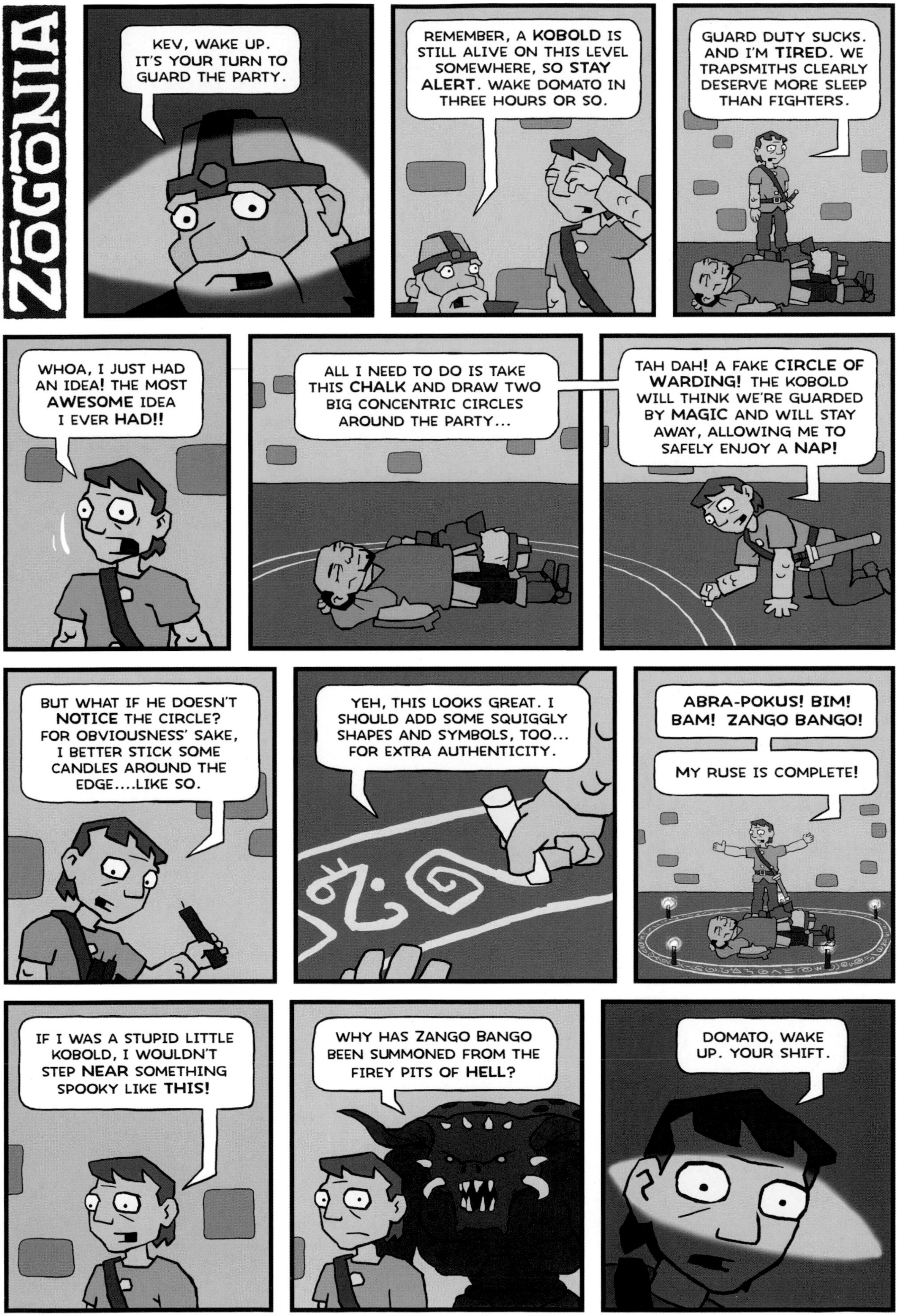
ZOGONIA
KEV, WAKE UP. IT'S YOUR TURN TO GUARD THE PARTY.
REMEMBER, A KOBOLD IS STILL ALIVE ON THIS LEVEL SOMEWHERE, SO STAY ALERT. WAKE DOMATO IN THREE HOURS OR SO.
GUARD DUTY SUCKS. AND I'M TIRED. WE TRAPSMITHS CLEARLY DESERVE MORE SLEEP THAN FIGHTERS.
WHOA, I JUST HAD AN IDEA! THE MOST AWESOME IDEA I EVER HAD!!
ALL I NEED TO DO IS TAKE THIS CHALK AND DRAW TWO BIG CONCENTRIC CIRCLES AROUND THE PARTY...
TAH DAH! A FAKE CIRCLE OF WARDING! THE KOBOLD WILL THINK WE'RE GUARDED BY MAGIC AND WILL STAY AWAY, ALLOWING ME TO SAFELY ENJOY A NAP!
BUT WHAT IF HE DOESN'T NOTICE THE CIRCLE? FOR OBVIOUSNESS' SAKE, I BETTER STICK SOME CANDLES AROUND THE EDGE....LIKE SO.
YEH, THIS LOOKS GREAT. I SHOULD ADD SOME SQUIGGLY SHAPES AND SYMBOLS, TOO... FOR EXTRA AUTHENTICITY.
ABRA-POKUS! BIM! BAM! ZANGO BANGO!
MY RUSE IS COMPLETE!
IF I WAS A STUPID LITTLE KOBOLD, I WOULDN'T STEP NEAR SOMETHING SPOOKY LIKE THIS!
WHY HAS ZANGO BANGO BEEN SUMMONED FROM THE FIREY PITS OF HELL?
DOMATO, WAKE UP. YOUR SHIFT.

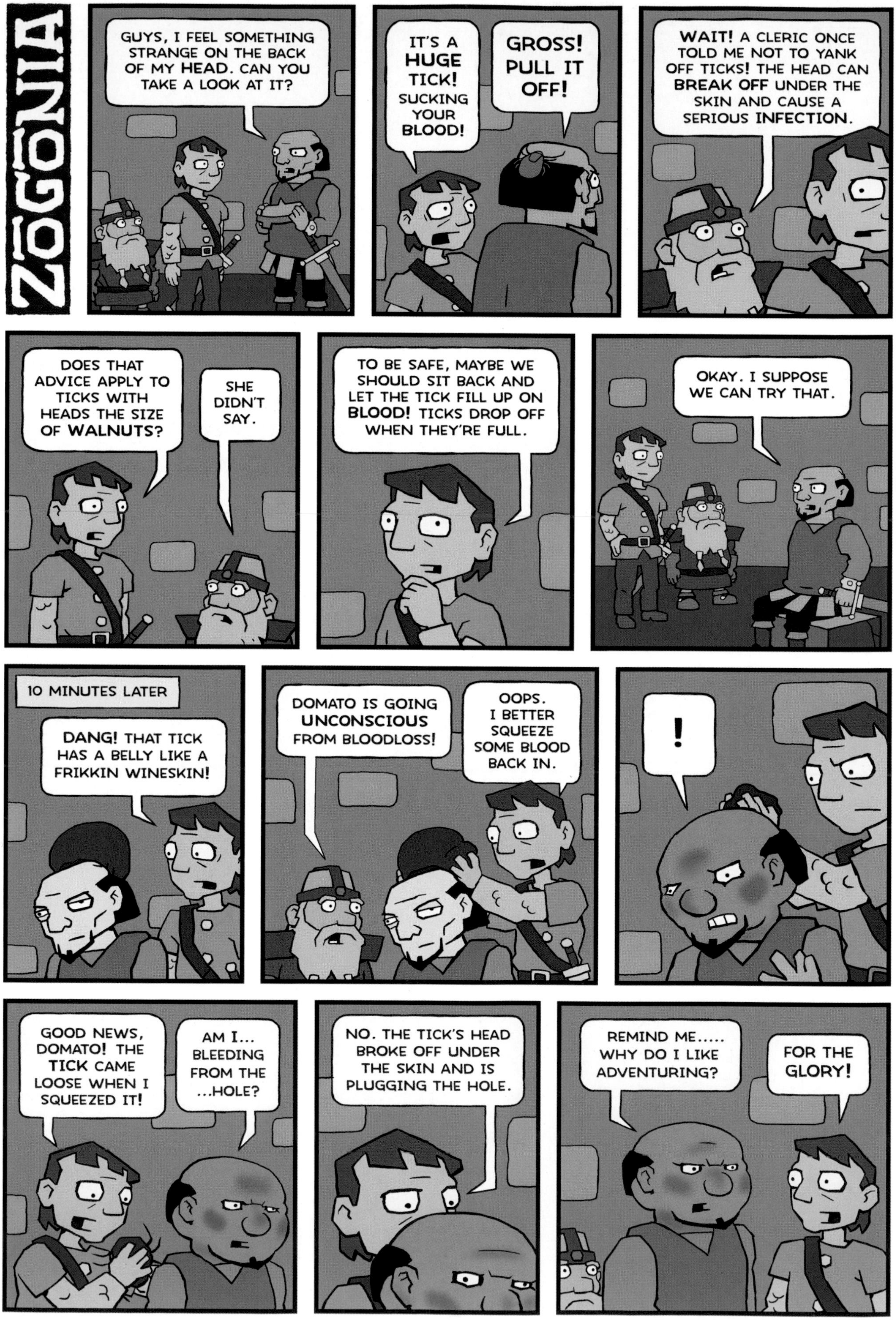
ZOGONIA
GUYS, I FEEL SOMETHING STRANGE ON THE BACK OF MY HEAD. CAN YOU TAKE A LOOK AT IT?
IT'S A HUGE TICK! SUCKING YOUR BLOOD!
GROSS! PULL IT OFF!
WAIT! A CLERIC ONCE TOLD ME NOT TO YANK OFF TICKS! THE HEAD CAN BREAK OFF UNDER THE SKIN AND CAUSE A SERIOUS INFECTION.
DOES THAT ADVICE APPLY TO TICKS WITH HEADS THE SIZE OF WALNUTS?
SHE DIDN'T SAY.
TO BE SAFE, MAYBE WE SHOULD SIT BACK AND LET THE TICK FILL UP ON BLOOD! TICKS DROP OFF WHEN THEY'RE FULL.
OKAY. I SUPPOSE WE CAN TRY THAT.
10 MINUTES LATER
DANG! THAT TICK HAS A BELLY LIKE A FRIKKIN WINESKIN!
DOMATO IS GOING UNCONSCIOUS FROM BLOODLOSS!
OOPS. I BETTER SQUEEZE SOME BLOOD BACK IN.
!
GOOD NEWS, DOMATO! THE TICK CAME LOOSE WHEN I SQUEEZED IT!
AM I... BLEEDING FROM THE ...HOLE?
NO. THE TICK'S HEAD BROKE OFF UNDER THE SKIN AND IS PLUGGING THE HOLE.
REMIND ME..... WHY DO I LIKE ADVENTURING?
FOR THE GLORY!

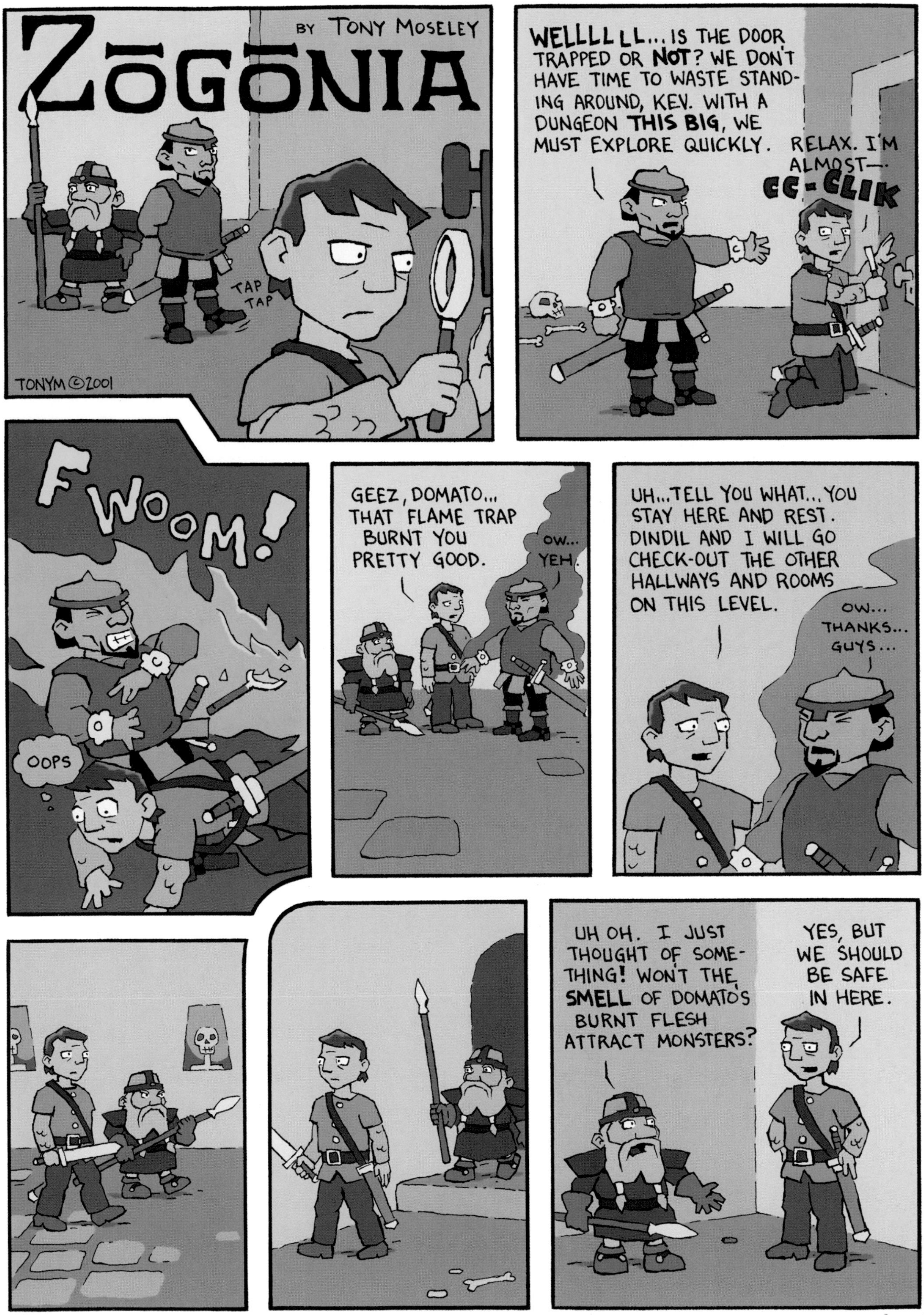
ZŌGŌNIA
BY TONY MOSELEY
TAP TAP
TONYM ©2001
WELLLLLL... IS THE DOOR TRAPPED OR NOT? WE DON'T HAVE TIME TO WASTE STANDING AROUND, KEV. WITH A DUNGEON THIS BIG, WE MUST EXPLORE QUICKLY.
RELAX. I'M ALMOST—
CC-CLIK
FWOOM!
OOPS
GEEZ, DOMATO... THAT FLAME TRAP BURNT YOU PRETTY GOOD.
OW... YEH.
UH... TELL YOU WHAT... YOU STAY HERE AND REST. DINDIL AND I WILL GO CHECK-OUT THE OTHER HALLWAYS AND ROOMS ON THIS LEVEL.
OW... THANKS... GUYS...
UH OH. I JUST THOUGHT OF SOMETHING! WON'T THE SMELL OF DOMATO'S BURNT FLESH ATTRACT MONSTERS?
YES, BUT WE SHOULD BE SAFE IN HERE.

The following three strips originally appeared in *Gaming Frontiers* magazine.

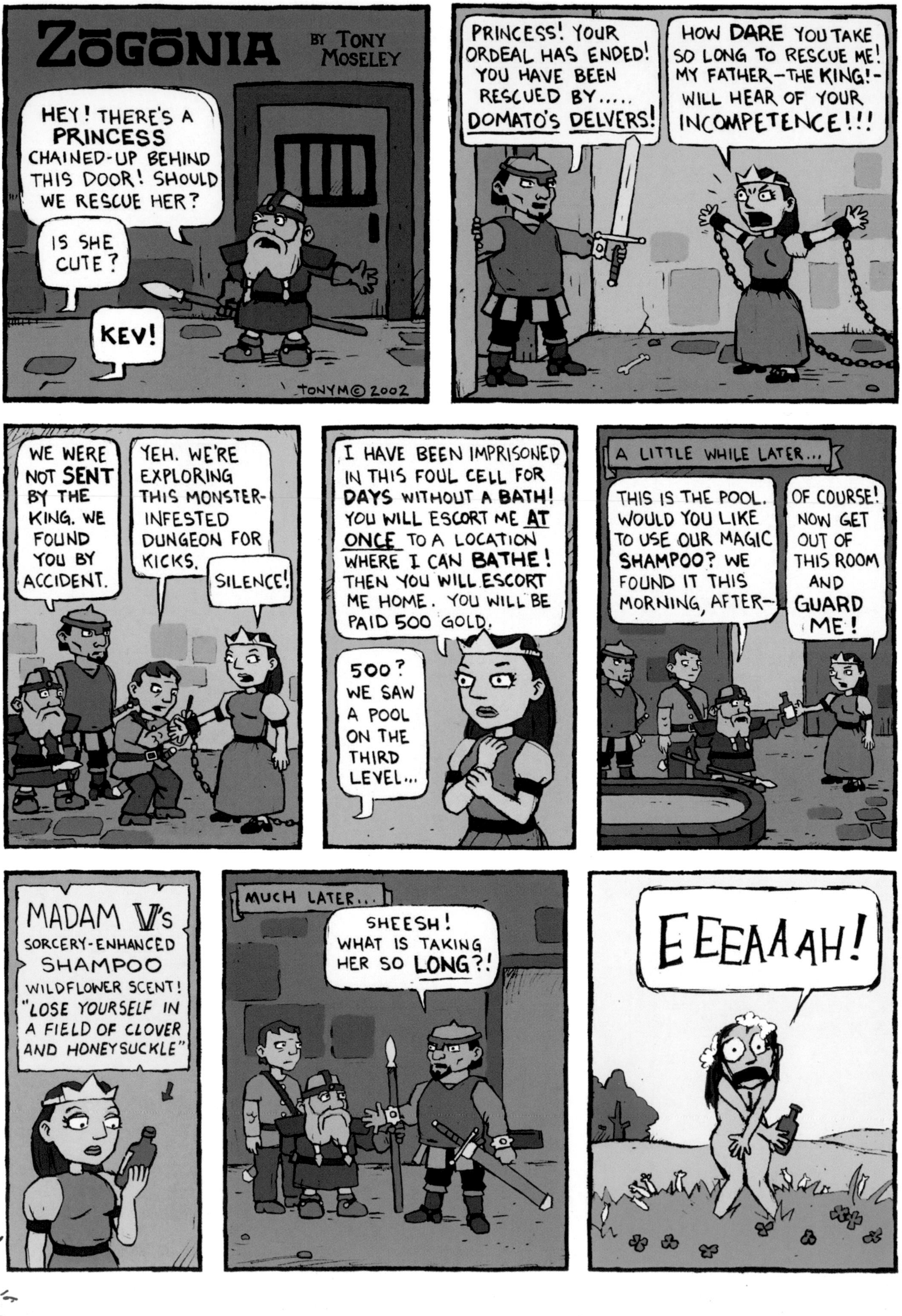
ZŌGŌNIA
BY TONY MOSELEY
HEY! THERE'S A PRINCESS CHAINED-UP BEHIND THIS DOOR! SHOULD WE RESCUE HER?
IS SHE CUTE?
KEV!
TONYM © 2002
PRINCESS! YOUR ORDEAL HAS ENDED! YOU HAVE BEEN RESCUED BY..... DOMATO'S DELVERS!
HOW DARE YOU TAKE SO LONG TO RESCUE ME! MY FATHER—THE KING!—WILL HEAR OF YOUR INCOMPETENCE!!!
WE WERE NOT SENT BY THE KING. WE FOUND YOU BY ACCIDENT.
YEH. WE'RE EXPLORING THIS MONSTER-INFESTED DUNGEON FOR KICKS.
SILENCE!
I HAVE BEEN IMPRISONED IN THIS FOUL CELL FOR DAYS WITHOUT A BATH! YOU WILL ESCORT ME AT ONCE TO A LOCATION WHERE I CAN BATHE! THEN YOU WILL ESCORT ME HOME. YOU WILL BE PAID 500 GOLD.
500? WE SAW A POOL ON THE THIRD LEVEL...
A LITTLE WHILE LATER...
THIS IS THE POOL. WOULD YOU LIKE TO USE OUR MAGIC SHAMPOO? WE FOUND IT THIS MORNING, AFTER—
OF COURSE! NOW GET OUT OF THIS ROOM AND GUARD ME!
MADAM V's SORCERY-ENHANCED SHAMPOO WILDFLOWER SCENT! "LOSE YOURSELF IN A FIELD OF CLOVER AND HONEYSUCKLE"
MUCH LATER...
SHEESH! WHAT IS TAKING HER SO LONG?!
EEEAAAAH!

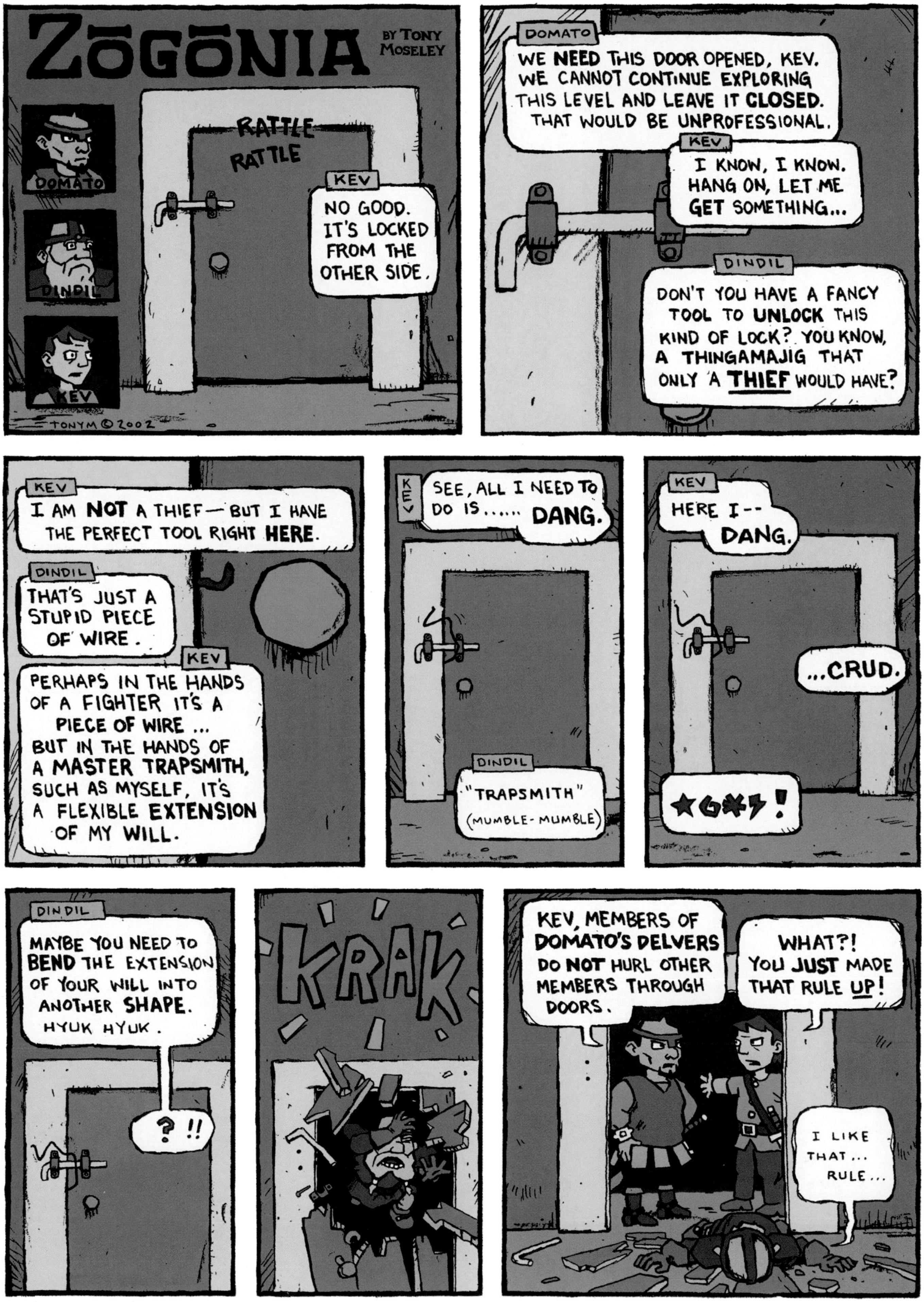
ZOGONIA
BY TONY MOSELEY
DOMATO
DINDIL
KEV
RATTLE RATTLE
KEV: NO GOOD. IT'S LOCKED FROM THE OTHER SIDE.
TONYM © 2002
DOMATO: WE NEED THIS DOOR OPENED, KEV. WE CANNOT CONTINUE EXPLORING THIS LEVEL AND LEAVE IT CLOSED. THAT WOULD BE UNPROFESSIONAL.
KEV: I KNOW, I KNOW. HANG ON, LET ME GET SOMETHING...
DINDIL: DON'T YOU HAVE A FANCY TOOL TO UNLOCK THIS KIND OF LOCK? YOU KNOW, A THINGAMAJIG THAT ONLY A THIEF WOULD HAVE?
KEV: I AM NOT A THIEF— BUT I HAVE THE PERFECT TOOL RIGHT HERE.
DINDIL: THAT'S JUST A STUPID PIECE OF WIRE.
KEV: PERHAPS IN THE HANDS OF A FIGHTER IT'S A PIECE OF WIRE ... BUT IN THE HANDS OF A MASTER TRAPSMITH, SUCH AS MYSELF, IT'S A FLEXIBLE EXTENSION OF MY WILL.
KEV: SEE, ALL I NEED TO DO IS...... DANG.
DINDIL: "TRAPSMITH" (MUMBLE-MUMBLE)
KEV: HERE I-- DANG.
...CRUD.
★@✱⚡!
DINDIL: MAYBE YOU NEED TO BEND THE EXTENSION OF YOUR WILL INTO ANOTHER SHAPE. HYUK HYUK.
? !!
KRAK
KEV, MEMBERS OF DOMATO'S DELVERS DO NOT HURL OTHER MEMBERS THROUGH DOORS.
WHAT?! YOU JUST MADE THAT RULE UP!
I LIKE THAT... RULE...

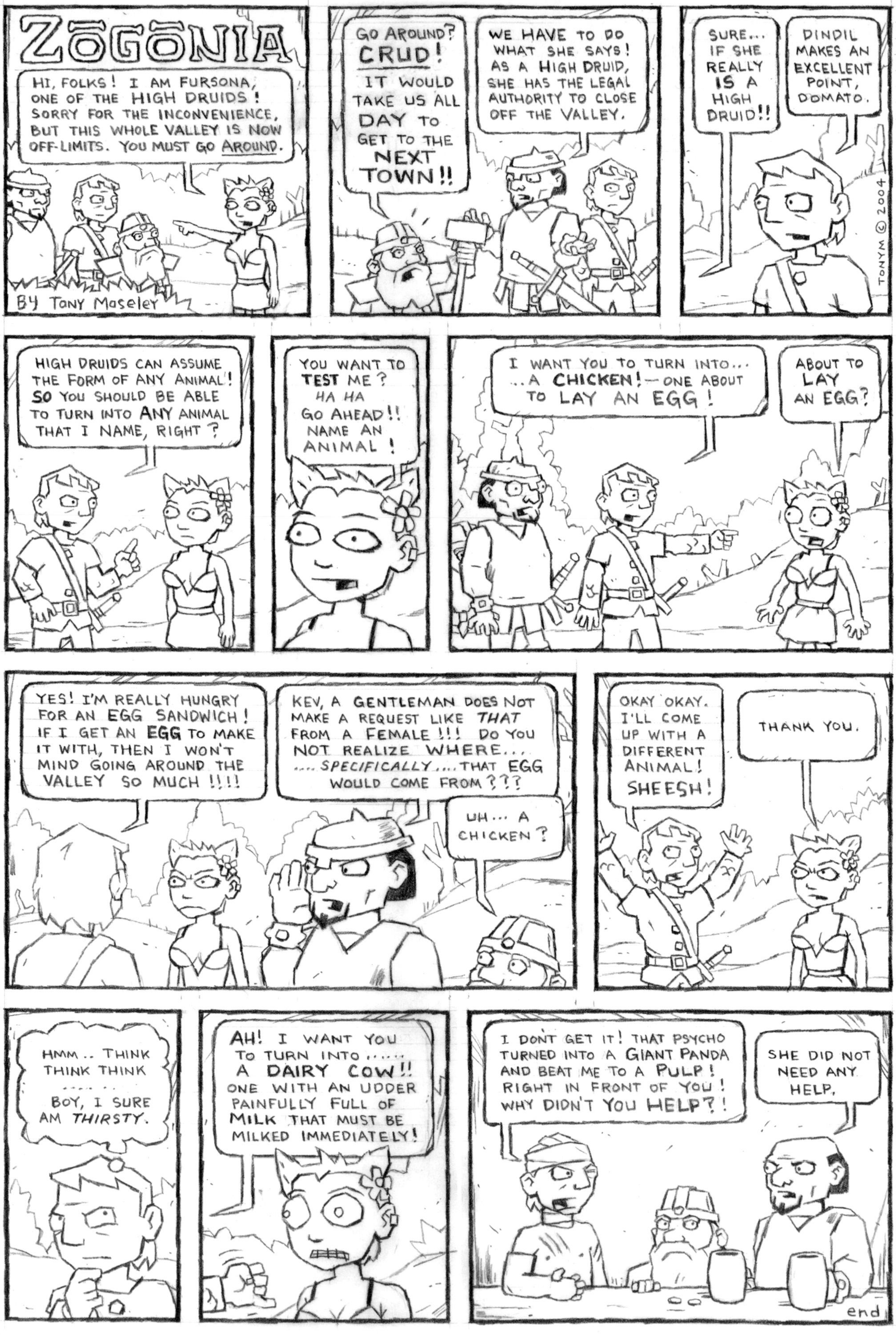
ZŌGŌNIA
HI, FOLKS! I AM FURSONA, ONE OF THE HIGH DRUIDS! SORRY FOR THE INCONVENIENCE, BUT THIS WHOLE VALLEY IS NOW OFF-LIMITS. YOU MUST GO AROUND.
BY TONY MOSELEY
GO AROUND? CRUD! IT WOULD TAKE US ALL DAY TO GET TO THE NEXT TOWN!!
WE HAVE TO DO WHAT SHE SAYS! AS A HIGH DRUID, SHE HAS THE LEGAL AUTHORITY TO CLOSE OFF THE VALLEY.
SURE... IF SHE REALLY IS A HIGH DRUID!!
DINDIL MAKES AN EXCELLENT POINT, DOMATO.
TONYM © 2004
HIGH DRUIDS CAN ASSUME THE FORM OF ANY ANIMAL! SO YOU SHOULD BE ABLE TO TURN INTO ANY ANIMAL THAT I NAME, RIGHT?
YOU WANT TO TEST ME? HA HA GO AHEAD!! NAME AN ANIMAL!
I WANT YOU TO TURN INTO... ...A CHICKEN!—ONE ABOUT TO LAY AN EGG!
ABOUT TO LAY AN EGG?
YES! I'M REALLY HUNGRY FOR AN EGG SANDWICH! IF I GET AN EGG TO MAKE IT WITH, THEN I WON'T MIND GOING AROUND THE VALLEY SO MUCH!!!!
KEV, A GENTLEMAN DOES NOT MAKE A REQUEST LIKE THAT FROM A FEMALE!!! DO YOU NOT REALIZE WHERE... ....SPECIFICALLY.... THAT EGG WOULD COME FROM???
UH... A CHICKEN?
OKAY OKAY. I'LL COME UP WITH A DIFFERENT ANIMAL! SHEESH!
THANK YOU.
HMM.. THINK THINK THINK ...... BOY, I SURE AM THIRSTY.
AH! I WANT YOU TO TURN INTO...... A DAIRY COW!! ONE WITH AN UDDER PAINFULLY FULL OF MILK THAT MUST BE MILKED IMMEDIATELY!
I DON'T GET IT! THAT PSYCHO TURNED INTO A GIANT PANDA AND BEAT ME TO A PULP! RIGHT IN FRONT OF YOU! WHY DIDN'T YOU HELP?!
SHE DID NOT NEED ANY HELP.
end

This previously unpublished strip was judged too risqué for *Dragon*.

Mt.Zogon

Due to the popularity of *Zogonia*, in issue #99 *Dragon*'s sister magazine *Dungeon* began running a four-panel companion strip entitled *Mt. Zogon*. This strip, set in Tony's same world of Zogonia, chronicled the adventures of Galeena, a morally questionable druid, and her talking mushroom as the two conquered the caves of the mysterious Mt. Zogon. What follows is a representative sample of the strip's blood-soaked history, including a bonus strip that was rejected as too edgy for publication—no small feat, given Galeena's sociopathic tendencies.

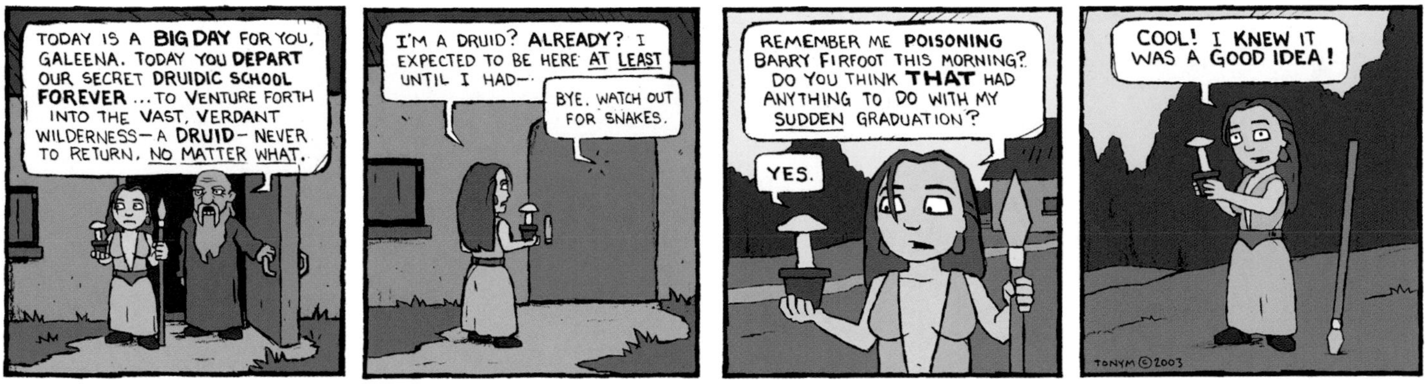
TODAY IS A BIG DAY FOR YOU, GALEENA. TODAY YOU DEPART OUR SECRET DRUIDIC SCHOOL FOREVER ...TO VENTURE FORTH INTO THE VAST, VERDANT WILDERNESS—A DRUID—NEVER TO RETURN. NO MATTER WHAT.
I'M A DRUID? ALREADY? I EXPECTED TO BE HERE AT LEAST UNTIL I HAD—
BYE. WATCH OUT FOR SNAKES.
REMEMBER ME POISONING BARRY FIRFOOT THIS MORNING? DO YOU THINK THAT HAD ANYTHING TO DO WITH MY SUDDEN GRADUATION?
YES.
COOL! I KNEW IT WAS A GOOD IDEA!
TONYM ©2003

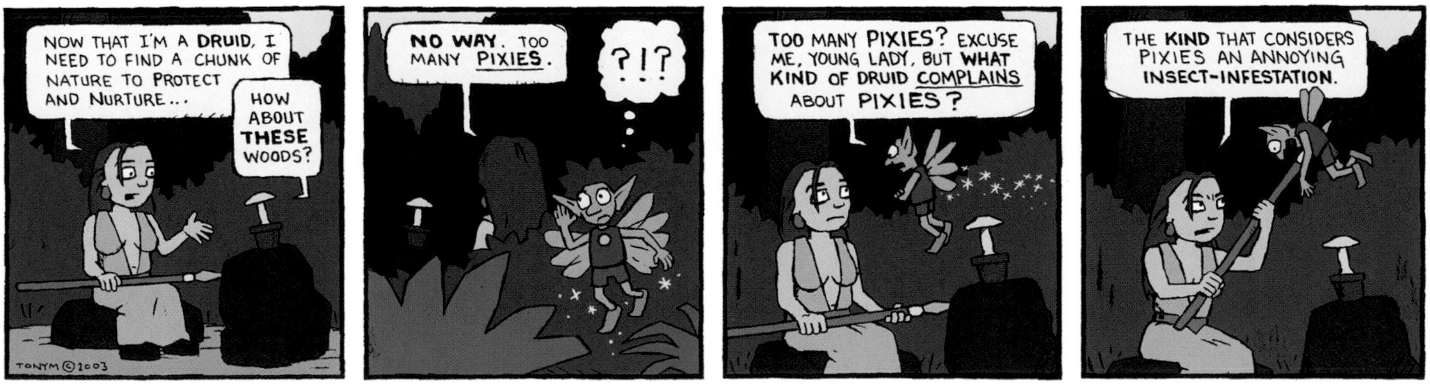
NOW THAT I'M A DRUID, I NEED TO FIND A CHUNK OF NATURE TO PROTECT AND NURTURE...
HOW ABOUT THESE WOODS?
TONYM ©2003
NO WAY. TOO MANY PIXIES.
?!?
TOO MANY PIXIES? EXCUSE ME, YOUNG LADY, BUT WHAT KIND OF DRUID COMPLAINS ABOUT PIXIES?
THE KIND THAT CONSIDERS PIXIES AN ANNOYING INSECT-INFESTATION.

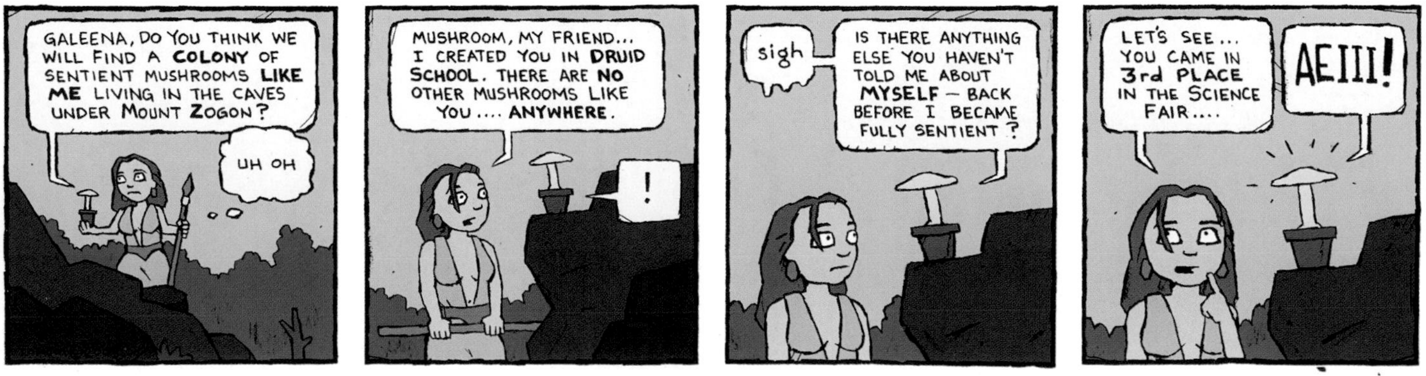
GALEENA, DO YOU THINK WE WILL FIND A COLONY OF SENTIENT MUSHROOMS LIKE ME LIVING IN THE CAVES UNDER MOUNT ZOGON?
UH OH
MUSHROOM, MY FRIEND... I CREATED YOU IN DRUID SCHOOL. THERE ARE NO OTHER MUSHROOMS LIKE YOU.... ANYWHERE.
!
sigh
IS THERE ANYTHING ELSE YOU HAVEN'T TOLD ME ABOUT MYSELF—BACK BEFORE I BECAME FULLY SENTIENT?
LET'S SEE... YOU CAME IN 3rd PLACE IN THE SCIENCE FAIR....
AEIII!

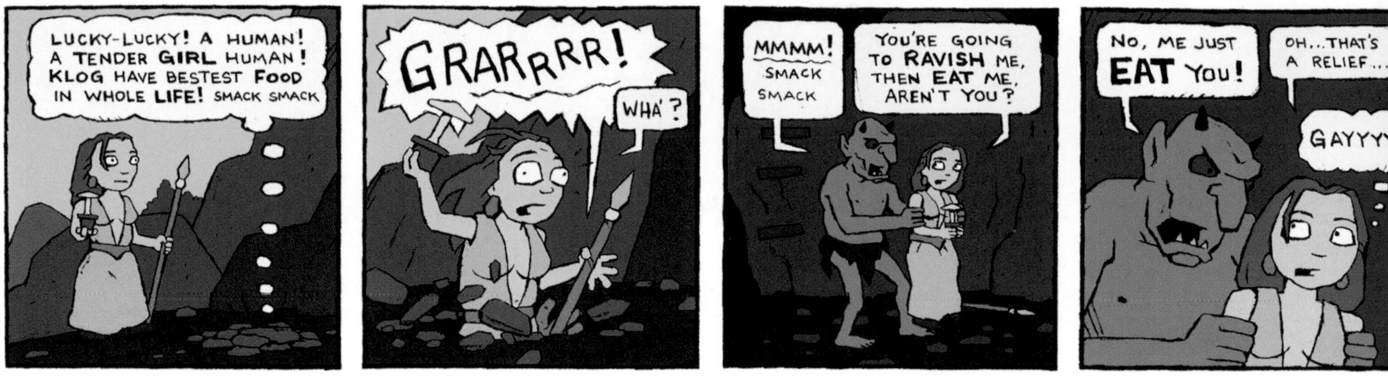
LUCKY-LUCKY! A HUMAN! A TENDER GIRL HUMAN! KLOG HAVE BESTEST FOOD IN WHOLE LIFE! SMACK SMACK
GRARRRR!
WHA'?
MMMM! SMACK SMACK
YOU'RE GOING TO RAVISH ME, THEN EAT ME, AREN'T YOU?
NO, ME JUST EAT YOU!
OH... THAT'S A RELIEF...
GAYYYY.

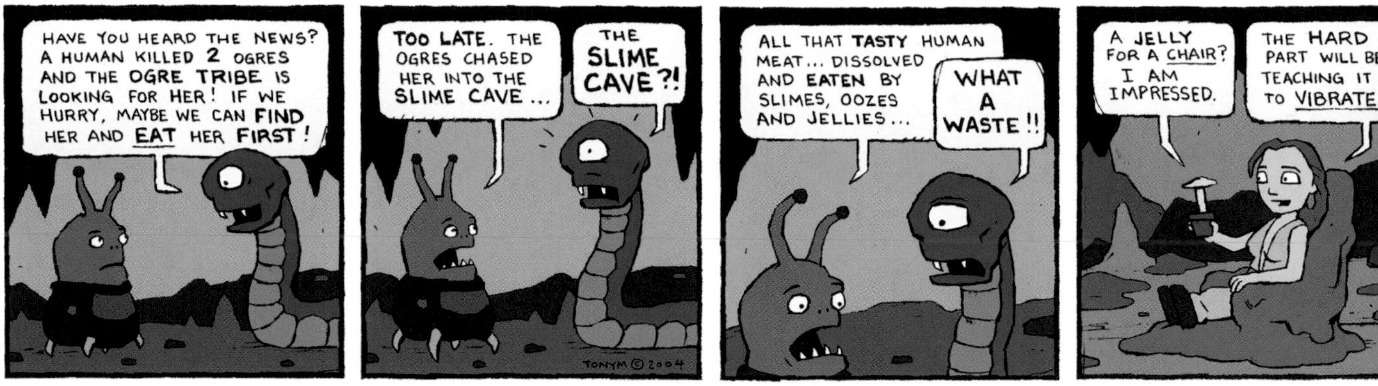
HAVE YOU HEARD THE NEWS? A HUMAN KILLED 2 OGRES AND THE OGRE TRIBE IS LOOKING FOR HER! IF WE HURRY, MAYBE WE CAN FIND HER AND EAT HER FIRST!
TOO LATE. THE OGRES CHASED HER INTO THE SLIME CAVE...
THE SLIME CAVE?!
TONYM © 2004
ALL THAT TASTY HUMAN MEAT... DISSOLVED AND EATEN BY SLIMES, OOZES AND JELLIES...
WHAT A WASTE!!
A JELLY FOR A CHAIR? I AM IMPRESSED.
THE HARD PART WILL BE TEACHING IT TO VIBRATE.

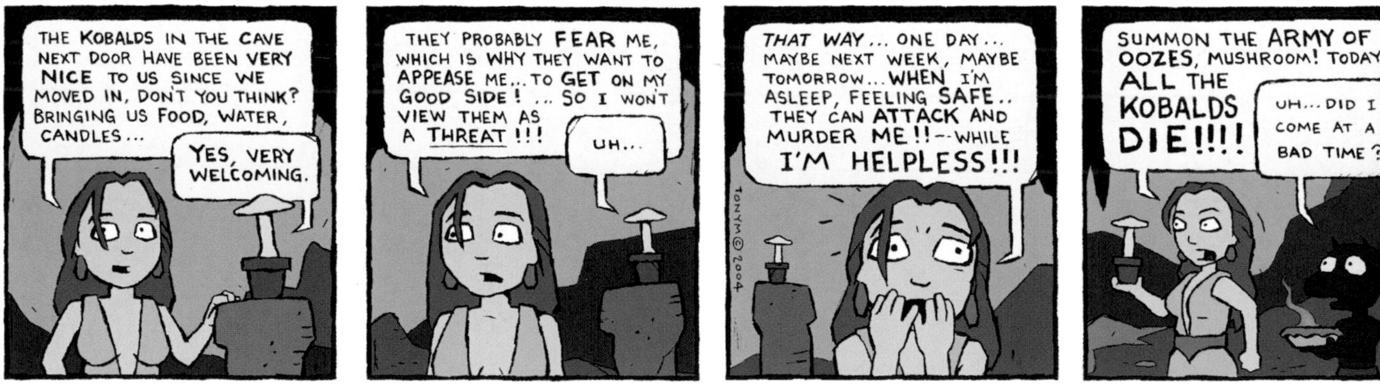
THE KOBALDS IN THE CAVE NEXT DOOR HAVE BEEN VERY NICE TO US SINCE WE MOVED IN, DON'T YOU THINK? BRINGING US FOOD, WATER, CANDLES...
YES, VERY WELCOMING.
THEY PROBABLY FEAR ME, WHICH IS WHY THEY WANT TO APPEASE ME... TO GET ON MY GOOD SIDE! ... SO I WON'T VIEW THEM AS A THREAT!!!
UH...
TONYM © 2004
THAT WAY... ONE DAY... MAYBE NEXT WEEK, MAYBE TOMORROW... WHEN I'M ASLEEP, FEELING SAFE.. THEY CAN ATTACK AND MURDER ME!!--WHILE I'M HELPLESS!!!
SUMMON THE ARMY OF OOZES, MUSHROOM! TODAY ALL THE KOBALDS DIE!!!!
UH... DID I COME AT A BAD TIME?

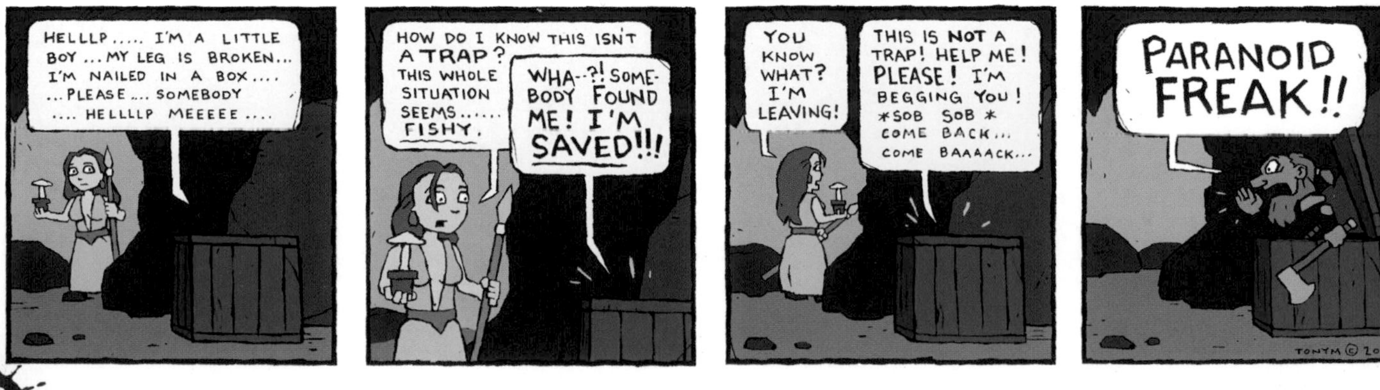
HELLLP..... I'M A LITTLE BOY... MY LEG IS BROKEN... I'M NAILED IN A BOX.... ...PLEASE... SOMEBODY .... HELLLLP MEEEEE....
HOW DO I KNOW THIS ISN'T A TRAP? THIS WHOLE SITUATION SEEMS...... FISHY.
WHA--?! SOMEBODY FOUND ME! I'M SAVED!!!
YOU KNOW WHAT? I'M LEAVING!
THIS IS NOT A TRAP! HELP ME! PLEASE! I'M BEGGING YOU! *SOB SOB* COME BACK... COME BAAAACK...
PARANOID FREAK!!
TONYM © 2004

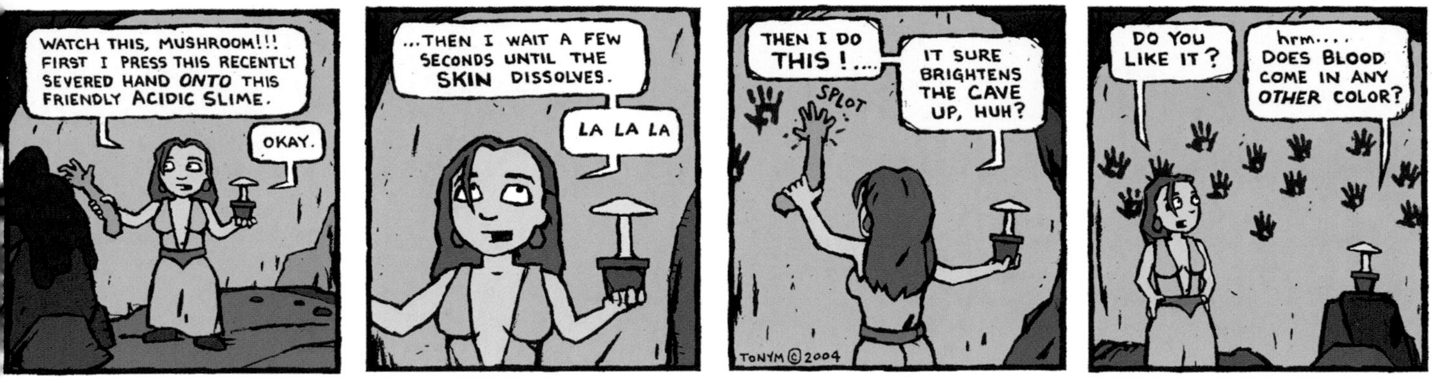
WATCH THIS, MUSHROOM!!! FIRST I PRESS THIS RECENTLY SEVERED HAND ONTO THIS FRIENDLY ACIDIC SLIME.
OKAY.
...THEN I WAIT A FEW SECONDS UNTIL THE SKIN DISSOLVES.
LA LA LA
THEN I DO THIS!....
SPLOT
IT SURE BRIGHTENS THE CAVE UP, HUH?
TONYM © 2004
DO YOU LIKE IT?
hrm.... DOES BLOOD COME IN ANY OTHER COLOR?

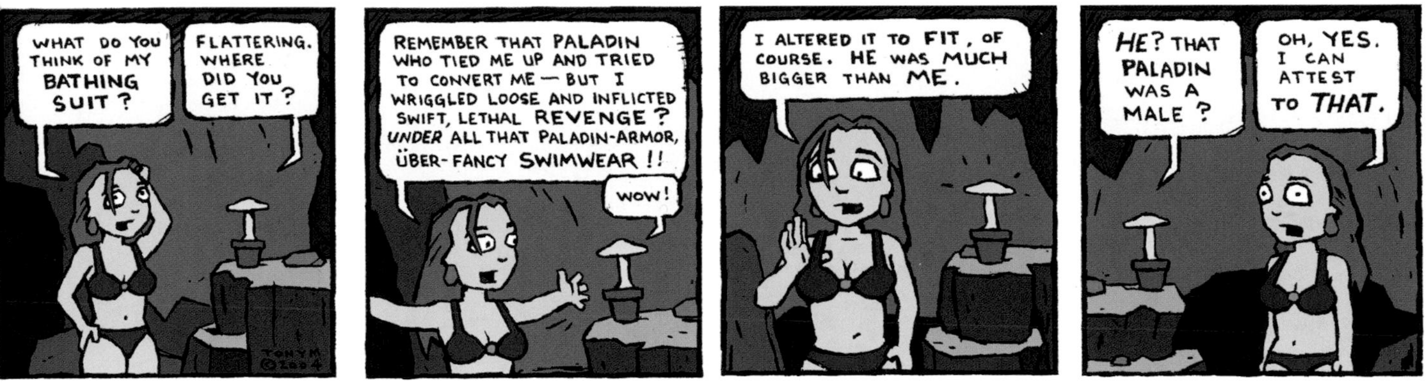
WHAT DO YOU THINK OF MY BATHING SUIT?
FLATTERING. WHERE DID YOU GET IT?
TONYM ©2004
REMEMBER THAT PALADIN WHO TIED ME UP AND TRIED TO CONVERT ME — BUT I WRIGGLED LOOSE AND INFLICTED SWIFT, LETHAL REVENGE? UNDER ALL THAT PALADIN-ARMOR, ÜBER-FANCY SWIMWEAR!!
WOW!
I ALTERED IT TO FIT, OF COURSE. HE WAS MUCH BIGGER THAN ME.
HE? THAT PALADIN WAS A MALE?
OH, YES. I CAN ATTEST TO THAT.

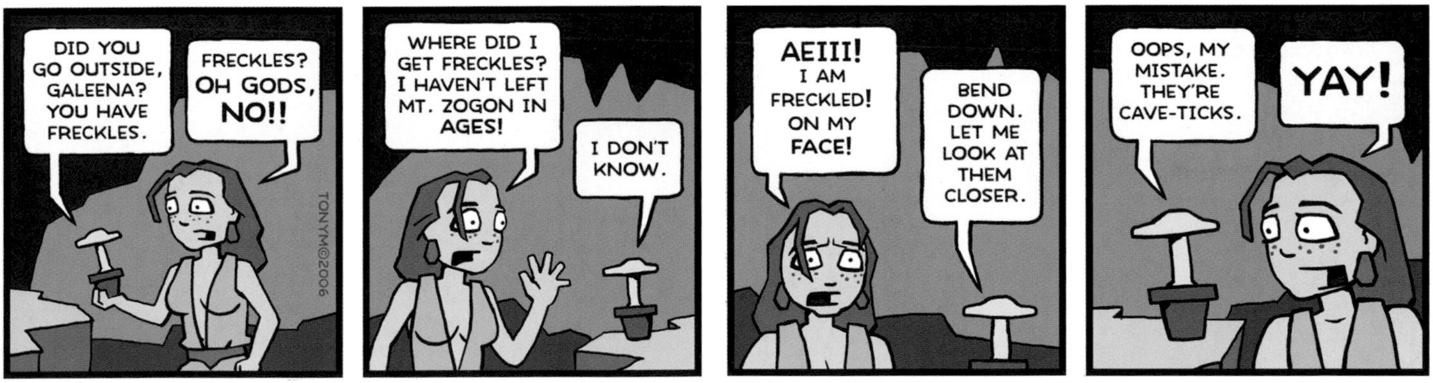
DID YOU GO OUTSIDE, GALEENA? YOU HAVE FRECKLES.
FRECKLES? OH GODS, NO!!
TONYM©2006
WHERE DID I GET FRECKLES? I HAVEN'T LEFT MT. ZOGON IN AGES!
I DON'T KNOW.
AEIII! I AM FRECKLED! ON MY FACE!
BEND DOWN. LET ME LOOK AT THEM CLOSER.
OOPS, MY MISTAKE. THEY'RE CAVE-TICKS.
YAY!

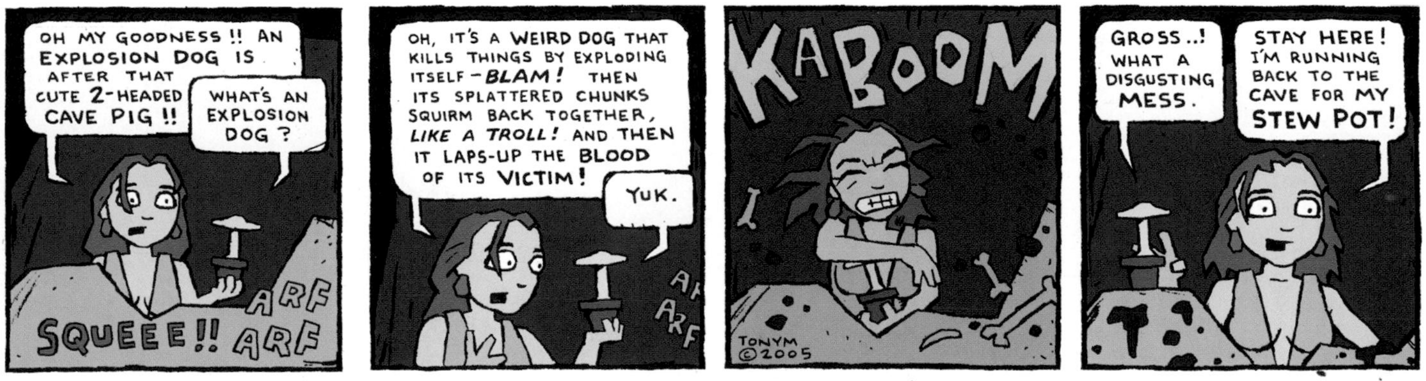
OH MY GOODNESS!! AN EXPLOSION DOG IS AFTER THAT CUTE 2-HEADED CAVE PIG!!
WHAT'S AN EXPLOSION DOG?
SQUEEE!! ARF ARF
OH, IT'S A WEIRD DOG THAT KILLS THINGS BY EXPLODING ITSELF — BLAM! THEN ITS SPLATTERED CHUNKS SQUIRM BACK TOGETHER, LIKE A TROLL! AND THEN IT LAPS-UP THE BLOOD OF ITS VICTIM!
YUK.
KABOOM
TONYM ©2005
GROSS..! WHAT A DISGUSTING MESS.
STAY HERE! I'M RUNNING BACK TO THE CAVE FOR MY STEW POT!

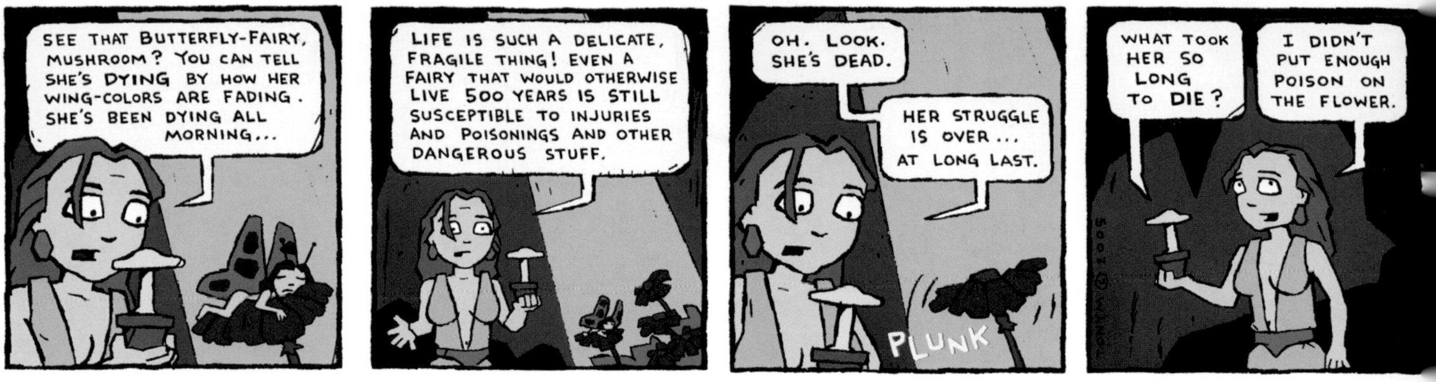
SEE THAT BUTTERFLY-FAIRY, MUSHROOM? YOU CAN TELL SHE'S DYING BY HOW HER WING-COLORS ARE FADING. SHE'S BEEN DYING ALL MORNING...
LIFE IS SUCH A DELICATE, FRAGILE THING! EVEN A FAIRY THAT WOULD OTHERWISE LIVE 500 YEARS IS STILL SUSCEPTIBLE TO INJURIES AND POISONINGS AND OTHER DANGEROUS STUFF.
OH. LOOK. SHE'S DEAD.
HER STRUGGLE IS OVER... AT LONG LAST.
PLUNK
WHAT TOOK HER SO LONG TO DIE?
I DIDN'T PUT ENOUGH POISON ON THE FLOWER.

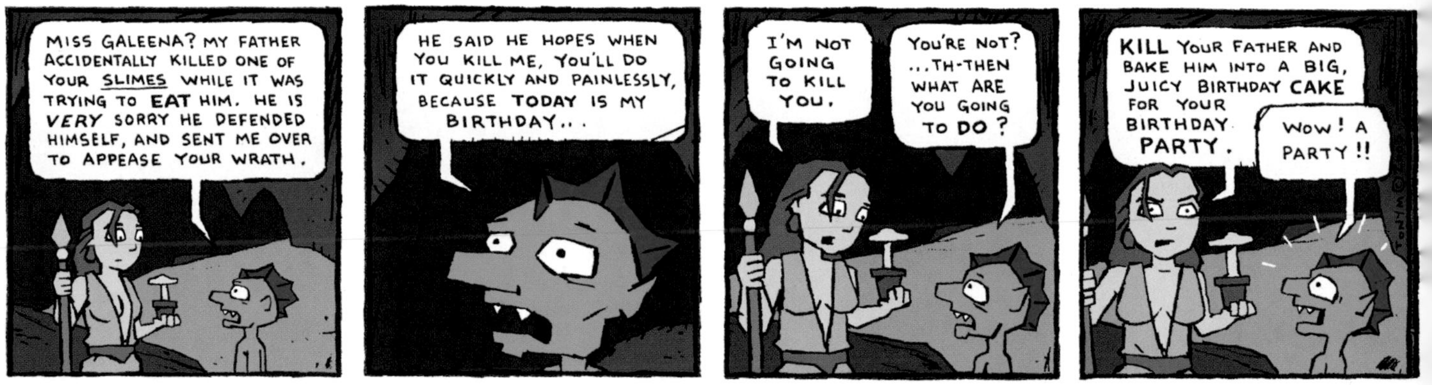
MISS GALEENA? MY FATHER ACCIDENTALLY KILLED ONE OF YOUR SLIMES WHILE IT WAS TRYING TO EAT HIM. HE IS VERY SORRY HE DEFENDED HIMSELF, AND SENT ME OVER TO APPEASE YOUR WRATH.
HE SAID HE HOPES WHEN YOU KILL ME, YOU'LL DO IT QUICKLY AND PAINLESSLY, BECAUSE TODAY IS MY BIRTHDAY...
I'M NOT GOING TO KILL YOU.
YOU'RE NOT? ...TH-THEN WHAT ARE YOU GOING TO DO?
KILL YOUR FATHER AND BAKE HIM INTO A BIG, JUICY BIRTHDAY CAKE FOR YOUR BIRTHDAY PARTY.
WOW! A PARTY!!

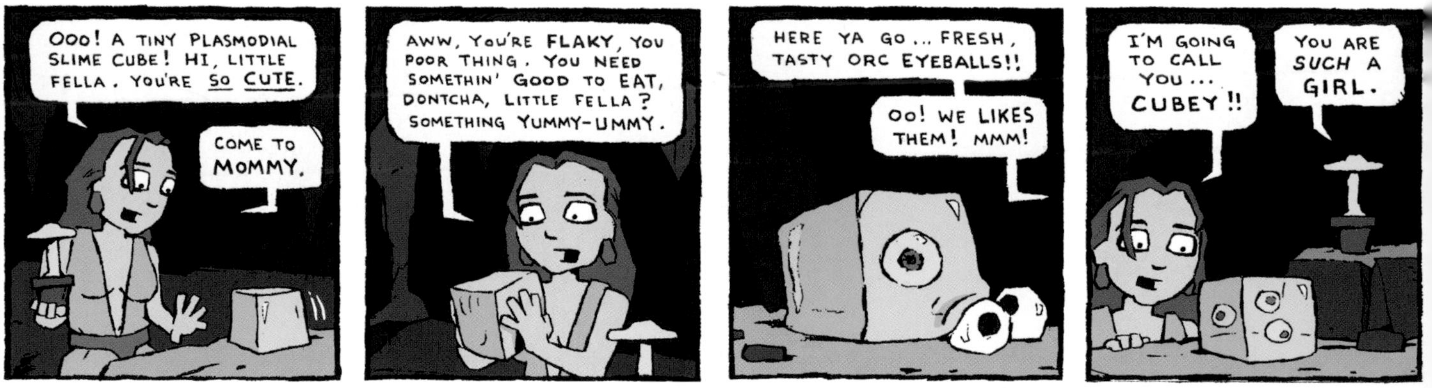
OOO! A TINY PLASMODIAL SLIME CUBE! HI, LITTLE FELLA. YOU'RE SO CUTE.
COME TO MOMMY.
AWW, YOU'RE FLAKY, YOU POOR THING. YOU NEED SOMETHIN' GOOD TO EAT, DONTCHA, LITTLE FELLA? SOMETHING YUMMY-UMMY.
HERE YA GO... FRESH, TASTY ORC EYEBALLS!!
OO! WE LIKES THEM! MMM!
I'M GOING TO CALL YOU... CUBEY!!
YOU ARE SUCH A GIRL.

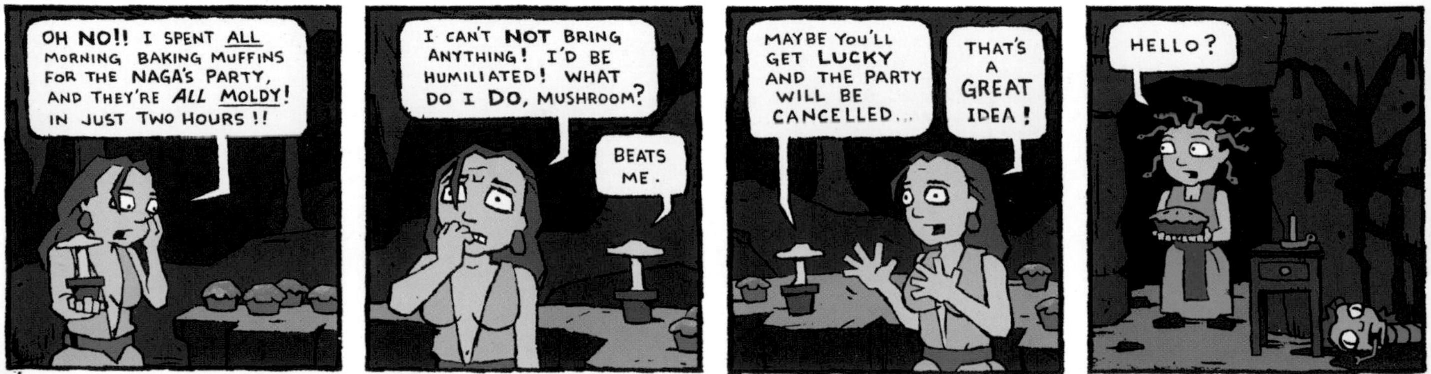
OH NO!! I SPENT ALL MORNING BAKING MUFFINS FOR THE NAGA'S PARTY, AND THEY'RE ALL MOLDY! IN JUST TWO HOURS!!
I CAN'T NOT BRING ANYTHING! I'D BE HUMILIATED! WHAT DO I DO, MUSHROOM?
BEATS ME.
MAYBE YOU'LL GET LUCKY AND THE PARTY WILL BE CANCELLED...
THAT'S A GREAT IDEA!
HELLO?

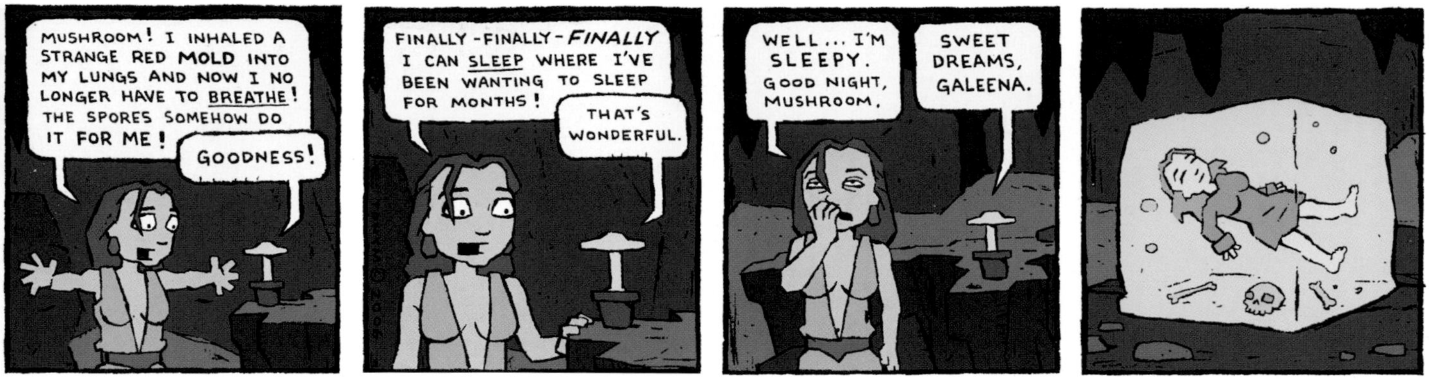
MUSHROOM! I INHALED A STRANGE RED MOLD INTO MY LUNGS AND NOW I NO LONGER HAVE TO BREATHE! THE SPORES SOMEHOW DO IT FOR ME!
GOODNESS!
FINALLY - FINALLY - FINALLY I CAN SLEEP WHERE I'VE BEEN WANTING TO SLEEP FOR MONTHS!
THAT'S WONDERFUL.
WELL... I'M SLEEPY. GOOD NIGHT, MUSHROOM.
SWEET DREAMS, GALEENA.

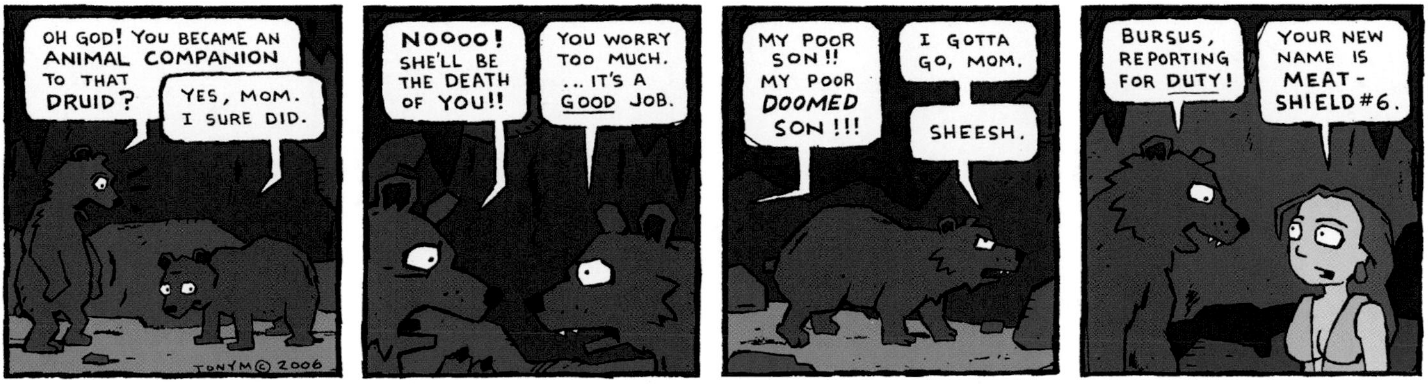
OH GOD! YOU BECAME AN ANIMAL COMPANION TO THAT DRUID?
YES, MOM. I SURE DID.
TONYM© 2006
NOOOO! SHE'LL BE THE DEATH OF YOU!!
YOU WORRY TOO MUCH. ... IT'S A GOOD JOB.
MY POOR SON!! MY POOR DOOMED SON!!!
I GOTTA GO, MOM.
SHEESH.
BURSUS, REPORTING FOR DUTY!
YOUR NEW NAME IS MEAT-SHIELD #6.

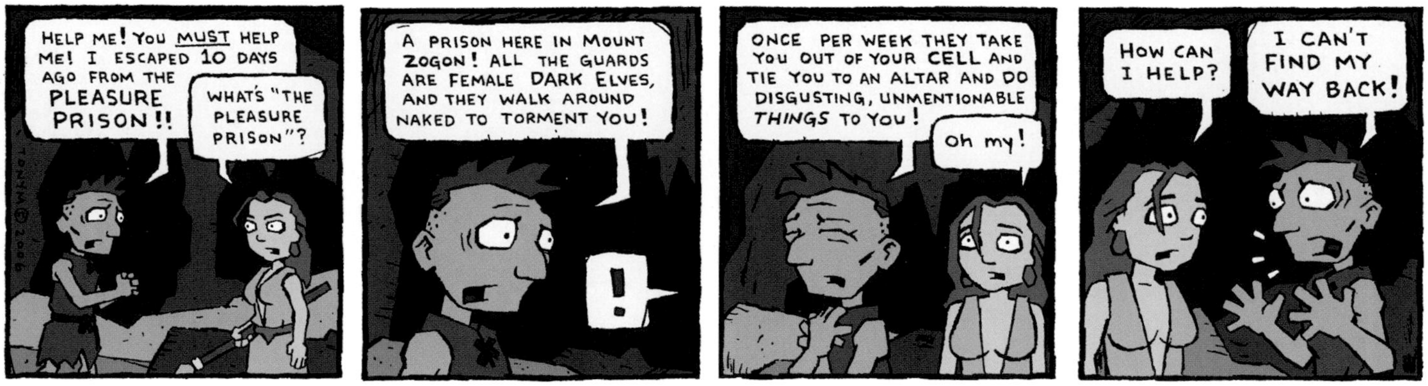
HELP ME! YOU MUST HELP ME! I ESCAPED 10 DAYS AGO FROM THE PLEASURE PRISON!!
WHAT'S "THE PLEASURE PRISON"?
A PRISON HERE IN MOUNT ZOGON! ALL THE GUARDS ARE FEMALE DARK ELVES, AND THEY WALK AROUND NAKED TO TORMENT YOU!
!
ONCE PER WEEK THEY TAKE YOU OUT OF YOUR CELL AND TIE YOU TO AN ALTAR AND DO DISGUSTING, UNMENTIONABLE THINGS TO YOU!
Oh my!
HOW CAN I HELP?
I CAN'T FIND MY WAY BACK!

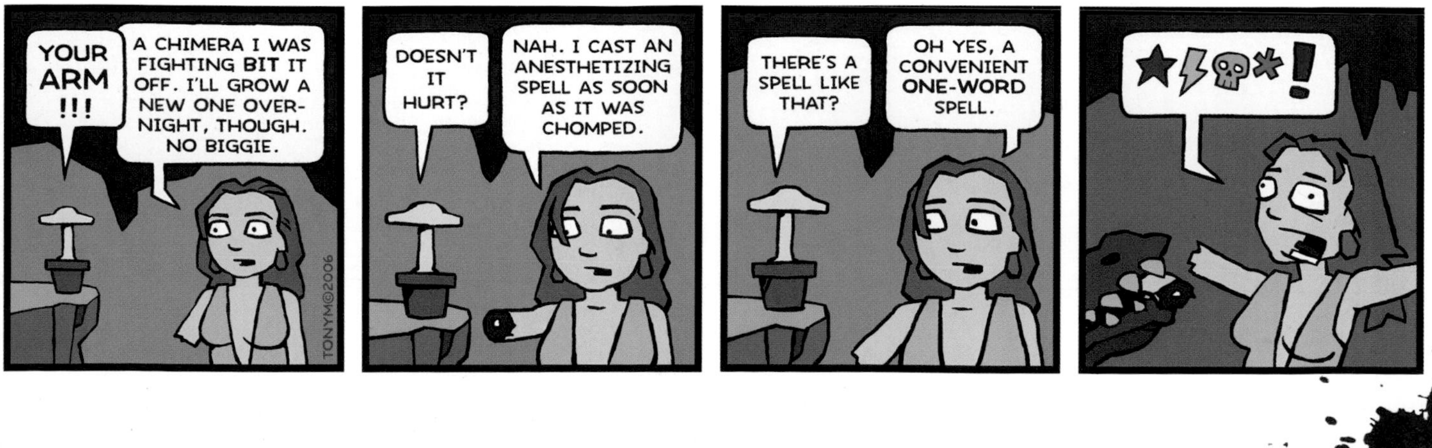
YOUR ARM !!!
A CHIMERA I WAS FIGHTING BIT IT OFF. I'LL GROW A NEW ONE OVER-NIGHT, THOUGH. NO BIGGIE.
TONYM©2006
DOESN'T IT HURT?
NAH. I CAST AN ANESTHETIZING SPELL AS SOON AS IT WAS CHOMPED.
THERE'S A SPELL LIKE THAT?
OH YES, A CONVENIENT ONE-WORD SPELL.

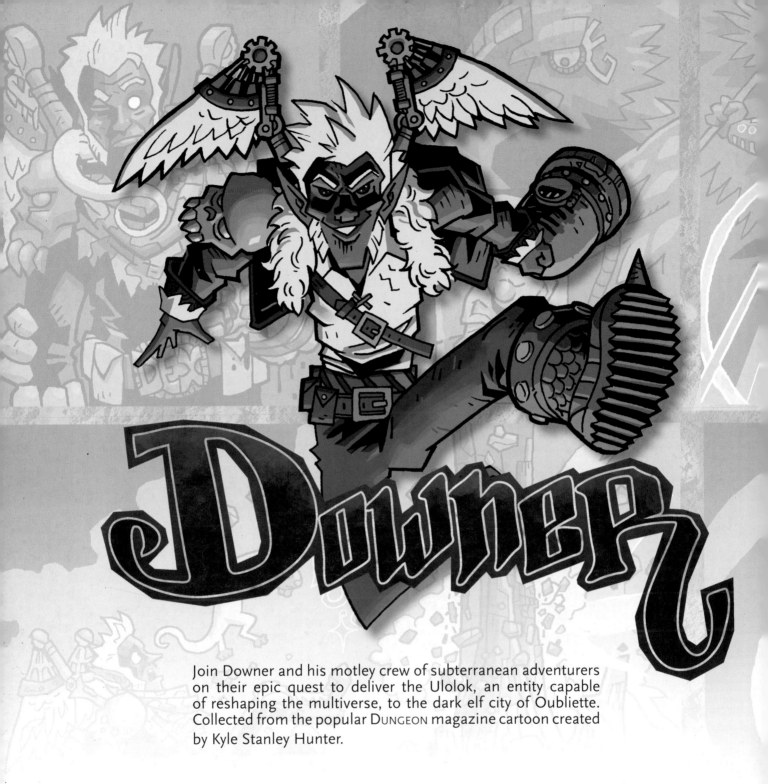

Join Downer and his motley crew of subterranean adventurers on their epic quest to deliver the Ulolok, an entity capable of reshaping the multiverse, to the dark elf city of Oubliette. Collected from the popular DUNGEON magazine cartoon created by Kyle Stanley Hunter.

Downer: Wandering Monster • $14.99
Available May 2007!

Introduce yourself to Downer online at

paizo.com

or at your local book or hobby store.